COMPILING FUNCTIONAL LANGUAGES

COMPILING FUNCTIONAL LANGUAGES

Antoni Diller

Department of Computer Science,
University of Birmingham

JOHN WILEY & SONS LTD
Chichester · New York · Brisbane · Toronto · Singapore

Library of Congress Cataloging-in-Publication Data
Diller, Antoni.
  Compiling functional languages.

  Bibliography: p.
  1. Functional programming languages.   2. Compiling
(Electronic computers)   I. Title.
QA76.73.F86D55   1988   005.13   88-14349
ISBN 0 471 92027 4 (pbk.)

British Library Cataloguing in Publication Data
Diller, Antoni
  Compiling functional languages.
  1. Computer systems. Functional programming
  Programming languages
  I. Title
  005.13

  ISBN 0 471 92027 4

Printed and bound in Great Britain
by Anchor Brendon, Tiptree, Essex

Contents

List of Figures

Preface

What I do in this book is to describe a number of different ways of implementing functional programming languages which bear a strong family resemblance to one another and which all have their origins in the work of Turner on combinator-based graph-reducers.

This book is aimed at final-year undergraduate or first-year graduate computer science students who are taking courses either in the principles of functional languages or in language translation, but I hope that other people will also find it interesting. In particular, I think that it might appeal to logicians—both mathematical and philosophical—because of the solid logical foundations of functional languages and their compilers in the theories of combinatory logic and the λ-calculus. It is mainly for the benefit of these readers that I include as an Appendix the Pascal source code for the compiler of a simple functional language, which they are urged to read, study, understand, criticize and improve upon.

Functional programming languages and their implementation techniques are a fascinating area of study. Here are used ideas and methods that range from the abstract logical disciplines of category theory and the model-theory of the λ-calculus to mindbogglingly abstruse examples of bit-twiddling in those translators which produce self-modifying assembler programs—whose jumps correspond to the arcs of the program graph they represent—as their object code. My own interests lie towards the logical end of this spectrum and I am frequently amazed that a number of esoteric logical systems have found their uses in this branch of computer science. To give just one example here, Yaghi (1983) shows how a functional language can be implemented by first being translated into an intensional logic—one developed by Carnap and Montague—and then evaluated.

One of the difficulties involved in writing any book on the translation of programming languages is that of choosing the language or languages that are to serve as examples of the implementation methods being described.

I have decided to begin by showing how to compile Henderson's language Lispkit Lisp, which I refer to as Lispkit. In common with other Lisps, both programs and data in Lispkit are represented by S-expressions. The choice of using Lispkit offers several advantages. Lispkit can be seen as a minimal functional programming language in that it is simply the type-free λ-calculus—extended with **let**- and **letrec**-clauses—dressed up in S-expressions. Therefore, its compilation—and the execution of the resulting object code—are easy to understand. Although this is true, Lispkit is not a toy language. It is extensively used by Henderson and his collaborators in various research projects, including being used as the foundation of the **me-too** specification language.

Chapters 2 to 5 are taken up, respectively, with a detailed account of Lispkit, combinatory logic, the translation of Lispkit into combinatory logic and the evaluation of the resulting object code by means of graph-reduction. The Appendix contains the Pascal source code of a compiler based on the material contained in these four Chapters. Once this material has been understood, then it will be easier for the reader to appreciate the developments and refinements that have been proposed in order to improve the efficiency of this implementation method and in order to handle more complicated language features. Some of these improvements are mentioned in later Chapters. I believe this approach—beginning with a simple implementation and then gradually improving it—to be pedagogically beneficial and it is one of the two main differences between this book and Peyton Jones (1987). His approach is to take a complicated functional language—in fact, a significant subset of Miranda—and show how that can be implemented. The danger of that method is that it is easy to lose sight of the wood for the trees.

The other main difference between this book and Peyton Jones's is that I explore various implementation techniques—combinator-based ones, supercombinator-based ones and those involving categorical combinators—whereas he sticks almost entirely to a method which uses supercombinators and the G-machine and, furthermore, I investigate the relationships that exist between implementing a functional language and such ideas as program transformation and partial evaluation, which he does not. (Partial evaluation is useful in providing meaningful error-messages for combinator-based compilers.) But having mentioned these two differences, I would like to point out that I do not see this book as rivalling Peyton Jones's, but rather as complementing it. In the remainder of this Preface I give a detailed account of the contents of each Chapter in this book.

Chapter 1: Introduction

I begin this Chapter by discussing the concepts of *referential opacity* and *referential transparency*, since it is the fact that a functional programming language is referentially transparent that allows it to be translated into a term of combinatory logic. Then I briefly discuss Turner's language KRC—as I find this very useful in expressing algorithms—and to conclude I make a few observations about the user-interfaces that some important functional languages have.

Chapter 2: Lispkit Lisp

Because every purely functional programming language is essentially a version of the λ-calculus coated in syntactic sugar, I begin this Chapter on Lispkit by giving an informal account of the λ-notation. Then I describe the abstract syntax of Lispkit and after that its concrete syntax. This is followed by some examples of programs written in Lispkit. To conclude I describe what an interactive programming system that makes use of Lispkit might look like and make a few observations on the development of functional programming languages.

Chapter 3: Combinatory Logic

In this Chapter I introduce the basic ideas of combinatory logic. In the implementation scheme that I describe in Chapters 2 to 5 combinatory logic functions as the machine code that a purely applicative language is translated into. Once the translation has taken place, the resulting machine code program is executed by repeatedly performing head reductions on it until something printable is produced. In this Chapter I describe the main operators found in combinatory logic and the process of reduction.

I begin by giving an informal account of some of the basic combinators and then I provide a more rigorous presentation in which I define such fundamental notions as those of *reduction, conversion* and *normal form*. Then I introduce the notions of a *reduction path* and a *reduction strategy* and following that I carefully state some important theorems of combinatory logic relating to those notions, namely the Semi-standardization Theorem, the Standardization Theorem and the second Church–Rosser Theorem. Then I define the important concept of a *head normal form* and state Wadsworth's corollary of Curry's Standardization Theorem, which is an important result about head normal forms. This is followed by an account of combinatorial completeness. It is because combinatory logic possesses this property that it can be used to remove all the bound variables from a functional program.

The remainder of the Chapter is devoted to explaining how combinatory logic can function as the machine code into which a purely functional language is compiled. First, I introduce fixed-point combinators—these are necessary in order to implement recursion—and then I show how the natural numbers, the basic list-manipulating operators, the booleans and the conditional can all be modelled in *pure* combinatory logic, that is to say, in that version of combinatory logic which only contains two primitive combinators, namely **S** and **K**. To conclude the Chapter I mention that it is better to use a version of *illative* combinatory logic as the machine code for a reduction machine and I list all the illative atoms—and their reduction properties—that are needed in order to compile and execute Lispkit programs.

Chapter 4: Translating Lispkit into Combinators

In Chapter 2 I discuss the functional language Lispkit and in Chapter 3 the various systems of combinatory logic. The version presented at the end of Chapter 3 is going to serve as the machine code of the reducer described in Chapter 5 and in this Chapter I explain how it is possible to translate all the different constructs of Lispkit into the terms of combinatory logic.

Chapter 5: Graph-reduction

In Chapter 4 I show how a program written in Lispkit could be translated into a term of combinatory logic. In this Chapter I look at the way in which this term is evaluated by the method of graph-reduction. To be more specific, I discuss the way in which a CL-term is represented as a program graph in a reduction machine and how the process of reduction can be turned into a series of graph-transformations. I show how the program graph can be efficiently manipulated if we maintain an auxiliary data structure known as the left ancestors' stack and I mention the desirability of using indirection nodes in order to avoid re-evaluating the same expression in certain circumstances. To conclude I say something about how the interactive Lispkit system, mentioned at the end of Chapter 2, can be implemented.

Chapter 6: The Lambda Calculus

The λ-calculus is very similar to combinatory logic and as I deal with that fully in Chapter 3 I am brief in my account of the λ-calculus. After explaining the basic ideas of *substitution, reduction* and *conversion,* I give a succinct account of the semantics of the λ-calculus—which I use to justify the graph-transformation corresponding to the fixed-point combinator **Y**—and I conclude by saying something about the relationship that exists between combinatory logic and the λ-calculus.

Chapter 7: Bracket Abstraction Algorithms

In this Chapter I discuss several bracket abstraction algorithms. Following the precedent set in Curry and Feys (1958), pp. 190ff., these are usually presented in the guise of Markov algorithms. I therefore begin by introducing the fundamental ideas of such algorithms and then go on to discuss abstraction methods that use only a finite number of primitive combinators. This is followed by a number of algorithms which use infinitely many combinators. Such algorithms can be divided into two distinct types. On the one hand, there are those proposed by Abdali and Piperno, for example, which use a *fixed* set of combinators, because they are generated from a finite base. On the other, there are algorithms based on Hughes's notion of a supercombinator. The class of supercombinators needed in a particular abstraction is not given in advance, it is rather determined by the structure of the term on which the abstraction is being carried out. Supercombinator algorithms are discussed in Chapter 8.

Chapter 8: Supercombinators

In this Chapter I look at algorithms that make use of supercombinators. To begin with, I describe Burton's balancing transformation which is applied to a term before that term is subjected to bracket abstraction. Burton introduced the notion of a supercombinator—under the name of autonomous function—but his algorithm leaves a lot to be desired. Then I discuss Hughes's work which has led to the most efficient implementations of purely functional languages, namely those based on the G-machine. To conclude I compare Hughes's supercombinator abstraction algorithm with the multi-sweep version of Piperno's compositive abstraction algorithm discussed in Chapter 7.

Chapter 9: Pattern-matching

In this Chapter I explain how to translate functions that are defined using patterns—as is allowed in KRC—into a version of combinatory logic that includes the combinators *MATCH*, *TRY* and *FAIL*.

Chapter 10: Categorical Combinators

To begin with, in this Chapter I briefly explain the ideas of a Cartesian closed category and then I give an account of Curien's system of categorical combinatory logic CCL_β and also of Lins's simplified version of this. Then I explain de Bruijn's namefree notation for the λ-calculus and show how a namefree λ-term can be compiled into Lins's simplified categorical combinators. The structure of this Chapter is, therefore, the reverse of a compiler based on categorical combinators, since I first explain how to evaluate a CCL-term and only then do I show how a λ-term can be compiled into a CCL-term.

Chapter 11: Reduction and Transformation

The method of graph-reduction as a technique of implementation was first applied to the λ-calculus by Wadsworth (1971) and later extended to combinatory logic by Turner (1979b), but it is possible to use the method directly on the abstract syntax graph of the applicative program being evaluated. In this case the implementation technique is referred to as *source reduction*. This is not a particularly efficient way of implementing a functional language; its interest lies in the fact that it can be easily incorporated into a program transformation system and also in the fact that it can be modified to perform *partial evaluation* or *mixed computation*. The phrase 'mixed computation' is particularly apt, because what it refers to is a mixture of program evaluation and transformation. In this Chapter I begin by describing how source reduction works and then I give a brief introduction to program transformation. This includes an account of Wadler's method of compiling ZF-expressions and also of dependency analysis. After that I explain what partial evaluation is and mention how similar ideas can be incorporated into a combinator-based compiler to give meaningful run-time error messages.

Chapter 12: Strictness Analysis

Strictness analysis is a form of abstract interpretation and that is a compile-time technique which works on the text of the program being analysed and derives properties of the program by executing it on a restricted domain of values. It is very useful in improving the efficiency of implementations of functional languages. The structure of this Chapter is as follows. First I say what abstract interpretation is by considering the example of the rule of signs for multiplication. Then I explain the basic ideas of domain theory, paying special attention to the finding of least fixed-points. After that I present the abstraction rules that are used in the simplest kinds of strictness analysis and illustrate their use by means by a few easy examples.

Chapter 13: Type Systems

I begin this Chapter by motivating the inclusion of a polymorphic type discipline in a functional programming language. I do this by pointing out the limitations of both a typeless language like Lispkit and a monomorphically typed language like Pascal. Then I discuss some of the choices that have to be made by designers of polymorphic type systems and that is followed by an example of type inference.

Appendix A: Simple Lispkit System

The Appendix contains the Pascal source of a compiler and reducer for Lispkit and also a brief description of the program included. The implementation method used is that which is fully presented in Chapters 2 to 5. I begin by giving my reasons for including this program in this book and then I describe its three main parts, namely the parser, the translator and the reducer.

Some people will no doubt criticize my decision to include such a straightforward compiler and reducer, but I believe that presenting such a system is pedagogically beneficial, since the reader can all the more easily concentrate on the principles underlying the compilation process rather than be distracted by all the frills that would have to be included in a production compiler intended for serious work. In making this decision I was strongly influenced by Terry (1987), but rather than present a series of ever more sophisticated implementations—as he does—I have described only how the improvements can be made and hope that the reader will implement them himself. If he does, then he will learn much more than he would by reading someone else's solution expressed in their source code.

Glossary

The Glossary contains the explanations of a large number of the terms that are found in the literature about combinatory logic, graph-reduction, functional languages and their implementation. If the reader comes across a word or phrase that he does not understand while reading this book, then there is a good chance of it being included in the Glossary.

Annotated Bibliography

The Bibliography contains a comprehensive selection of the material that has been published on applicative languages and the various ways in which they can be implemented. I also include a Chapter by Chapter discussion of the relevant publications dealing with issues raised in each Chapter. This should help the reader to follow up any idea that he finds interesting.

Acknowledgements

I would like to thank Rachid Anane, Tom Axford, Chris Kindberg and Mike Joy for reading through drafts of parts of the material contained here and for making many helpful comments. They have saved me from making a number of mistakes, but—needless to say—I am solely responsible for any remaining errors.

Parts of Chapters 1 and 10 were presented as seminars at Leeds University and I am grateful for the comments of those who participated. Some of the material contained in Chapters 2 to 6 is based on my M.Sc. dissertation—Diller (1985)—which was supervised by Phil Wadler, from whom I learnt a lot. I am grateful to the SERC for financial support at that time.

Most of what I know about Lisp is due to numerous animated conversations with György Lajos and Mark Tarver.

The following trademarks are used in this book: 'Miranda' is a trademark of Research Software Ltd. 'Unix' is a trademark of AT & T Bell Laboratories. 'Ada' is a registered trademark of the US Government (Ada Joint Program Office).

Chapter 1

Introduction

1.1   Introduction

This book is about the compilation of functional programming languages. Such languages come in several varieties, as do their implementations. Here, I concentrate on purely functional languages which have a non-strict semantics. I restrict myself to a small number of implementation methods, all of whose origins can be traced back to a technique introduced by Turner (1979b), in which an applicative program is first translated into a term of combinatory logic (CL-term)—which is stored in the form of a graph—and then that "machine-code" program is executed by repeatedly performing graph-transformations on it until something printable—like a number or a list—is produced. This corresponds to successively carrying out head reductions on the non-graphical version of the CL-term involved. This execution strategy is known as lazy evaluation.

A *pure* functional language is one which has no assignment statement, is free from side effects and is referentially transparent. The characterization of applicative languages as lacking an assignment statement puts the emphasis on something negative and is about as useful in trying to understand the value of such languages as saying that structured programming is a good thing just because it avoids **goto** statements. Hughes (1984a, 1984b) has forcefully put the case for writing programs in a functional language because of the high-level structuring constructs that these contain, but it would be out of place to rehearse his arguments here as this is a book about implementation and not programming style. The fact that functional languages are referentially transparent is, however, of crucial importance to the implementation methods described here. I will, therefore, explain what referential

1

transparency means in greater detail later on in this Introduction.

A function is *strict* if its value is undefined whenever any of its arguments are, whereas a non-strict function can sometimes return a value even when some of its arguments are undefined.

Combinatory logic is a formal system devised by Curry in order to study the properties of functions and especially the properties of higher-order functions, that is to say, functions whose values and/or arguments are themselves functions. It is similar to Church's λ-calculus. One of the main differences is that combinators in combinatory logic are constants without a logically relevant internal structure, whereas combinators in the λ-calculus—that is to say, certain closed λ-terms—are made up out of simpler constituents.

The *reduction* process is similar to the method we use to calculate the value of an arithmetical expression, say $(7+81 \div 3) \times (253-45)$, by repeatedly evaluating parts of it to give, for example, the sequence of results $(7+27) \times (253-45)$, $34 \times (253-45)$, 34×208 and 7072. In the functional language case this "calculation" is carried out by a reducer. This is usually an abstract reduction machine simulated in software, but hardware implementations also exist.

Graph-reduction was introduced by Wadsworth (1971) in his doctoral dissertation. If a CL-term contains several identical occurrences of the same sub-expression, then the graphical representation of that term need only contain one node corresponding to that sub-expression, but that node will have as many edges leading to it as the number of its occurrences in the original term. Thus, evaluating that single node corresponds to evaluating each of its multiple occurrences in the original term and is, therefore, a more efficient method of reduction. Note that the evaluation of such shared sub-expressions is only possible in a referentially transparent notation.

The organization of this Chapter is as follows. In the next Section I explain what is meant by saying that a notation is referentially transparent and then I describe Turner's language KRC. This is done for two main reasons. The first is that I think its user-interface is superior to that of every other purely functional language that I know of and the second is that I express many algorithms in this book in a KRC-like notation, so—just in case the reader is unfamiliar with KRC—I describe its main features here.

1.2 Referential Transparency and Opacity

1.2.1 Referential Opacity in Philosophical Logic

The reason why a program written in a functional language can be translated into a term of combinatory logic is that such languages are *referentially transparent*. The concept of *referential transparency*—and its opposite, the concept of *referential opacity*—are taken over from the philosophy of language, where they are used to distinguish between two kinds of context.[1] A context here is to be understood as a sentence with a gap in it. A predicate, for example, is a context which has been formed from a sentence by the omission of a singular term. I will use the Greek letter ξ to indicate such gaps. A context $F\xi$ is, therefore, a function from singular terms to whole sentences.

An opaque context $F\xi$ is one which can result in a true sentence when its gap is filled by one singular term, say a, and in a false sentence when its gap is filled by another singular term, say b, even though it is true that $a = b$. Thus, substituting equals for equals in a sentence made up out of an opaque context does not necessarily preserve the meaning of that sentence. To put this more formally, an opaque predicate F is one for which the following inference schema does *not* hold:

$$Fa, a = b \vdash Fb,$$

where the turnstyle $\vdash$ is read 'therefore'. This schema yields valid inferences only if F is replaced by a predicate with a transparent argument-place.

As an illustration of this phenomenon I will use an example that occurs in Russell (1956a), p. 47. Consider the sentence:

> George IV wished to know whether Scott was the author of *Waverley*.

From this we can form the predicate:

> George IV wished to know whether Scott was ξ.

The argument-place in this predicate is referentially opaque because the following argument is invalid:

---

[1] The notion of transparency in this sense was introduced into logic by Whitehead and Russell (1925). See Appendix 3, entitled "Truth-Functions and Others", on pp. 659–666.

> George IV wished to know whether Scott was the author of *Waverley*,
>
> Scott was indeed the author of *Waverley*,
>
> therefore, George IV wished to know whether Scott was Scott.

This is invalid, for—as Russell adds on p. 48—'an interest in the law of identity can hardly be attributed to the first gentleman of Europe'.

Referential opacity is not, however, restricted to argument-places that are fitting for singular terms. The notion can be applied to any sort of argument-place. For example, if we remove the predicate 'ξ is a female fox' from the proposition:

> Jack believes that the animal in his garden is a female fox,

we get a referentially opaque context whose argument-place is fitting for a predicate:

> Jack believes that the animal in his garden is ϕ.

This context is referentially opaque because the following argument is not necessarily valid:

> Jack believes that the animal in his garden is a female fox,
>
> an animal is a female fox iff it is a vixen,
>
> therefore, Jack believes that the animal in his garden is a vixen.

This argument would be invalid if Jack did not know that a female fox was a vixen. The concepts *vixen* and *female fox* are extensionally identical, but they have different senses or intensions.

Needless to say, the notion of a referentially opaque context can be extended to argument-places that are fitting for expressions belonging to any syntactic category.

There are a large number of operators that create opaque contexts. As well as the epistemic operators *believes that*, *knows that* and *thinks that*, there are modal operators like *it must be the case that* and *it might be the case that* and deontic operators like *it ought to be the case that* and *it is permitted to be the case that*, to give just a few examples.

Although programming languages do not contain the sort of intensional operators that create the opaque contexts that I have been discussing, the terms *opacity* and *transparency* can still be used to describe them. An opaque construct in a programming language is one which cannot be used confidently in equational reasoning, whereas a transparent one does allow equals to be substituted for equals without change of meaning. It is the failure of equational reasoning that opaque notations share in logical systems and in programming languages.

1.2.2   Opaque Features of Imperative Languages

The first kind of opacity in imperative programming languages that I am going to consider arises because functions and procedures in such languages can have side effects, that is to say, they can alter variables which are not local to them. Consider, for example, the following global declarations in a Pascal program:

```
var
   x, y, global: Integer;
   b1, b2, b3, b4: Boolean;

function IsFunny (i: Integer): Boolean;
begin
   global := global + 1;
   IsFunny := i = global;
end;
```

Now consider the effect of the following compound statement:

```
begin
   global := 0;
   x := 1;
   y := 1;
   b1 := x = y;
   b2 := IsFunny (x);
   b3 := IsFunny (y);
   b4 := IsFunny (y);
end;
```

After this has been executed *b1* and *b2* are both true, but *b3* and *b4* are both false.

This feature of imperative programming languages is something that is completely alien to the language of mathematics. In mathematics functions

5

always return the same value if they are called with identical arguments. You do not expect $sin\ (\pi)$ to be 0 on one occasion and 1 on another, whereas this is a possibility that we must always be on the look out for in procedural languages.

The second kind of opacity that I want to consider arises in imperative languages because of the way they handle input and output operations. Consider, for example, the following global declarations in a Pascal program:

```
var
   sample: Text;

function MyRead (var f: Text): Char;
   var k: Char;
begin
   Read (f, k);
   MyRead := k;
end;
```

Now consider the following statement:

```
begin
   while not Eof (sample) do
      if MyRead (sample) = MyRead (sample) then
         WriteLn ('same')
      else
         WriteLn ('different')
end;
```

To begin with, it should be noted that a run-time error will occur if the file *sample* does not contain an even number of characters. The execution of the above statement will only result in the output

```
same
same
same
same
. . .
```

if the file *sample* is made up out of pairs of letters as, for example, in the file 'xxyyzzaa'. But the expression

6

```
MyRead (sample) = MyRead (sample)
```

cannot in general be guaranteed to be true.

The third source of opacity in imperative languages that I want to look at is the phenomenon of aliasing. This occurs when two variables both name the same cell in the computer's memory. The following example is derived from Axford (1986), p. 5. Consider these two Pascal functions:

```
procedure One (var x, y, z: Integer);
   var t: Integer;
begin
  t := x;
  x := y;
  y := z;
  z := t;
 end;
```

```
procedure Two (var x, y, z: Integer);
   var t: Integer;
begin
  t := y;
  y := z;
  z := x;
  x := t;
 end;
```

It may appear at first sight as if *One* and *Two* have the same effect, but the procedure call *One* (a, b, a) has no net effect on the global integer variables a and b—the values of a and b after the procedure call are the same, respectively, as their values before the procedure call—whereas after a call of *Two* (a, b, a) the values of a and b have been swapped. This is because in this case x and z are aliases for the same cell.

1.2.3 Opaque Features of Functional Languages?

Some functional languages contain opaque features because of the way in which they handle input and output. In Wadler's language Orwell, for example, there is a built-in function *keyboard*, of type *bool* → *list char*, such that *keyboard b* returns a list of what is typed on the keyboard until the next interrupt, that is to say, *control–A*. If *b* is true, then the typed characters are echoed to the screen; otherwise they are not. The function *keyboard* is opaque. The expression

$$keyboard\ True = keyboard\ True$$

is not necessarily true. It is so only if pairs of identical characters are typed on the keyboard, as in '$xxyyzzaa \uparrow A \uparrow A$'.[2] But there is no necessity for functional languages to deal with input and output operations in an opaque way. This matter is dealt with, for example, in Henderson and Jones (1984). They discuss other ways of handling interactive programs based on streams, that is to say, infinite sequences of characters or other data items.

1.3   Turner's Language KRC

In this Section I describe the KRC programming language and the way in which it is used in an interactive session. The material is based on Turner (1982b) and Bird and Hughes (1984).

There are four types of object in the KRC universe and these are integers, strings, lists and functions. Each of these is a first-class citizen in that any object of each type can be the value of an expression, the argument of a function, the value of a function or one of the elements of a list.

The usual operations on integers are provided, with % signifying the remainder operation. Strings are sequences of characters enclosed in double quotation marks and the standard operations on strings are provided.

1.3.1   Functions

Functions are defined by means of higher-order recursion equations. This can be done either interactively or by reading in the function definitions from a file. If you are using the KRC system interactively, then in order to enter a definition of a function you simply type it in. Using the sign '>' as the KRC prompt, in order to set up the definition of a function to calculate the greatest common divisor of two number *a* and *b*, you would type:

---

[2]This account is based on the 1985 version of Orwell, described in Wadler (1985a), but may not necessarily be true of later versions as the language is—at present—in a state of development.

$$
\begin{aligned}
>\ \ gcd\ a\ b\ &=\ gcd\ (a-b)\ b,\ a>b,\\
>\qquad\qquad &=\ gcd\ a\ (b-a),\ b>a,\\
>\qquad\qquad &=\ a.
\end{aligned}
$$

It should be noted that the punctuation marks at the extreme right of the lines in this definition—commas in the case of the first two lines and a full stop at the end of the third line—are not part of KRC syntax, but are added to clarify the discussion of KRC programs by making it clear which sentence they occur in and where in that sentence they occur. The expressions after the first comma in the first two lines are *guards*.

Function application is represented by juxtaposition, with a space separating the function from its argument, and it is the most tightly binding operation. It should be noted that the function *gcd* is a higher-order function of type $int \rightarrow (int \rightarrow int)$. Thus, *gcd* 7 is a function which makes integers out of integers. Note that brackets are not needed on the left-hand side of the definition of *gcd* as function application associates to the left. It is also possible for the arguments in a function definition to be place holders for functions as well as for objects, like integers.

KRC does not allow local definitions to be made, but the language can be easily extended to include them. The layout convention for such **whererec**-clauses should follow Landin's offside rule. Thus, a function *product*, which returns the product of all the integers in a list, can be defined using the function *foldright* as follows:

$$
\begin{aligned}
foldright\ f\ b\ &=\ g,\\
&\textbf{whererec}\\
&g\ [\ ] = b,\\
&g\ (a:x) = f\ a\ (g\ x),\\
mul\ x\ y\ &=\ x*y,\\
product\ &=\ foldright\ mul\ 1.
\end{aligned}
$$

1.3.2 Lists

Lists are just sequences of elements and in KRC they are represented by enclosing the members of the list in square brackets and separating them with commas. Thus, $[1,3,7,8,19]$ is a list of integers and $["feb","mar","dec"]$ is a list of strings. The elements of a list need not all be of the same type, but it is considered good programming practice not to construct lists with elements of different types.

Various operations on lists are provided. The infix operator : is the list constructor. List addition is represented by the infix operator $++$ and list subtraction by $--$. The prefix operator $\#$ returns the length of a list, *hd* returns its first element and *tl* the list consisting of everything except the first element. The use of *hd* and *tl* can generally be avoided because patterns are allowed on the left-hand sides of equations defining functions. A pattern is an expression made up out of variables, constants and the list constructor. Thus, the function *sum*, which returns the sum of all the integers in a list, can be defined as

$$sum\ [\ ]\ =\ 0,$$
$$sum\ (a:x)\ =\ a + sum\ x,$$

which is preferable to the definition involving *hd*, *tl* and explicit guards, namely

$$sum\ x\ =\ 0,\ x = [\ ],$$
$$=\ hd\ x + sum\ (tl\ x).$$

In the case of lists of integers the notation $[a..b]$ represents the list of length $b - a + 1$ whose first element is a and whose last element is b and in which each element, except the first, is one more than its predecessor. Lists made up of integers satisfying a different arithmetical progression are depicted by including a second element, thus $[3, 7..18]$ is $[3, 7, 11, 15]$. Note that the final integer in an abbreviated list need not be an element of the expanded list. Infinite lists can be represented in this way by leaving off the last element. Thus $[2, 4..]$ is the infinite list of even numbers.

1.3.3   ZF-expressions

ZF-expressions are derived from set comprehensions in set theory.[3] Set comprehensions allow sets to be formed from other sets. For example,

$$\{x | x \in female \wedge x \in married\},$$

is the set of all married women. Sometimes a colon is used instead of the vertical line, but mathematical notation is more fluid than a programming

---

[3]According to Wadler—in Peyton Jones (1987), p. 127—they were first incorporated into a functional language by Burstall in NPL.

language. KRC uses a semi-colon for this separator. ZF-expressions allow lists to be formed from other lists. For example, the KRC ZF-expression

$$\{x * x; x \leftarrow [1..10]; even\ x\},$$

evaluates to the list $[4, 16, 36, 64, 100]$, that is to say, the list of squares of all even numbers between 1 and 10. The above ZF-expression can be read: 'The list of all numbers $x * x$ such that x is drawn from the list $[1..10]$ and x is even'.

The general form of a ZF-expression in KRC is

$$\{e; q_1; q_2; \ldots; q_n\},$$

where e is an expression and each of the qualifiers q_i is either a generator or a filter. A *filter* is a predicate or boolean-valued expression and a *generator* is an expression of the form $a \leftarrow x$, where x must evaluate to a list, but a can be either a variable or a pattern.

Several abbreviations are allowed. If q_1 is a generator whose left-hand side is the same as e, then e can be omitted. If several generators $q_i ; \ldots ; q_{i+j}$ have the same right-hand side—so, for example, they are of the form $a \leftarrow x; b \leftarrow x; c \leftarrow x$—they can be combined to $a, b, c \leftarrow x$.

Some more examples of the use of ZF-expressions should clarify the above general discussion. The expression

$$\{[i, j]; i \leftarrow [1..10]; prime\ i; j \leftarrow [7..11]\},$$

evaluates to the list whose first few elements are

$$[[2, 7], [2, 8], [2, 9], [2, 10], [2, 11], [3, 7], [3, 8], \ldots].$$

Note that the variable in the rightmost generator, here j, varies most rapidly.

The next example comes from the KRC prelude, see Turner (1982b), p. 25:

$$perms\ [\ ] = [[\ ]],$$
$$perms\ x = \{a : p; a \leftarrow x; p \leftarrow perms\ (x - -[a])\}.$$

The function *perms* when applied to an arbitrary list y returns the list of all the permutations of elements of y. Thus, *perms* $[1, 2, 3]$ is

$$[[1, 2, 3], [1, 3, 2], [2, 1, 3], [2, 3, 1], [3, 1, 2], [3, 2, 1]],$$

The following program

$$primes \quad = \quad sieve\ [2..],$$

$$\textbf{whererec}$$

$$sieve\ (a:x) = a : sieve\ \{b \leftarrow x; b\%a \neq 0\},$$

defines the list *primes* of all the prime numbers.

1.3.4   The User-interface

KRC is particularly easy to use. It is even easier to use than, say, BASIC on a micro. I have already described how functions can be defined in an interactive KRC session. Assuming that the function *gcd* has been defined as described, then in order to execute a program you just enter the name of a function, followed by the appropriate number and type of arguments, and terminated by either an exclamation mark or a question mark (depending on how you want the output to be formatted). For example, entering:

$$> gcd\ 544\ 119?$$

results in the system responding with 17.

In order to display the definition of an already defined function you simply type that function name. For example, in order to display the definition of the function used to calculate the greatest common divisor of two numbers, you would type $>$ *gcd* and KRC would respond with

$$
\begin{aligned}
1)\quad gcd\ a\ b\ &=\ gcd\ (a-b)\ b,\ a > b,\\
2)\quad\quad\quad &=\ gcd\ a\ (b-a),\ b > a,\\
3)\quad\quad\quad &=\ a.
\end{aligned}
$$

Notice the presence of numerical labels on the extreme left of these equations. These are used in editing function definitions. The order of equations can be altered by the command */reorder*. Thus, */reorder gcd* 2 puts the second equation first. To delete a line in a function definition the command */delete* is used. Thus, */delete gcd* 3 would remove the third equation in the definition of *gcd*. Lines can be inserted by prefixing them by a number followed by a right parenthesis. Thus, 1.5) *gcd a b* = 1, *a* = 1 would insert a line in the definition of *gcd* between the first two lines. There are also other system commands available, but these should be sufficient to give you the flavour of the interactive system.

12

Miranda and Orwell can both be thought of as extensions of KRC—the major addition in both cases being the provision of a type system based on Milner (1978)—but, in my opinion, their user-interfaces are not as good as that of KRC. In Miranda a program is created using an editor and then that is compiled by the Miranda system, thus program development is very similar to that used in writing imperative programs, following an edit-compile-execute cycle. Orwell, on the other hand, is built on top of a screen editor—which is similar to that described in Sufrin (1982)—and you can ask for expressions to be evaluated from within an editor session. This is a novel way of using a functional language, but it is not one that I found particularly helpful in developing programs. At present, functional languages are mainly used for experimental programming, therefore their user-interfaces should be designed to facilitate such programming and not hinder it.

Chapter 2

Lispkit Lisp

2.1 Introduction

The functional language that I have chosen to serve as an example for a combinator-based implementation is a slight variant of Lispkit Lisp, which is described fully in Henderson (1980) and in Henderson, Jones and Jones (1983a, 1983b). I shall refer to this language as Lispkit and in this Chapter I briefly describe its main features.

Every purely functional programming language is essentially a version of the λ-calculus covered in syntactic sugar. Usually, the λ-calculus kernel is enriched in various ways, such as by the introduction of **let**- and **letrec**-clauses or by incorporating some form of type discipline. Henderson's language Lispkit is no exception to this. It is, in fact, simply a version of the type-free λ-calculus, with **let**- and **letrec**-clauses added, dressed up in the form of S-expressions, which should be familiar to anyone acquainted with Lisp. I, therefore, begin this Chapter by giving an informal account of the λ-notation. Then I describe the abstract syntax of Lispkit and after that I give its concrete syntax and some examples of programs written in it. To conclude I describe what an interactive programming system that makes use of Lispkit might look like.

2.2 Informal λ-notation

Later on in Chapter 6 I give a formal account of the λ-calculus; here, I just want to motivate the notation and introduce it informally. There are a number of differences between the λ-notation used in this Chapter and the

14

formal λ-calculus. In the informal λ-notation infix operators, like $+$ and $\div$, are used and arbitrary n-place functions are allowed, whereas in the formal calculus all operators are prefix and all functions are one-place ones. There are also some minor differences in the concrete syntax used.

The λ-notation is a way of making explicit that we are dealing with functions. Thus, Geach (1972), p. 119, suggests that the λ-expression

$$\lambda(x).(2x^2 + 3x^3),$$

should be read as 'this function of a number: twice its square *plus* thrice its cube'. There are many occasions when it is helpful to be aware that we are dealing with a function. Consider, for example, the following mathematical expression:

$$x^7 + y^2 x^5 + y^3. \tag{2.1}$$

This can be construed as a function of x or as a function of y or, indeed, as a function of both x and y simultaneously. If we differentiate the expression (2.1) with respect to x, keeping y constant, then we are treating it as a function of x:

$$\frac{d}{dx}(x^7 + y^2 x^5 + y^3) = 7x^6 + 5y^2 x^4. \tag{2.2}$$

But if we differentiate it with respect to y, keeping x constant, then we are treating it as a function of y:

$$\frac{d}{dy}(x^7 + y^2 x^5 + y^3) = 2y\dot{x}^5 + 3y^2. \tag{2.3}$$

Using the λ-notation we can easily distinguish between these cases. In the first case, when we treat expression (2.1) as a function of x, we are dealing with the function

$$\lambda(x).(x^7 + y^2 x^5 + y^3),$$

and in the second, when we treat expression (2.1) as a function of y, we are dealing with the function:

$$\lambda(y).(x^7 + y^2 x^5 + y^3).$$

Using the λ-notation equation (2.2) can be written in the form:

$$D(\lambda(x).(x^7 + y^2 x^5 + y^3)) = \lambda(x).(7x^6 + 5y^2 x^4),$$

where D is the differentiation operator, whose type is $(\mathbb{R} \to \mathbb{R}) \to (\mathbb{R} \to \mathbb{R})$, assuming that we are dealing with real functions as opposed, say, to complex ones. Equation (2.3) is transformed into

$$D(\lambda(y).(x^7 + y^2 x^5 + y^3)) = \lambda(y).(2yx^5 + 3y^2).$$

In the case when expression (2.1) is construed as a function of both x and y simultaneously it is represented in the λ-notation by the following term:

$$\lambda(x, y).(x^7 + y^2 x^5 + y^3).$$

In order to further motivate the use of the λ-notation I shall consider two more mathematical examples. In the first of these the λ-notation makes the presentation of the facts more perspicuous, whereas in the second it enables us to disambiguate standard mathematical notation.

The traditional notation for differentiation is cumbersome and unperspicuous in certain circumstances.[1] Say we want to know the value of the derivative of x^3 when $x = 4$. We have to resort to such notation as:

$$\left(\frac{d}{dx}x^3\right)_{x=4} = 3 \times 4^2.$$

Using the λ-notation this is easily expressed as:

$$D(\lambda(x).x^3)4 = 3 \times 4^2.$$

Since $D(\lambda(x).x^3)$ is $\lambda(x).3x^2$ the result of applying this to 4 is 3×4^2.[2]

There are cases when the λ-notation is useful in disambiguating standard mathematical idioms.[3] Consider, for example, the higher-order operator P, defined as follows:

$$P[f(x)] = \frac{f(x) - f(0)}{x}, \text{ if } x \neq 0.$$

What does $P[f(x + 1)]$ mean? There are two possibilities. In order to clearly state what these are using normal mathematical language we would have to introduce temporary function names. (a) To bring out the first way of construing $P[f(x + 1)]$, let $g(x) = f(x + 1)$, then $P[f(x + 1)]$ can be

---

[1] The following example is derived from Dummett (1981), pp. 40–43.

[2] In the formal λ-calculus the transition from $(\lambda(x).3x^2)4$ to 3×4^2 would be an instance of β-reduction.

[3] The following example is a slight simplification of one found in Curry and Feys (1958), pp. 81–83.

read as $P[g(x)]$. (b) To bring out the second way of reading $P[f(x+1)]$, let $h(x) = P[f(x)]$, then $P[f(x+1)]$ can be construed as $h(x+1)$.

There are circumstances when these two interpretations give different results, for example, when $f(x) = x^2$. Under interpretation (a) we have that $P[f(x+1)]$ is $x+2$, if $x \neq 0$. But under interpretation (b) we have that $P[f(x+1)]$ is $x+1$, if $x \neq 0$. These can be easily distinguished if we introduce an operator E defined as:

$$E(\lambda(x).f(x)) = \lambda(x).f(x+1).$$

Then, interpretation (a) of $P[f(x+1)]$ is represented by:

$$P[E(\lambda(x).f(x))],$$

and interpretation (b) by

$$E[P(\lambda(x).f(x))].$$

Equating $\lambda(x).f(x)$ with f, these are, respectively, $P(Ef)$ and $E(Pf)$.[4]

In most of the above examples of the usefulness of the λ-notation I have made use of the operation of differentiation. This is well suited to bringing out the utility of the λ-notation because differentiation is a higher-order function. Its type is, as already mentioned, $(\mathbb{R} \to \mathbb{R}) \to (\mathbb{R} \to \mathbb{R})$, that is to say, it yields a function of type $(\mathbb{R} \to \mathbb{R})$ when applied to another function of this type. In other words, both its arguments and values are functions from real numbers to real numbers. Higher-order functions are not very common in mathematics—as well as differentiation we could mention integration, summation and the various forms of taking limits—but they are commonplace in functional programming. In fact, this style of programming would be crippled if higher-order functions were not allowed to be first-class citizens along with constants and first-order functions. The use of higher-order functions leads to well-structured, modular and perspicuous functional programs.[5] It is not surprising, therefore, that applicative programming languages should be so intimately related to the λ-calculus, as one of the reasons that led Church to design this logical system was his interest in formalizing higher-order logics, that is to say, logics in which it is allowed to quantify over functions, predicates and propositions, as well as individuals.[6]

---

[4]In the formal λ-calculus the rule which allows us to equate $\lambda(x).f(x)$ with f is known as η-conversion.

[5]See, for example, Hughes (1984b) for good illustrations of these points.

[6]See Church (1956) and Andrews (1986) for accounts of higher-order logics.

17

2.3 The Abstract Syntax of Lispkit

Lispkit makes use of the integers, that is to say, the negative and positive whole numbers together with zero. It also uses variables and literal or symbolic constants. For the time being I shall use alphanumeric identifiers consisting entirely of lower-case letters for variables, whereas constants will be represented by sequences of upper-case letters. Thus, *alpha* and *beta* are variables, whereas *GAMMA* and *DELTA* are constants. Built-in functions represented by alphanumeric identifiers will also be written in lower-case.

The constants *TRUE* and *FALSE* are booleans which, not surprisingly, stand for truth and falsity, respectively. The built-in function *not* negates its single argument, which must evaluate to a boolean, and the truth-functions *and* and *or* have their usual meanings.

Lispkit contains a number of built-in numeric functions, such as addition $+$, subtraction $-$, multiplication $\times$, (integer) division $\div$ and the remainder operation, symbolized here as % and defined so that:

$$x \% y = x - y(x \div y).$$

There is also a one-place function *sq* which returns the square of its argument. The one-place numeric predicates *odd* and *even* have the obvious meanings as does the two-place predicate $\leq$.[7] The two-place identity predicate $=$ is also provided.

The only data structure supported in Lispkit is the list, which is represented as a sequence of items, separated by blanks, and enclosed in parentheses. The constant *NIL* represents the empty list and the primitive list destructors—*head* and *tail*—and the list constructor *cons* are provided. The predicate *null* tests to see whether its single argument is the empty list and returns *TRUE* if it is. The one-place predicate *atom* only returns *TRUE* if its argument is atomic. The identity predicate $=$ can be used to test two arbitrary lists for equality.

The final built-in function is *chr* which takes a numerical argument in the range 0 to 127 and returns the corresponding ASCII character.

Not all of these functions are primitives in Henderson's version of Lispkit. In particular, his implementation does not support primitive versions of *not, and, or, null, odd, even* and *sq*. Furthermore, the version of Lispkit described here does not contain the functions *explode* and *implode*, which

---

[7]A predicate is just a boolean-valued function none of whose arguments are themselves booleans.

Henderson's does. Also the semantics of the identity predicate are different. It corresponds to Henderson's *equal*, rather than to his *eq*.

2.3.1 Function Application

When the five arithmetical functions—namely $+, -, \times, \div$ and %—and the two predicates $\leq$ and $=$ are applied to their arguments this is depicted simply by placing the operator in question between its two arguments as, for example, in the cases $9 \leq maximum$, $5 \div size$ and $17 + 37$.

In the case of all the other two-place functions their arguments are written—enclosed in parentheses and separated by a comma—after the name of the function that is being applied to them. Examples of this are *cons* $(7, NIL)$ and *cons* (x, y).

In the case of a one-place function, application is represented by juxtaposition with the function-name appearing on the left. The argument can be enclosed in parentheses, but it does not have to be. Examples of this are: *sq* (7), *tail* $(ALPHA\ BETA\ GAMMA)$ and *odd* 8.

2.3.2 The Conditional

The abstract syntax of the conditional in Lispkit is

$$\textbf{if } b \textbf{ then } p \textbf{ else } q,$$

where b is an expression that evaluates to a truth-value. If b evaluates to *TRUE*, then the expression p is evaluated and if b evaluates to *FALSE*, then q is evaluated. For example, the conditional:

$$\textbf{if } 3 = 5 \textbf{ then } 7 \textbf{ else } 9,$$

is simply equivalent to 9.

2.3.3 Lambda Abstraction

The simplest form of lambda abstraction is that in which only a single variable is abstracted, as in $\lambda(x).e$. Here, the variable x immediately following the letter λ is said to be the *binding* occurrence of that variable and it *binds* any occurrences of x that might occur in e.[8] These occurrences—if any—of x are, thus, said to be *bound* by that binding occurrence. Any variable y, distinct from x, that occurs in e is said to be *free* in e.

---

[8]There is, of course, no necessity for e to contain any occurrences of x whatsoever.

19

The general form of a function abstraction looks like this:

$$\lambda(x_1, x_2, \ldots, x_n).e,$$

and it is a straightforward matter to extend the notions of *binding*, *bound* and *free* occurrences of variables to the n variables $x_1, x_2, \ldots, x_n$.

An example of the use of function abstraction is the expression:

$$\lambda(h).7 \div h, \qquad\qquad (2.4)$$

which defines a function that returns seven times the reciprocal of its argument h. The first occurrence of h in (2.4) is the *binding* occurrence and the second occurrence of h in (2.4) is *bound* by this binding occurrence.

As another example, consider the abstraction:

$$\lambda(x, y).\textbf{if } x \leq y \textbf{ then } y - x \textbf{ else } x - y,$$

which returns the absolute value of the difference between the two numbers x and y.

As already mentioned, Lispkit supports arbitrary n-place functions as well as higher-order functions. Therefore, we need to distinguish between the two-place function:

$$\lambda(x, y).(x - y) + (x \times y), \qquad\qquad (2.5)$$

and the higher-order one-place function:

$$\lambda(x).\lambda(y).(x - y) + (x \times y). \qquad\qquad (2.6)$$

The difference between these two can be brought out by realizing that the higher-order one-place function (2.6) can be partially parameterized by applying it to a single argument, whereas the two-place function cannot be applied to a single argument. Thus, applying (2.6) to the argument 7 yields:

$$(\lambda(x).\lambda(y).(x - y) + (x \times y))7,$$

which is the same as $\lambda(y).(7 - y) + (7 \times y)$, but (2.5) has to be applied to two arguments *simultaneously* to yield a meaningful result.

2.3.4 Let-clauses

The abstract representation of **let**-clauses can take two forms. It can be written as:

$$\text{let } x_1 = e_1 \text{ and } x_2 = e_2 \text{ and } \ldots \text{ and } x_n = e_n \text{ in } e, \qquad (2.7)$$

or it can be depicted in the following way:

$$e \text{ where } x_1 = e_1 \text{ and } x_2 = e_2 \text{ and } \ldots \text{ and } x_n = e_n. \qquad (2.8)$$

In both of these it is possible for n to be 0. An expression of the form $x_j = e_j$ in either (2.7) or (2.8) is known as either a *definition* or a *declaration*. The occurrences of the x_j on the left of the declarations in (2.7) and (2.8) are the *binding* occurrences. Any occurrences of the x_j in e are said to be *bound* by those binding occurrences, but any occurrences of the x_j in the e_k are *free*, even when $j = k$.

Such **let**-clauses are used to make non-recursive local definitions as, for example, in the case:

$$\text{let } y = 9 - 4 \text{ and } x = 5 \times 7 \text{ in } x + y.$$

This is equivalent to the expression formed by substituting $9 - 4$ for y and 5×7 for x in $x + y$, namely $(5 \times 7) + (9 - 4)$. Such substitutions can be represented by means of the notation:

$$[(9 - 4)/y, (5 \times 7)/x]x + y,$$

and this way of understanding **let**-clauses is true in general. Both of the expressions (2.7) and (2.8) are equivalent to:

$$[e_1/x_1, e_2/x_2, \ldots, e_n/x_n]e,$$

where it is to be understood that the substitutions of the e_j for the x_j are all to be performed simultaneously.

The above account of **let**-clauses has the consequence that:

$$\text{let } y = y - 4 \text{ and } x = y \times 7 \text{ in } x + y,$$

is equivalent to:

$$(y \times 7) + (y - 4), \qquad (2.9)$$

where y is assumed to be bound by some enclosing expression. If we do not perform the substitutions simultaneously but first substitute $y \times 7$ for x and then substitute $y - 4$ for y, that is to say, evaluate:

$$[y - 4/y]([y \times 7/x]x + y),$$

then we obtain:

$$((y - 4) \times 7) + (y - 4),$$

and this is not equivalent to (2.9). It is, of course, possible that there should be occasions on which this last expression is exactly what we wish to achieve. In that case, we have to use some nested **let**-clauses, as follows:

$$\textbf{let } y = y - 4 \textbf{ in } (\textbf{let } x = y \times 7 \textbf{ in } x + y). \tag{2.10}$$

Simultaneous declarations in a single **let**-clause should, therefore, be contrasted with nested **let**-clauses, since the two constructions can have different meanings.

Lispkit makes use of static binding. Under this binding mechanism the meaning of a variable is determined when it is defined and not when it is used. It is usually contrasted with dynamic binding in which the value of a variable is only fixed in the calling environment. Consider, for example, the Lispkit clause:

$$\textbf{let } x = 7 \textbf{ in } (\textbf{let } g = \lambda(z).(x \times z) \textbf{ in } (\textbf{let } x = 3 \textbf{ in } g(5))).$$

Under static binding the result is 35, but in dynamic binding the result would be 15.

The version of Lispkit that I am considering is also a lazily implemented language and that affects the way in which **let**-clauses are to be interpreted. For example, an expression **let** $x = e$ **in** f can have a meaning even if e is meaningless. A concrete example of this is the expression **let** $x = 7 \div 0$ **in** $3 + y$, which is equivalent to $3 + y$ although $7 \div 0$ is undefined, that is to say, meaningless. In a language with a strict semantics expressions like **let** $x = 7 \div 0$ **in** $3 + y$ are themselves undefined.

2.3.5   Letrec-clauses

The abstract representation of **letrec**-clauses can take two forms. It can be written as:

$$\textbf{letrec } x_1 = e_1 \textbf{ and } x_2 = e_2 \textbf{ and } \ldots \textbf{ and } x_n = e_n \textbf{ in } e,$$

or it can be depicted in the following way:

$$e \text{ whererec } x_1 = e_1 \text{ and } x_2 = e_2 \text{ and } \ldots \text{ and } x_n = e_n.$$

In either of these it is possible for n to be 0.

Such **letrec**-clauses are used to make recursive local definitions, and—apart from the fact that the keyword is either **letrec** or **whererec** and neither **let** nor **where**—the syntax of **letrec**-clauses is exactly the same as that of **let**-clauses. Also—just as in **let**-clauses—the x_j on the left of the declarations are the *binding* occurrences. They bind any occurrences of the x_j in e, which are thus said to be *bound*, but—unlike **let**-clauses—they also bind any occurrences of the x_j in the e_k. Thus allowing recursive functions and mutually recursive functions to be defined. For example, the factorial function *fact* can be defined and used in this way:

$$\text{letrec } fact = \lambda(i).\textbf{if } i = 0 \textbf{ then } 1 \textbf{ else } fact\,(i-1) \textbf{ in } fact\,(7).$$

The implementation of Lispkit being discussed here uses lazy evaluation. One of the consequences of this is that it is possible to define and manipulate infinite data structures. The function *cons*, for example, is not strict in either of its argument-places. Thus, we can define the infinite list of non-negative natural numbers as:

$$\text{letrec } from = \lambda(i).cons\,(i, from\,(i+1)) \textbf{ in } from\,(0).$$

2.4 The Concrete Syntax of Lispkit

2.4.1 S-expressions

In common with other dialects of Lisp, a Lispkit program is written in the form of an S-expression, which is either an atom or a dotted pair, each of whose components is an S-expression. Dotted pairs are enclosed in parentheses and separated by a full stop in the concrete syntax. There are two sorts of atom, namely the literal and the numeric. In the version of Lispkit used here only whole numbers are supported. This restriction was adopted in order to make the implementation more straightforward. Thus, the following are examples of numeric atoms: 15, 7, -8 and 985.

A literal atom is an alphabetic character followed by zero, one or more alphanumeric characters. Thus, the following are examples of literal atoms: *alpha*, *x*, *Thing567* and *BIG*. Note that lower-case and capital letters are considered to be different from one another.

The following are examples of S-expressions:

```
alpha,

(alpha . beta),

(alpha . (beta . gamma)),

((alpha . (beta . gamma)) . delta),

(alpha . (beta . (gamma . delta))).
```

So far each dotted pair has been enclosed in a single pair of parentheses, but there is an abbreviatory convention in Lispkit—as there is in other Lisps—which allows certain combinations of full stops and parentheses to be omitted. The rule in question states that the combination of signs '.(', together with the corresponding closing bracket ')', may be removed as many times as we wish from any S-expression in which they occur.[9] Making use of this rule we can abbreviate:

```
(alpha . (beta . gamma)),
```

to the simpler form:

```
(alpha  beta . gamma),
```

and the S-expression:

```
(alpha . (beta . (gamma . delta))),
```

becomes—after two applications of the rule—the simpler:

```
(alpha  beta  gamma . delta).
```

---

[9]See Danicic (1983), pp. 1–2, for a clear statement of this and the next abbreviatory convention.

The literal atom *NIL* plays a special role in Lispkit. It represents the empty list. S-expressions containing *NIL* can sometimes be written in a more succinct way. It is allowed to replace the S-expression

```
(alpha  beta  gamma . NIL),
```

by

```
(alpha  beta  gamma).
```

That is to say, it is possible to remove the combination of signs '. *NIL*' from the end of a larger expression. An S-expression of the form:

```
(alpha  beta  gamma  delta),
```

is known as a *list*.

2.4.2 Application Clauses

In the abstract syntax of Lispkit if we want to express the fact that the n-place function f is applied to n arguments $e_1, e_2, \ldots, e_n$, we write:

$$f(e_1, e_2, \ldots, e_n),$$

whereas in the concrete syntax this is written as $(n + 1)$-list:

$$(f' \ e_1' \ e_2' \ \ldots \ e_n' \ ),$$

where e' indicates the concrete version of the abstract item e. For example, Lispkit contains the predefined function *chr*, which takes a numeric atom as its single argument and returns the character which has that number as its ASCII code as its value. So,

```
(chr (quote 71)),
```

is the character F. Note that I have written:

25

```
(quote 71).
```

This is how constants are expressed in Lispkit.

2.4.3 Built-in Lispkit Functions

The account of function application just given explains how all the prefix operators in the abstract syntax are represented in the concrete syntax. The only thing that remains to be shown is how to represent the infix operators. This is entirely straightforward. The arithmetical expressions $x + y$, $x \times y$, $x - y$, $x \div y$ and $x \% y$ become, respectively, $(add\ x'\ y')$, $(mul\ x'\ y')$, $(sub\ x'\ y')$, $(div\ x'\ y')$ and $(rem\ x'\ y')$, where x' represents the concrete version of x. Similarly, the relational expression $x = y$ becomes $(eq\ x'\ y')$ and $x \leq y$ becomes $(leq\ x'\ y')$.

2.4.4 The Conditional

Because Lispkit is implemented here in a lazy fashion, the conditional can be thought of as just a three-place function. Thus, the abstract conditional

$$\textbf{if } b \textbf{ then } p \textbf{ else } q,$$

becomes the S-expression

$$(if\ b'\ p'\ q').$$

In strict languages, like Franz Lisp and Scheme, the conditional has to be thought of as a special form, because it cannot be evaluated in the usual way, which is to first evaluate the arguments of a function and then to apply the function to those arguments.

2.4.5 Lambda Clauses

The abstract form of a λ-abstraction:

$$\lambda(x_1, x_2, \ldots, x_n).e,$$

becomes in the concrete syntax the following S-expression:

$$(lambda\ (x_1\ x_2\ \ldots\ x_n)\ e'),$$

where e' represents the concrete form of the abstract e. Atoms are assumed to be the same in both abstract and concrete versions.

26

2.4.6 Let-clauses

The abstract form of a **let**-clause, namely either:

$$\text{let } x_1 = e_1 \text{ and } x_2 = e_2 \text{ and } \ldots \text{ and } x_n = e_n \text{ in } e,$$

or the equivalent:

$$e \text{ where } x_1 = e_1 \text{ and } x_2 = e_2 \text{ and } \ldots \text{ and } x_n = e_n,$$

becomes in the concrete syntax the S-expression:

$$(\textit{let } e' \, . \, ((x_1.e_1') \, (x_2.e_2') \, \ldots \, (x_n.e_n'))),$$

which is equivalent to:

$$(\textit{let } e' \, (x_1.e_1') \, (x_2.e_2') \, \ldots \, (x_n.e_n')).$$

2.4.7 Letrec-clauses

The abstract form of a **letrec**-clause, namely either:

$$\text{letrec } x_1 = e_1 \text{ and } x_2 = e_2 \text{ and } \ldots \text{ and } x_n = e_n \text{ in } e,$$

or the equivalent:

$$e \text{ whererec } x_1 = e_1 \text{ and } x_2 = e_2 \text{ and } \ldots \text{ and } x_n = e_n,$$

becomes in the concrete syntax the S-expression:

$$(\textit{letrec } e' \, . \, ((x_1.e_1') \, (x_2.e_2') \, \ldots \, (x_n.e_n'))),$$

which is equivalent to:

$$(\textit{letrec } e' \, (x_1.e_1') \, (x_2.e_2') \, \ldots \, (x_n.e_n')).$$

2.4.8 A Grammar for Lispkit

Although every Lispkit program is an S-expression, not every S-expression is a meaningful Lispkit program. A Lispkit program is an S-expression of a certain form. The forms in question are defined by singling out a certain class of symbolic atoms as reserved words or standing for built-in functions. In Lispkit these are:

```
let       add       rem       leq       atom      and       NIL
letrec    sub       sq        eq        null      or        TRUE
lambda    mul       odd       head      if        chr       FALSE
quote     div       even      tail      not       cons
```

In terms of these a Lispkit program can be defined as follows:

```
<program> ::= <application-clause>

    | <letrec-clause>

    | <let-clause>

    | <quote-clause>

<application-clause> ::= <clause-list>

<clause-list> ::= (quote NIL)

    | (<one-place-op> <clause>)

    | (<two-place-op> <clause> <clause>)

    | (<three-place-op> <clause> <clause> <clause>)

    | (<non-empty-clause-seq>)

<non-empty-clause-seq> ::= <clause>

    | <clause> <non-empty-clause-seq>

<one-place-op> ::= sq | odd | even | head

    | tail | atom | null | not | chr

<two-place-op> ::= add | sub | mul | div | rem
```

28

```
      | leq | eq | and | or | cons

<three-place-op> ::= if

<clause> ::= <letrec-clause>

      | <let-clause>

      | <lambda-clause>

      | <quote-clause>

      | <application-clause>

      | <name>

<letrec-clause> ::= (letrec <clause> . <declaration-list>)

<let-clause> ::= (let <clause> . <declaration-list>)

<lambda-clause> ::= (lambda <argument-list> <clause>)

<quote-clause> ::= (quote <S-expression>)

<declaration-list> ::= (quote NIL)

      | (<non-empty-declaration-seq>)

<non-empty-declaration-seq> ::= (<name> . <clause>)

      | (<name> . <clause>) <non-empty-declaration-seq>

<argument-list> ::= (quote NIL)

      | (<non-empty-argument-seq>)

<non-empty-argument-seq> ::= <name>

      | <name> <non-empty-argument-seq>
```

```
<S-expression> ::= <atom>

    | (<S-expression-seq>)

<S-expression-seq> ::= <S-expression>

    | <S-expression> . <S-expression>

    | <S-expression> <S-expression-seq>

<atom> ::= <name> | <numeral>

<name> ::= <letter> | <digit> <name> | <letter> <name>

<numeral> ::= <digit> | <digit> <numeral>

<letter> ::= a | b | ... | z | A | B | ... | Z

<digit> ::= 0 | 1 | ... | 9
```

2.5   Some Examples of Lispkit Programs

In order to illustrate the above discussion of the syntax of Lispkit I will give some examples of Lispkit programs. The purpose of this Section is not that of being an introduction to programming in a functional language[10] but, rather, to illustrate the syntactic constructs available in Lispkit. The programs are not necessarily the most efficient possible; they have been chosen just to illustrate Lispkit's capabilities.

2.5.1   The Fibonacci Numbers

The Fibonacci numbers are defined in the following way:

$$fib\ 0 \ = \ 0,$$

---

[10] The books by Bird and Wadler (1988), Henderson (1980) and Henson (1987) contain good introductions to functional programming. Both Abelson and Sussman (1985) and Wikström (1987) are also useful, although neither use a lazy language.

30

$$fib\ 1\ =\ 1,$$
$$fib\ n\ =\ fib\ (n-1) + fib\ (n-2), n > 1.$$

This can be easily translated into Lispkit and incorporated into a program to calculate, for example, the seventh Fibonacci number. In the abstract syntax the program is:

$$fib\ (7)\ \textbf{whererec}$$
$$fib\ =\ \lambda(n).\textbf{if}\ n = 0\ \textbf{then}\ 0\ \textbf{else if}\ n = 1\ \textbf{then}\ 1$$
$$\textbf{else}\ fib\ (n-1) + fib\ (n-2).$$

The concrete form of this program is represented by the following S-expression:

```
(letrec
  (fib (quote 7))
    (fib lambda (n)
      (if (eq n (quote 0))
          (quote 0)
          (if (eq n (quote 1))
              (quote 1)
              (add (fib (sub n (quote 1)))
                   (fib (sub n (quote 2)))))))))).
```

A more efficient definition of the Fibonacci numbers makes use of an auxiliary function, say, f:

$$fib\ n = f\ 0\ 1\ n,$$

where f is defined in this way:

$$f\ a\ b\ 0\ =\ f\ a,$$
$$f\ a\ b\ n\ =\ f\ b\ (a+b)\ (n-1), n > 0.$$

This method of calculating the Fibonacci numbers illustrates the programming technique of *accumulating parameters* and the variables a and b in the definition of f are known as *accumulators*.[11] Whereas the previous algorithm has an exponential time complexity, this one is linear. It is used in the following Lispkit program, which again calculates the seventh Fibonacci number:

[11] For further discussion of this see Allen (1978), pp. 443–50, and Henderson (1980), pp. 33–37.

```
(letrec
  (let
    (fib (quote 7))
      (fib lambda (n)
        (f (quote 0) (quote 1) n)))
    (f lambda (a b n)
      (if (eq n (quote 0))
          a
          (f b (add a b)
            (sub n (quote 1))))))).
```

Yet another efficient way of defining the Fibonacci numbers makes use of the potentially infinite list of these numbers. The idea involved is closely related to that of memo functions, as introduced by Michie (1968) and used, for example, by Turner (1981c), p. 92. In KRC this would be programmed as:

$$
\begin{aligned}
fib\ 0 &= 0, \\
fib\ 1 &= 1, \\
fib\ n &= select\ (n-1)\ fiblist + select\ (n-2)\ fiblist, \\
\\
fiblist &= map\ fib\ [0..], \\
\end{aligned}
$$

$$
\begin{aligned}
select\ 0\ (a:x) &= a, \\
select\ n\ (a:x) &= select\ (n-1)\ x,\ n > 0.
\end{aligned}
$$

In Lispkit the relevant program to calculate the seventh Fibonacci number using this technique is:

```
(letrec (fib (quote 7))
  (fib lambda (n)
    (if (eq n (quote 0))
        (quote 0)
        (if (eq n (quote 1))
            (quote 1)
            (add (select (sub n (quote 1)) fiblist)
```

32

```
                  (select (sub n (quote 2)) fiblist)))))
    (fiblist map fib (from (quote 0)))
    (select lambda (n x)
       (if (eq n (quote 0))
            (head x)
            (select (sub n (quote 1)) (tail x))))
    (map lambda (f x)
       (if (eq x (quote NIL))
            (quote NIL)
            (cons (f (head x))
                  (map f (tail x)))))
    (from lambda (i)
       (cons i (from (add i (quote 1)))))))).
```

The algorithm used here to calculate Fibonacci numbers is again linear, but it has the advantage—according to Turner—of preserving the structure of the "obvious" mathematical definition of these numbers.

Yet another way of calculating the Fibonacci numbers involves the use of continuations.[12] This definition of the Fibonacci numbers makes use of an auxiliary function f of type $int \to (int \to int) \to int$. The second argument to f is the continuation.

$$
\begin{aligned}
\text{fib } n &= f\, n\, \mathbf{I}, \\
f\, 0\, g &= g\, 0, \\
f\, 1\, g &= g\, 1, \\
f\, n\, g &= f\, (n-1)\, (\mathbf{B}\, g\, (\lambda(i).i + \text{fib}\, (i-2))), \\
\mathbf{I}\, x &= x, \\
\mathbf{B}\, f\, g\, x &= f\, (g\, x).
\end{aligned}
$$

This can be coded in Lispkit as follows, using *id* for **I** and *comp* for **B**:

```
(letrec
   (fib (quote 7))
      (fib lambda (n) (f n id))
      (id lambda (x) x)
```

---

[12]See Henderson (1980), pp. 250–251 and 269–272, Henson (1987), pp. 190–209, and Wand (1980) for the use of continuations in functional programming.

```
(f lambda (n) (lambda (g)
   (if (eq n (quote 0))
       (g (quote 0))
       (if (eq n (quote 1))
           (g (quote 1))
           (f (sub n (quote 1))
              (comp g (lambda (i)
                 (add i (fib (sub n (quote 2)))))))))))
(comp lambda (f) (lambda (g) (lambda (x) (f (g x)))))).
```

2.5.2 Programs Involving Homomorphisms

An important and very useful higher-order function in applicative programming is *foldright*, which can be defined in KRC as:

$$
\begin{aligned}
foldright\ f\ b\ [\ ] &= b,\\
foldright\ f\ b\ (a:x) &= f\ a\ (foldright\ f\ b\ x).
\end{aligned}
$$

This is just a special case of the list homomorphism operator *hom*, since

$$foldright\ f = hom\ f\ \mathbf{I},$$

where $\mathbf{I}$ is the identity function.[13] The homomorphism *hom* is defined in the following way:

$$
\begin{aligned}
hom\ f\ g\ b\ [\ ] &= b,\\
hom\ f\ g\ b\ (a:x) &= f\ (g\ a)\ (hom\ f\ g\ b\ x).
\end{aligned}
$$

The function *foldright* can be used in the definition of many other functions. For example, in the following Lispkit program it is used in the definition of the function *sum* which adds together all the arguments in a list of numbers:

```
(letrec (sum (quote (1 2 3 4 5 6 7)))
   (plus lambda (x) (lambda (y) (add x y)))
   (sum lambda (z) (foldright plus (quote 0) z))
   (foldright lambda (f b xs)
```

---

[13] In fact, it suffices to use just the *right* identity of f here, that is to say, the function $\mathbf{I}_R$ such that $f \circ \mathbf{I}_R = f$, where $\circ$ is functional composition. The Glossary contains more information about homomorphisms in functional programming.

```
(if (eq xs (quote NIL))
    b
    (f (head xs) (foldright f b (tail xs)))))).
```

In the next Lispkit program *foldright* is used in the definition of *product*, which returns the product of all the arguments in a list:

```
(letrec (product (quote (1 2 3 4 5 6 7)))
   (times lambda (x) (lambda (y) (mul x y)))
   (product lambda (z) (foldright times (quote 1) z))
   (foldright lambda (f b xs)
              (if (eq xs (quote NIL))
                  b
                  (f (head xs) (foldright f b (tail xs)))))).
```

2.5.3 Linear Search

The Lispkit function *member* is a predicate which returns *TRUE* only if a is an element in the list x and the function *search*, when applied to an object a and a list x, returns 0 if a is not in x but otherwise returns the index of a's location in x.

```
(letrec
   (search (quote gg) (quote (fg sd cg vh vh tg ss dd ff)))
   (search lambda (a x)
              (if (member a x)
                  (if (eq a (head x))
                      (quote 1)
                      (add (quote 1)
                           (search a (tail x))))
                  (quote 0)))
   (member lambda (a x)
              (if (eq (quote NIL) x)
                  (quote FALSE)
                  (if (eq a (head x))
                      (quote TRUE)
                      (member a (tail x)))))).
```

2.5.4 Quicksort

The following Lispkit version of Hoare's Quicksort algorithm makes use of the auxiliary functions *append*, which joins two lists together, *lt*, which, when applied to a number a and a list of numbers x, returns the list of all those numbers in x that are less than or equal to a, and *gt*, which, when applied to a number a and a list of numbers x, returns the list of all those numbers in x that are greater than a. This version of Quicksort can only be used to sort numbers. It is a fairly straightforward translation into Lispkit of the KRC definition of Quicksort involving ZF-expressions, namely[14]

$$qs\,[\,] \;=\; [\,],$$
$$qs\,(a:x) \;=\; \{b; b \leftarrow x; b \leq a\} + +[a] + +\{b; b \leftarrow x; a < b\}.$$

In the following Lispkit program the Quicksort function qs is used to sort a list of eight numbers.

```
(letrec
   (qs (quote (7 1 3 4 8 6 22 8)))
     (qs lambda (ys)
           (if (eq (quote NIL) ys)
               ys
               (append (qs (lt (head ys) (tail ys)))
                       (cons (head ys)
                             (qs (gt (head ys) (tail ys)))))))))
     (append lambda (z y) (foldright kons y z))
     (kons lambda (x) (lambda (y) (cons x y)))
     (foldright lambda (f b xs)
                   (if (eq xs (quote NIL))
                       b
                       (f (head xs)
                          (foldright f b (tail xs)))))
     (lt lambda (a x)
           (if (eq (quote NIL) x)
               (quote NIL)
```

---

[14]This definition is from Meira (1983), p. 16. For a different Lispkit version of Quicksort see Henderson, Jones and Jones (1983b), p 103.

```
              (if (leq (head x) a)
                  (cons (head x) (lt a (tail x)))
                  (lt a (tail x)))))
(gt lambda (a x)
      (if (eq (quote NIL) x)
          (quote NIL)
          (if (leq (head x) a)
              (gt a (tail x))
              (cons (head x) (gt a (tail x))))))))).
```

2.6   An Improved Lispkit System

So far I have only described a programming environment for Lispkit in which
a program has to be a single S-expression which evaluates either to an atom
or to a list. In a combinator-based compiler, as described in the Appendix,
this S-expression will be translated into a term of combinatory logic and
that will be evaluated by repeatedly performing head reductions on it until
a term in head normal form is encountered. If no programming errors have
been made, the result will be something printable. Such a system has many
limitations and in practice it is better to build a programming environment
in which it is possible to define functions interactively and also to ask for
them to be evaluated interactively, as in most Lisp systems. In such an
environment a function definition would be entered in as, say:

```
(def <name> <lambda-clause>),
```

where *def* is a new reserved word indicating that a definition is being made
and <*name*> is the name of the function being defined. So, the definition
of a function which cubes its argument would be:

```
(def cube (lambda (x) (mul x (mul x x)))).
```

It is permissible to include the name of the function being defined in its
body, thus:

```
(def factorial
  (lambda (x)
    (if (eq x (quote 0))
        (quote 1)
        (mul x (factorial (sub x (quote 1)))))))).
```

It is also possible to define functions that are mutually recursive. Thus, the following would be a legitimate terminal session. Here, the symbol ==> is to be understood as the system's prompt.

```
==> (def gt (lambda (x xs)
          (if (eq (quote NIL) xs)
              (quote NIL)
              (if (leq (head xs) x)
                  (gt x (tail xs))
                  (cons (head xs) (gt x (tail xs))))))

==> (def foldright (lambda (f b xs)
                  (if (eq xs (quote NIL))
                      b
                      (f (head xs)
                         (foldright f b (tail xs))))))

==> (def kons (lambda (x) (lambda (y) (cons x y))))

==> (def append (lambda (z y) (foldright kons y z)))

==> (def lt (lambda (x xs)
          (if (eq (quote NIL) xs)
              (quote NIL)
              (if (leq (head xs) x)
                  (cons (head xs) (lt x (tail xs)))
                  (lt x (tail xs))))))

==> (def qs (lambda (ys)
          (if (eq (quote NIL) ys)
              ys
```

38

```
                (append (qs (lt (head ys) (tail ys)))
                        (cons (head ys)
                              (qs (gt (head ys) (tail ys)))))))))

==> (qs (quote (5 4 9 2 33 66 1 3)))

(1 2 3 4 5 9 33 66)
```

Although the syntax for *def* is taken from Franz Lisp, the syntax for the
defining bodies is just the Lispkit that I have already explained. In such a
system we could also define atoms to be constants and not just functions,
thus:

```
==> (def two (quote 2)),
```

and possibly other Lispkit objects, such as infinite lists, thus:

```
==> (def from (lambda (x) (cons x (from (add x (quote 1)))))),

==> (def ones (from (quote 1))).
```

In the sample terminal session given above involving the Quicksort function
qs the series of function definitions can be schematically represented as

$$(def\ f_1\ e_1)$$
$$(def\ f_2\ e_2)$$
$$...$$
$$(def\ f_n\ e_n)$$
$$(f_i\ a_1\ a_2\ ...\ a_m)$$

and this is equivalent to the following Lispkit program:

$f_i(a_1, a_2, \ldots, a_m)$ **whererec** $f_1 = e_1$ **and** $f_2 = e_2$ **and** $\ldots$ $f_n = e_n$.

This is true in general only in those cases in which $f_i = f_j$ only if $i = j$. A
question that needs to be resolved, therefore, is what happens if we redefine
a function or constant in a single interactive session. For example, in this
way:

```
(def x (quote 3))
(def f (lambda (y) (add y x)))
(def x (quote 5))
(f (quote 4))
```

Should we insist on static binding or not? In the static case the result would be 7, but in the dynamic situation it would be 9. It seems to make sense to allow dynamic binding at the top level of an interactive system, but to retain static binding within each function definition. This can be seen as a concession to the interactive environment. In practice it means that if the function f is defined more than once, then the latest one is the only one that is used in any evaluation request.

Although the interactive programming environment just described will—superficially—resemble a Franz Lisp system, there are a number of significant differences. In the first place, the enhanced Lispkit system supports lazy evaluation, whereas Franz Lisp uses applicative order reduction. In the second place, it is possible to have local **let**- and **letrec**-clauses inside the defining body of a function. Thirdly, no imperative features—such as *setq* or *prog*—are supported; the language is entirely free from opaque constructs.

2.7 The Development of Functional Languages

Above I described an interactive Lispkit system in which function definitions were given in the form

$$(\mathit{def}\ f\ (\mathit{lambda}\ (x_1\ x_2\ \ldots\ x_n)\ e)).$$

Some Lisp systems allow you to define the function f in this way

$$(\mathit{define}\ (f\ x_1\ x_2\ \ldots\ x_n)\ e),\qquad(2.11)$$

and this is closer to the syntax of a function definition in KRC, which is

$$f\ x_1\ x_2\ \ldots\ x_n = e.\qquad(2.12)$$

One of the differences between (2.11) and (2.12) is that (2.11) defines an n-place function, whereas (2.12) defines a higher-order one-place function.

One way of looking at the developments of functional languages in recent years is that, as time goes by, increasingly complicated expressions are

40

allowed on the left-hand sides of function definitions. In KRC, for example, the x_i in (2.12) can be arbitrary patterns made up out of variables, constants and the list constructor. Thus, a function *length* to find the length of a list could be defined as:

$$\begin{aligned} length\ x &= len\ x\ 0, \\ len\ [\ ]\ n &= n, \\ len\ (a:x)\ n &= len\ x\ (n+1). \end{aligned}$$

In Miranda, the x_i in (2.12) can be arbitrary patterns as in KRC, but also user-defined type constructors are allowed to occur in the terms x_i and they can also be of the form $n+1$. Thus, factorial can be defined as

$$\begin{aligned} fact\ 0 &= 1, \\ fact\ (n+1) &= (n+1)*fact\ n. \end{aligned}$$

It is possible to have even more complicated expressions on the left in a function "definition". In a subtree replacement system—as described in O'Donnell (1977), for example—user-defined function symbols can occur in the terms x_i in (2.12). For example, if we were defining a group of functions dealing with stacks, we could have

$$top\ (push\ a\ x) = x, \tag{2.13}$$

where *top* and *push* have been previously defined as

$$\begin{aligned} top\ (a:x) &= a, \tag{2.14} \\ push\ a\ x &= a:x. \tag{2.15} \end{aligned}$$

In such circumstances (2.13) can no longer be viewed as a function definition, since (2.14) defines *top*. Here, we are moving into the area of general rewrite systems and algebraic specification languages, such as OBJ2, described in Sridhar (1986).

Chapter 3

Combinatory Logic

3.1 Introduction

In this Chapter I introduce the basic ideas of combinatory logic. In the
implementation scheme that I describe in Chapters 2 to 5 combinatory logic
functions as the machine code that a purely applicative language is translated into.[1] Once the translation has taken place, the resulting machine
code program is executed by repeatedly performing head reductions on it
until something printable is produced. In this Chapter I describe the main
operators found in combinatory logic and the process of reduction.

I begin by giving an informal account of some of the basic combinators
and then I provide a more rigorous presentation in which I define such fundamental notions as those of *reduction, conversion* and *normal form*. Then
I introduce the notions of a *reduction path* and a *reduction strategy* and
following that I carefully state some important theorems of combinatory
logic relating to those notions, namely the Semi-standardization Theorem,
the Standardization Theorem and the Second Church–Rosser Theorem. After that I define the important concept of a *head normal form* and state
Wadsworth's corollary of Curry's Standardization Theorem, which is an important result about head normal forms. This is followed by an account
of combinatorial completeness. It is because combinatory logic possesses
this property that it can be used to remove all the bound variables from a
functional program.

---

[1] According to Turner (1984), p. 5.28, it was Petznick (1970) who first had the idea of
using combinatory logic as the machine code of an abstract machine, but it was Turner
(1979a, 1979b, 1981a) who made it into a practicable implementation method.

The remainder of the Chapter is devoted to explaining how combinatory logic can function as the machine code into which a purely functional language is compiled. First, I introduce fixed-point combinators—these are necessary in order to implement recursion—and then I show how the natural numbers, the basic list-manipulating operators, the booleans and the conditional can all be modelled in *pure* combinatory logic, that is to say, in that version of combinatory logic which only contains two primitive combinators, namely **S** and **K**. To conclude the Chapter I mention that it is better to use a version of *illative* combinatory logic as the machine code for a reduction machine and I list all the illative atoms—and their reduction properties—that are needed in order to compile and execute Lispkit programs.

3.2   A Plea for Combinatory Logic

Pure combinatory logic is that branch of mathematical logic concerned with investigating the properties of combinators. These are very general functions which are implicitly made use of in many branches of mathematics and even in some elementary mathematics. A very simple example is functional composition. This is often represented in mathematical books by means of a small circle written as an infix operator between the expressions for its two functional operands. It is defined in the following way:

$$(f \circ g)(x) \stackrel{\wedge}{=} f(g(x)).$$

In combinatory logic functional composition is represented by the capital letter **B**, which is written as a prefix operator before the expressions for its functional arguments. Its fundamental property is:

$$\mathbf{B}fgx \to f(gx). \tag{3.1}$$

You should notice that the combinator **B** is printed in boldface type. This is how you can distinguish combinators from other sorts of operators. The combinator **B** is known as the *elementary compositor* and equation (3.1) is read as '**B**fgx *reduces to* $f(gx)$'.

It is necessary at this stage to mention some of the assumptions and notational conventions of combinatory logic. It only deals with one-place functions, but as functions are allowed to be both the arguments and values of other functions it is possible to "simulate" a function of type $(J \times J) \to J$, say, by one of type $J \to (J \to J)$, where J is the type of individuals. Two-place functions—and n-place functions in general—are curried. Currying is

43

the process of replacing a function of several variables by a (higher-order) one-place function. For example, let $f(x, y)$ be a two-place function. First, we define $f_x \triangleq \lambda y.f(x, y)$ and then $g \triangleq \lambda x.f_x$. Here, g is the *curried* version of f and the following holds:

$$(gx)y = f_x(y) = f(x, y).$$

The general case of an n-place function is treated similarly.

Concerning notation, in combinatory logic almost all functional signs are prefix operators and juxtaposition represents functional application. Parentheses are used to distinguish between $(ab)c$ and $a(bc)$, for example. In order to avoid having to write lots of parentheses they can be left out on the assumption that they associate to the left. That is to say, $abcd$ is the same as $((ab)c)d$.

I will now introduce some more combinators. This can be done conveniently by analysing a suitable piece of mathematical discourse. I shall consider the proposition:

$$\frac{d}{dx}(16x) = 16. \tag{3.2}$$

Differentiation is here understood as being a higher-order function whose arguments and values are both functions from real numbers to real numbers. The first thing to note about (3.2) is that it looks as if the right-hand side (RHS) is just a number, but mathematicians would construe the RHS of (3.2) as that function which for any real number taken as argument has the value 16. In informal mathematics there is no notational difference between the representation of this function and that of the number 16. Menger (1955) uses the combination of symbols '16' to stand for that function which for any real number taken as argument has the value 16. In combinatory logic there is a combinator $\mathbf{K}$ which makes the function $\underline{16}$ out of the number 16. That is to say, the combinator $\mathbf{K}$ takes a real number, say 16, as its argument and returns as its value that function which for any real number taken as argument has the value 16. Thus, $\mathbf{K}$ 16 7 is 16 and $\mathbf{K}$ 16 11 is 16 and $\mathbf{K}$ 16 17 is 16. Thus it is easy to see that the combinator $\mathbf{K}$ has the following fundamental property:

$$\mathbf{K}ab \to a.$$

In other words, the *elementary cancellator* $\mathbf{K}$ discards its second argument, returning its first.

In informal mathematics the argument of the differential operator in (3.2) would be said to be $16x$. This is because it is conventional in informal

44

mathematics to name a function after its value for the indeterminate x. $16x$ is understood as being that function which for any given number taken as argument returns 16 times that number. Juxtaposing symbols has many meanings in mathematics and here it represents multiplication. Multiplication is a two-place function which returns the product of its arguments, but here it looks as if its value is a function from reals to reals. Moreover, the arguments to the multiplication here are both functions and not numbers. Let us use the symbol M' to represent this function. Now we have to investigate what its two arguments are.

The number 16 represents the function $\mathbf{K}$ 16 x and x the identity function, which returns its argument unchanged. In combinatory logic this is represented by the combinator $\mathbf{I}$ and its fundamental property is:

$$\mathbf{I}a \to a.$$

The combinator $\mathbf{I}$ is known as the *elementary identificator*.

Summarizing, the notation $16x$ represents the combination by means of M' of the two functions $\mathbf{K}$ 16 x and $\mathbf{I}$ x. M' is closely related to multiplication. Let us write M for multiplication. If we think about what the function M' does, we see that the following equivalence holds:

$$M(\mathbf{K}16x)(\mathbf{I}x) = M'(\mathbf{K}16)\mathbf{I}x.$$

Thus $16x$ is more appropriately expressed as $M'(\mathbf{K}$ 16$)$ $\mathbf{I}$ x. There is a combinator $\mathbf{S}'$ which makes M' out of M. Its fundamental property is:[2]

$$\mathbf{S}'abcd \to a(bd)(cd).$$

Putting all this together we have instead of (3.2) the logically preferable (from the point of view of combinatory logic):

$$\frac{d}{dx}(\mathbf{S}'M(\mathbf{K}16)\mathbf{I}x) = \mathbf{K}16. \qquad (3.3)$$

Variables-binding operators can be eliminated in combinatory logic. In (3.3) we see that the variable x bound by the differential operator is at the extreme right of the expression for the argument of the differential operator on the LHS of the equation. I will later show that in combinatory logic it is always possible to move variables to this position and to coalesce multiple

---

[2] $\mathbf{S}'$ is the name given to this combinator by Turner and it is used in the computing literature; in logical texts it is denoted by the symbol Φ.

occurrences of the same variable.[3] Thus we can replace the usual differential operator by Arbogast's symbol for differentiation D and we can leave off the rightmost variable x on the LHS of the equation, giving:

$$D(\mathbf{S}'M(\mathbf{K}16)\mathbf{I}) = \mathbf{K}16.$$

This completes my analysis of the proposition (3.2).

There are a number of other useful combinators. To justify the combinator $\mathbf{W}$ let us consider the connection between the multiplication function M and the square function, which I shall denote by Q for the time being. These are related as follows:

$$Qa = Maa.$$

$\mathbf{W}$ is the combinator that makes Q out of M and its fundamental property is:

$$\mathbf{W}ab \rightarrow abb.$$

Thus, we have that Q is $\mathbf{W}M$. The combinator $\mathbf{W}$ is known as the *elementary duplicator*.

Another common combinator is $\mathbf{C}$, which Curry and Feys (1958), p. 152, call the *elementary permutator*. This is because it permutes its second and third arguments, as shown by the following reduction relation:

$$\mathbf{C}fxy \rightarrow fyx.$$

The final combinator that I want to introduce at this point is used extensively, but—unfortunately—it does not have as simple an intuitive meaning as the previous combinators. This is the *substitution and composition* combinator $\mathbf{S}$ which has the following fundamental property:

$$\mathbf{S}fgx \rightarrow fx(gx).$$

Several further combinators will be introduced in what follows.

3.3 Reduction in Pure Combinatory Logic

3.3.1 Fundamental Ideas

In this Section I give a more rigorous account of the basic ideas of combinatory logic than that contained in the previous Section. The syntactic

---

[3]This is possible in all systems of combinatory logic that are combinatorially complete. This is explained later in this Chapter.

categories that pure combinatory logic makes use of are those of constants, variables and terms. The category *Con* of constants will just contain— to begin with—the combinators **S** and **K**.[4] The category *Var* of variables is to be understood as being ordered in some definite way, so that we can meaningfully talk, for example, about the first unused variable—in the given ordering—that occurs in a particular expression, and so on. The abstract syntax of terms is given in this way:

$$\epsilon ::= \kappa \mid \xi \mid \epsilon\epsilon',$$

where $\kappa \in Con$, $\xi \in Var$ and $\epsilon, \epsilon' \in Ter$, the category of terms. This says that a term is either a variable or a constant or a combination $\epsilon\epsilon'$, where both ϵ and ϵ' are terms. An *atom* is either a constant or a variable. Unless otherwise stated, in what follows it should be assumed that lower-case letters are variables and capital letters are arbitrary CL-terms.

There may be occasions on which it is necessary to distinguish terms as just defined from other expressions that are also called terms. On such occasions I will refer to these terms as *terms of combinatory logic* or simply as *CL-terms*. Sometimes I will use the expression *CL-term* rather than *term* in order to emphasize that we are dealing with combinatory logic.

Now—having defined the category of CL-terms—it is possible to state the reduction rules for performing transformations on CL-terms. I shall write $M \to N$ to mean that the term M *reduces to* N. The reduction rules for **S** and **K** are:

$$\mathbf{S}PQR \quad \to \quad PR(QR),$$
$$\mathbf{K}PQ \quad \to \quad P.$$

Any term of the form $\mathbf{S}PQR$ or $\mathbf{K}PQ$ is known as a *redex*—short for reducible expression—and to distinguish between them we call a term of the form $\mathbf{S}PQR$ an **S**-*redex* and one of the form $\mathbf{K}PQ$ a **K**-*redex*. The right-hand side of either of these reductions is known as a *contractum* and the replacement of a redex by its contractum is known as a *contraction*. (The converse transformation is known—according to Curry and Feys (1958), p. 91—as an *expansion.*) Thus, $M \to N$, means that there exists a finite number of CL-terms $M_0, M_1, \ldots, M_n$—where n can, of course, be 0—such that $M \equiv M_0$ and $M_n \equiv N$ and for all i between 1 and n, M_i is obtained from M_{i-1} by

---

[4]In systems of *illative* combinatory logic the set *Con* will also contain illative atoms relating to such things as the arithmetical operators and the list-manipulating operators.

replacing a single redex in M_{i-1} by its corresponding contractum.[5] A reduction is, therefore, the transformation of a CL-term into another to which it is reducible.[6]

Two CL-terms M and N are said to be *convertible* if it is possible to transform M into N by means of a finite number of contractions or expansions. (In general there will be some contractions and some expansions.) To signify that M and N are convertible we write $M = N$.

A term M is *in normal form* if it contains no redexes. If $M \rightarrow N$ and N is in normal form, then N is *a normal form* of M. A fundamental result in combinatory logic is the (First) Church–Rosser Theorem. This states that if two CL-terms P and Q, say, are convertible, then there exists a term to which they can both be reduced. This can be expressed as follows:[7]

$$P = Q \Rightarrow (\exists N)(P \rightarrow N \wedge Q \rightarrow N).$$

One of the consequences of the (First) Church–Rosser Theorem is that normal forms are unique.

3.3.2 Defining Combinators in Terms of S and K

From the combinators **K** and **S** it is possible to define all the other combinators that there are, for example:

$$\mathbf{I} \triangleq \mathbf{SKK},$$
$$\mathbf{B} \triangleq \mathbf{S(KS)K},$$
$$\mathbf{C} \triangleq \mathbf{S(BBS)(KK)},$$
$$\mathbf{W} \triangleq \mathbf{CSI},$$
$$\mathbf{B}' \triangleq \mathbf{BB},$$
$$\mathbf{C}' \triangleq \mathbf{B(BC)B},$$
$$\mathbf{S}' \triangleq \mathbf{B(BS)B}.$$

---

[5] The sign $\equiv$ means syntactic identity.

[6] The reduction relation $\rightarrow$ introduced in this paragraph is *weak* reduction; *strong* reduction also contains what is known as rule (ξ), which is that if $M \rightarrow N$, then $[x]M \rightarrow [x]N$, where $[x]$ denotes bracket abstraction. Strong reduction is discussed in more detail in the Glossary. Bracket abstraction will be explained in due course.

[7] A proof of the Church–Rosser Theorem for the λ-calculus can be found in Chapter 4 of Curry and Feys (1958) and several proofs occur in Barendregt (1984). The most accessible proof is contained in the Appendix to Hindley, Lercher and Seldin (1972).

For reference the reduction properties of all the combinators mentioned so far are given here:

$$
\begin{aligned}
\mathbf{I}P &\rightarrow P, \\
\mathbf{K}PQ &\rightarrow P, \\
\mathbf{B}PQR &\rightarrow P(QR), \\
\mathbf{C}PQR &\rightarrow PRQ, \\
\mathbf{S}PQR &\rightarrow PR(QR), \\
\mathbf{W}PQ &\rightarrow PQQ, \\
\mathbf{B'}PQRS &\rightarrow PQ(RS), \\
\mathbf{C'}PQRS &\rightarrow P(QS)R, \\
\mathbf{S'}PQRS &\rightarrow P(QS)(RS).
\end{aligned}
$$

Although all combinators are one-place functions, it is possible to associate different *arities* with different combinators. The *arity* of a combinator is the number of CL-terms that it has to be followed by in order for it to be possible for a reduction to take place. Thus, the combinator $\mathbf{I}$ has arity 1, $\mathbf{K}$ and $\mathbf{W}$ have arity 2, $\mathbf{B}$, $\mathbf{C}$ and $\mathbf{S}$ have arity 3, and $\mathbf{B'}$, $\mathbf{C'}$ and $\mathbf{S'}$ have arity 4. When a combinator is followed by enough CL-terms to allow a reduction to take place it is said to be *saturated*. The terminology of *saturation* comes from Frege (1893)—see, for example, §1, "The Function is Unsaturated"—though he used it slightly differently.

3.3.3 Free Variables and Substitution

Because combinatory logic contains no variable-binding operators every variable that occurs in a CL-term is *free*. I use the notation $FV(M)$ to denote the set of free variables in the term M. This is defined as follows:

$$
\begin{aligned}
FV(k) &= \{\ \}, \text{ if } k \in Con, \\
FV(x) &= \{x\}, \text{ if } x \in Var, \\
FV(MN) &= FV(M) \cup FV(N).
\end{aligned}
$$

Similarly, because combinatory logic does not contain any variable-binding operators the definition of substitution in it is very simple. I use the notation $[M/x]N$ to mean that term that is the result of substituting M for every occurrence of x in N. It is defined thus:

$$
[M/x]y \equiv y, \text{ if } y \in Var \text{ and } x \not\equiv y,
$$

49

$$[M/x]x \equiv M,$$
$$[M/x]PQ \equiv ([M/x]P)([M/x]Q).$$

Unfortunately, there is no standard notation for substitution. I have come across the following notations used to represent the idea of substituting M for x in N: $N[x := M]$,[8] $N[M/x]$[9] and $N[x \leftarrow M]$.[10] As substitution is a function it makes sense to write it as a prefix operator—as I do following Curry and Feys (1958) and Stoy (1977)—rather than as a postfix operator of some kind.

Simultaneous substitution is also easy to define in combinatory logic. The notation $[M_1/x_1, M_2/x_2, \ldots, M_n/x_n]N$ means N with every free occurrence of x_i in N replaced by M_i, for $1 \leq i \leq n$.

$$[M_1/x_1, M_2/x_2, \ldots, M_n/x_n]y \equiv y, \text{if } y \not\equiv x_i \text{ for all } i,$$
$$[M_1/x_1, M_2/x_2, \ldots, M_n/x_n]y \equiv M_i, \text{if } y \equiv x_i \text{ for some } i,$$
$$[M_1/x_1, M_2/x_2, \ldots, M_n/x_n]PQ \equiv ([M_1/x_1, M_2/x_2, \ldots, M_n/x_n]P)$$
$$([M_1/x_1, M_2/x_2, \ldots, M_n/x_n]Q).$$

3.4   Reduction Strategies

3.4.1   Reduction Paths

A *reduction path* σ is a finite or infinite sequence of the form:

$$M_0 \rightarrow M_1 \rightarrow M_2 \rightarrow M_3 \rightarrow \ldots,$$

where each step $M_i \rightarrow M_{i+1}$, for $i \geq 0$, is such that a single redex in M_i is replaced by its corresponding contractum. Thus, for no $i \geq 0$ is it true that $M_i \equiv M_{i+1}$. A reduction path is also known as a *reduction sequence* or simply as a *reduction*. If we want to make explicit which redex is being contracted, this can be done by writing it over the arrow, as in:

$$\mathbf{C}f(\mathbf{K}cx)y \overset{\mathbf{K}cx}{\rightarrow} \mathbf{C}fcy.$$

This is sometimes necessary as there are occasions on which it cannot be inferred from the context. An example of such a situation is attributed to

---

[8] Barendregt (1984), p. 27.

[9] Paulson (1987), p. 25, which he reads as 'N putting M for x' and Peyton Jones (1987), p. 22.

[10] O'Donnell (1977), p. 7.

Lévy by Barendregt (1984), p. 56. We have both that:

$$\mathbf{I}(\mathbf{I}x) \overset{\mathbf{I}x}{\rightarrow} \mathbf{I}x,$$

and that:

$$\mathbf{I}(\mathbf{I}x) \overset{\mathbf{I}(\mathbf{I}x)}{\rightarrow} \mathbf{I}x.$$

Not all CL-terms have a normal form. To see that this is so, first consider the combination $\mathbf{CSI}fx$. This reduces to a normal form, as the following reduction path shows:

$$
\begin{aligned}
\tau : \mathbf{CSI}fx \quad &\rightarrow \quad \mathbf{S}f\mathbf{I}x, \\
&\rightarrow \quad fx(\mathbf{I}x), \\
&\rightarrow \quad fxx.
\end{aligned}
$$

Now consider the CL-term $\mathbf{CSI}(\mathbf{CSI})(\mathbf{CSI})$. Substituting $\mathbf{CSI}$ for both f and x in the reduction path τ we get:

$$
\begin{aligned}
\tau' : \mathbf{CSI}(\mathbf{CSI})(\mathbf{CSI}) \quad &\rightarrow \quad \mathbf{S}(\mathbf{CSI})\mathbf{I}(\mathbf{CSI}), \\
&\rightarrow \quad \mathbf{CSI}(\mathbf{CSI})(\mathbf{I}(\mathbf{CSI})), \\
&\rightarrow \quad \mathbf{CSI}(\mathbf{CSI})(\mathbf{CSI}).
\end{aligned}
$$

Clearly this gives rise to an infinite reduction path, since the final term of τ' is the same as the first.

Let us define $\mathbf{W} \overset{\Delta}{=} \mathbf{CSI}$. Now consider $\mathbf{K}x(\mathbf{WWW})$. If we choose to always reduce the first occurrence of $\mathbf{W}$, then we get the following reduction path:

$$
\begin{aligned}
\mathbf{K}x(\mathbf{WWW}) \quad &\rightarrow \quad \mathbf{K}x(\mathbf{WWW}), \\
&\rightarrow \quad \mathbf{K}x(\mathbf{WWW}), \\
&\rightarrow \quad \mathbf{K}x(\mathbf{WWW}), \\
&\rightarrow \quad \ldots
\end{aligned}
$$

But if we decide to reduce the $\mathbf{K}$-redex first, we get:

$$\mathbf{K}x(\mathbf{WWW}) \rightarrow x,$$

and x is in normal form.

Let us give the name *reduction strategy* to any policy for constructing a reduction path by always contracting the redex satisfying a particular property, if such a redex exists. An example of such a policy is that reduction strategy in which the leftmost redex is always contracted first. This is known as *normal order reduction*.

The above discussion has shown that some reduction strategies find normal forms while others do not. This raises the question whether or not there exists a reduction strategy that always finds a normal form, if one exists. The answer to this question is that such a strategy does exist and is, in fact, normal order reduction. This result is known as the Second Church–Rosser Theorem, which is a consequence of Curry's Standardization Theorem, which itself is a consequence of what I propose to call the Semi-standardization Theorem. What I intend to do next is to state each of these theorems in the order of their logical dependence.

3.4.2   The Semi-standardization Theorem

In order to state the Semi-standardization Theorem it is first necessary to define some terms. It is easy to see—and straightforward to prove by induction on its length—that every CL-term X can be expressed in the form:

$$X \equiv aX_1 \ldots X_n,$$

where a is an atom—possibly a combinator—and $n \geq 0$. This occurrence of a is called the *head* or *leading element* of X.

Let R be a redex in Y, then R is a *head redex* if the head of R and the head of Y are the same. Clearly, if a CL-term has a head redex at all, then it has to be unique. As an example, consider the term $\mathbf{S}(\mathbf{BCI})\mathbf{I}x(\mathbf{K}yz)$. This has a head redex and it is $\mathbf{S}(\mathbf{BCI})\mathbf{I}x$. In contrast, the term $xy(\mathbf{I}x)$ does not have a head redex at all.

A *head contraction* is one in which the head redex is contracted and a *head-reduction path* is one that only involves head contractions. The following path is an example of a head-reduction path:

$$\tau_1 : \mathbf{S}(\mathbf{CK}b)(\mathbf{B}(\mathbf{I}x)c)\mathbf{I} \quad \rightarrow \quad \mathbf{CK}b\mathbf{I}(\mathbf{B}(\mathbf{I}x)c\mathbf{I}),$$
$$\rightarrow \quad \mathbf{KI}b(\mathbf{B}(\mathbf{I}x)c\mathbf{I}),$$
$$\rightarrow \quad \mathbf{I}(\mathbf{B}(\mathbf{I}x)c\mathbf{I}).$$

If the redex $\mathbf{I}x$ that occurs in every term of this reduction path had been contracted at any stage, then the resulting path would no longer be a head-reduction one. Similarly, if the redex $\mathbf{B}(\mathbf{I}x)c\mathbf{I}$ that occurs in every term of this reduction path except the first had been contracted at any stage, then the resulting path would not be a head-reduction one.

A redex S in Y is called an *internal redex* only in those cases when it is not a head redex of Y. An *internal contraction* is one in which an internal redex is contracted and an *internal reduction path* is one that only involves internal contractions. The path:

$$\tau_2 : \; \mathbf{I}(\mathbf{B}(\mathbf{I}x)c\mathbf{I}) \to \mathbf{I}(\mathbf{I}x(c\mathbf{I})) \to \mathbf{I}(x(c\mathbf{I})),$$

is an example of an internal reduction path and so is:

$$\tau_3 : \; \mathbf{I}(\mathbf{B}(\mathbf{I}x)c\mathbf{I}) \to \mathbf{I}(\mathbf{B}xc\mathbf{I}) \to \mathbf{I}(x(c\mathbf{I})).$$

A *semi-standard reduction path* is a reduction path in which no head contraction follows an internal contraction. What may be called the *Semi-standardization Theorem* states that if $M \to N$, then there exists a semi-standard reduction path σ from M to N.[11] The following is an example of a semi-standard reduction path:

$$
\begin{aligned}
\tau_4 : \; \mathbf{S}(\mathbf{CK}b)(\mathbf{B}(\mathbf{I}x)c)\mathbf{I} \;&\to\; \mathbf{CK}b\mathbf{I}(\mathbf{B}(\mathbf{I}x)c\mathbf{I}), \\
&\to\; \mathbf{KI}b(\mathbf{B}(\mathbf{I}x)c\mathbf{I}), \\
&\to\; \mathbf{I}(\mathbf{B}(\mathbf{I}x)c\mathbf{I}), \\
&\to\; \mathbf{I}(\mathbf{B}(\mathbf{I}x)c\mathbf{I}), \\
&\to\; \mathbf{I}(\mathbf{I}x(c\mathbf{I})), \\
&\to\; \mathbf{I}(x(c\mathbf{I})).
\end{aligned}
$$

Notice that this is just the path τ_1 followed by τ_2. Another example of a semi-standard reduction is that obtained by appending τ_3 to τ_1. In neither of these reduction paths are all of the redexes contracted. Both of them terminate with the CL-term $\mathbf{I}(x(c\mathbf{I}))$, which is a redex. The Semi-standardization Theorem applies to any reduction $M \to N$ and not just those in which N is in normal form.

Thus, what the Semi-standardization Theorem states is that if τ is a reduction path from M to N, then there exists a CL-term P and reduction paths τ_1 and τ_2 such that τ_1 is a head-reduction path from M to P and τ_2 is an internal reduction path from P to N.

---

[11] For a proof, see Curry, Hindley and Seldin (1972), p. 32.

3.4.3 The Standardization Theorem

In order to precisely state the *Standardization Theorem* for combinatory logic it is necessary to understand the concepts of a *residual* and those of the *i-th stage* and *i-th step* in a reduction path and also the relation of *seniority* between redexes. I now explain each of these in turn.

A rigorous definition of a *residual* can be found in Curry, Hindley and Seldin (1972), p. 29, but I will introduce the idea by means of some examples. Consider the CL-term:

$$X \equiv \mathbf{S}(\mathbf{S}abc)(\mathbf{S}pqr)(\mathbf{S}xyz).$$

This has four redexes, namely $\mathbf{S}abc$, $\mathbf{S}pqr$, $\mathbf{S}xyz$ and X itself. Now consider any two—not necessarily distinct—redexes in X. Let these be R and S, where R is the redex that is going to be reduced next. There are now four ways in which these two redexes can be related to each other and these are:

1. R and S are the same.

2. R and S have no part in common.

3. R is part of S.

4. S is part of R.

In order to understand what the residuals of S with respect to R are we have to consider each of these cases separately. We denote the residuals of S with respect to R by the combination of signs $S|R$, and this is to be understood as a set of *occurrences* of redexes.

Case 1 R and S are the same. One of the ways in which this can happen is when R and S are both $\mathbf{S}xyz$:

$$\mathbf{S}(\mathbf{S}abc)(\mathbf{S}pqr)\underbrace{\overbrace{(\mathbf{S}xyz)}^{S}}_{R} \rightarrow \mathbf{S}(\mathbf{S}abc)(\mathbf{S}pqr)(xz(yz)).$$

In this case the set of residuals of S with respect to R, $S|R$, is the empty set.

Case 2 R and S have no part in common. This can happen as follows:

$$\mathbf{S}(\mathbf{S}abc)\overbrace{(\mathbf{S}pqr)}^{S}\underbrace{(\mathbf{S}xyz)}_{R} \rightarrow \mathbf{S}(\mathbf{S}abc)\overbrace{(\mathbf{S}pqr)}^{S'}\underbrace{(xz(yz))}_{T}.$$

54

In this case the set $S|R$ contains the trace of S in Y, represented by S', where Y is the term such that $X \rightarrow Y$ by replacing the redex R by its contractum T. Let $X \rightarrow Y$. Then the trace in Y of the subexpression M of X is that subexpression N of Y which occurs in the same position of the parse tree of Y as M occurs in X.

Case 3 R is part of S. One way in which this can happen is as follows:

$$\overbrace{\mathbf{S}(\mathbf{S}abc)(\mathbf{S}pqr)\underbrace{(\mathbf{S}xyz)}_{R}}^{S} \rightarrow \overbrace{\mathbf{S}(\mathbf{S}abc)(\mathbf{S}pqr)\underbrace{(xz(yz))}_{T}}^{S'}.$$

In this case the set $S|R$ contains the trace of S in Y. This is represented as S' and it is different from S itself, because it contains T where X contained R. As in the previous case, T is the contractum of R and Y is obtained from X by replacing R with T.

Case 4 S is part of R. One way in which this can happen in X is as follows:

$$\underbrace{\mathbf{S}(\mathbf{S}abc)(\mathbf{S}pqr)\overbrace{(\mathbf{S}xyz)}^{S}}_{R} \rightarrow \mathbf{S}abc\,\overbrace{(\mathbf{S}xyz)}^{S'}(\mathbf{S}pqr\,\overbrace{(\mathbf{S}xyz)}^{S''}).$$

In this case the set $S|R$ contains two members. It contains S' and S'', which are distinct occurrences of the same term $\mathbf{S}xyz$.

Let M and N be CL-terms such that $M \rightarrow N$. Then there must be a finite sequence of CL-terms, $M_0, M_1, \ldots, M_n$, such that $M_0 \equiv M$ and $M_n \equiv N$ and:

$$\sigma : M_0 \rightarrow M_1 \rightarrow M_2 \rightarrow \ldots \rightarrow M_n,$$

where each step $M_i \rightarrow M_{i+1}$, for $0 \leq i \leq n - 1$, is such that M_{i+1} is obtained from M_i by the replacement of a single redex by its corresponding contractum. The term M_i is known as the i-th *stage* in the reduction path σ and the one-step reduction $M_{i-1} \rightarrow M_i$, for $i > 0$, is the i-th *step* of the path. As an example, consider the reduction path:

$$\mathbf{C}\mathbf{I}(\mathbf{K}cx)y \xrightarrow{\quad} \overbrace{\mathbf{C}\mathbf{I}cy}^{\text{2nd step}} \rightarrow \underbrace{\mathbf{I}yc}_{\text{3rd step}} \rightarrow yc.$$

The term $\mathbf{CI}(\mathbf{K}cx)y$ is the first stage, $\mathbf{CI}cy$ is the second, $\mathbf{I}yc$ is the third and yc the fourth.

Let R and S be any two distinct redexes in a CL-term Y. Then R is *senior* to S if the head of S is to right of the head of R. There are two different ways in which this can happen and I will illustrate them both by considering the term:

$$X \equiv \mathbf{S}(\mathbf{S}abc)(\mathbf{S}pqr)(\mathbf{S}xyz).$$

1. It is possible for the whole of R to be to the left of the whole of S. This happens in X if we take R to be $\mathbf{S}abc$ and S to be $\mathbf{S}pqr$:

$$\mathbf{S}\overbrace{(\mathbf{S}abc)}^{R}\overbrace{(\mathbf{S}pqr)}^{S}(\mathbf{S}xyz).$$

2. It can happen that S is an argument of R or part of an argument of R. In this case R and S overlap. This happens in X, for example, if we let R be X itself and if S is $\mathbf{S}abc$:

$$\overbrace{\mathbf{S}\underbrace{(\mathbf{S}abc)}_{S}(\mathbf{S}pqr)(\mathbf{S}xyz)}^{R}.$$

Note that in this case the rightmost part of R is to the right of S, but what is important is that the head of R is to the left of the head of S.

Let R_i, where $1 \leq i \leq n$, be the redex contracted in the i-th step $M_{i-1} \to M_i$, of the reduction path σ. Then σ is a *standard reduction path* if, for $1 \leq i \leq n$, the redex contracted in the $(i+1)$-th step, namely R_{i+1}, is never a residual of a redex S in M_{i-1} which is senior to R_i.

Some examples may clarify this idea. The path:

$$\mathbf{C}f(\mathbf{K}cx)y \overset{\mathbf{K}cx}{\to} \mathbf{C}fcy \overset{\mathbf{C}fcy}{\to} fyc,$$

is not a standard one because the redex $\mathbf{C}fcy$ contracted in the second step is the residual of the redex $\mathbf{C}f(\mathbf{K}cx)y$, which is senior to the redex $\mathbf{K}cx$, which is contracted in the first. The path:

$$\mathbf{C}f(\mathbf{K}cx)y \overset{\mathbf{C}f(\mathbf{K}cx)y}{\to} fy(\mathbf{K}cx) \overset{\mathbf{K}cx}{\to} fyc,$$

however, is a standard reduction path, because the redex $\mathbf{K}cx$ is not a residual of a redex in $\mathbf{C}f(\mathbf{K}cx)y$, which is senior to the redex $\mathbf{C}f(\mathbf{K}cx)y$.

Intuitively, a standard reduction is one in which the redexes occurring in a CL-term are contracted from left to right, possibly with some redexes remaining uncontracted. (A *normal reduction* is a standard one in which no redex is left uncontracted.) The *Standardization Theorem* simply states that if $M \rightarrow N$, then there exists a standard reduction path from M to N.[12]

3.4.4 The Second Church–Rosser Theorem

The *Second Church–Rosser Theorem* states that if $M \rightarrow N$ and N is in normal form, then there exists a normal reduction sequence starting from M and terminating in N. This follows fairly straightforwardly from the Standardization Theorem.

Although normal order reduction always finds a normal form, if one exists, it is not an efficient way of locating normal forms. Let $\alpha M_1 M_2 \ldots M_n$ be the leftmost redex in a CL-term M, with α a combinator of arity n. Then *applicative order reduction* is that reduction strategy in which the M_i are all reduced as much as possible before $\alpha M_1 M_2 \ldots M_n$. Applicative order reduction is more efficient than normal order reduction, although there are circumstances in which applicative order reduction will give rise to an infinite reduction path even though the initial term has a normal form.

If we represent a CL-term as a graph in which common sub-expressions are shared, then *normal order graph-reduction* is a reduction strategy that combines the efficiency of applicative order reduction with the property possessed by normal order reduction of always finding normal forms, if they exist. (Normal order *graph-reduction* is just normal order reduction applied to CL-terms represented as graphs.)

If we want to build a reducer that employs lazy evaluation, then—rather than implementing normal order graph-reduction—we should implement a reduction strategy in which only the head redex—with two qualifications—is ever contracted. The two qualifications are that internal contractions are performed when the head redex is shared and also when a strict operator occurs as the head of a head redex. In these circumstances, Wadsworth's corollary of the Standardization Theorem is useful.

---

[12]For a proof, see Curry, Hindley and Seldin (1972), p. 33. The proof makes use of the Semi-standardization Theorem and structural induction.

3.4.5 A Corollary of the Standardization Theorem

Recall the definition of the *head* of a CL-term X. Every CL-term X can be expressed in the form:

$$X \equiv aX_1 \ldots X_n,$$

where a is an atom—possibly a combinator—and $n \geq 0$. This occurrence of a is called the *head* of X. A term $X \equiv aX_1 \ldots X_n$ is in *head normal form* if either a is not a combinator or it is one, but it is followed by too few terms to allow a contraction to take place. In other words, a term X is in head normal form if it does not have a head redex, but—clearly—it may still contain internal redexes. Examples of terms in head normal form are $y(\mathbf{B}fgx)z$, because y is not a combinator with an associated reduction property, and $\mathbf{S}f\mathbf{I}$, because $\mathbf{S}$ is here only followed by two arguments.

One and the same CL-term may have several distinct head normal forms. Consider the term $\mathbf{B}y(\mathbf{I}x)(\mathbf{K}cz)$. This has at least the following three head normal forms: $y(\mathbf{I}x(\mathbf{K}cz))$, $y(x(\mathbf{K}cz))$ and $y(xc)$.

For some purposes it is necessary to single out a particular head normal form as being of special significance. This is the *principal head normal form* of a term X and it is only defined in those cases that X has at least one head normal form. If it has, then the principal head normal form is the final term in the head reduction path starting from X. For example, the principal head normal form of the term $\mathbf{B}y(\mathbf{I}x)(\mathbf{K}cz)$ is $y(\mathbf{I}x(\mathbf{K}cz))$.

A corollary of Curry's Standardization Theorem—first proved for the λ-calculus by Wadsworth—states that M has a head normal form iff the head reduction path of M terminates.[13]

3.5 Combinatorial Completeness

Certain sets of combinators possess the property of *combinatorial completeness*. In order to explain this it is necessary to go over some of the basic facts of combinatory logic. There is only one mode of combination used in combinatory logic and that is function application which is symbolized by juxtaposition. Thus, if f is a function and x is its argument, then the value of f for the argument x is fx. This is also known as a *combination* of f and x, and in general if M' has been obtained by repeated uses of function

---

[13]Henson (1987), p. 27, contains what is there called Theorem 2.2.3 (xxv): 'If M has a HNF, N, then the head reduction sequence of M terminates with N.' This is false. A counterexample is easily found because head normal forms are not unique. See, for example, Barendregt (1984), p. 177. *Principal* head normal forms are, however, unique.

application out of $x_1, x_2, \ldots, x_n$, then M' is said to be a *combination* of $x_1, x_2, \ldots, x_n$.

Let M' be a combination of the variables $x_1, x_2, \ldots, x_n$ and combinators from the set G^*. The set G^* is said to be *combinatorially complete* iff there exists a combination of combinators from the set G^*, say M, such that:

$$M x_1 x_2 \ldots x_n \to M'.$$

Many sets possess this property. I shall here consider the set G^* consisting of the combinators $\mathbf{K}, \mathbf{I}, \mathbf{B}, \mathbf{C}$ and $\mathbf{S}$.[14] To prove that the set G^* is combinatorially complete it is obviously sufficient to prove that if M' is a combination of x and the elements of G^*, then there exists a combination M of the elements of G^* (hence M does not contain x) such that:

$$M x \to M'.$$

This is proved by giving an algorithm ALG such that given any combination M', applying ALG to M' yields M. The result of applying the algorithm ALG to M' is written $[x]M'$ and the process is known as *bracket abstraction*. One such algorithm is the following:[15]

$$
\begin{array}{llll}
[x]E & = & \mathbf{K}E, & \text{(a)} \\
[x]x & = & \mathbf{I}, & \text{(b)} \\
[x]Ex & = & E, & \text{(c)} \\
[x]EX & = & \mathbf{B}E([x]X), & \text{(d)} \\
[x]XE & = & \mathbf{C}([x]X)E, & \text{(e)} \\
[x]XY & = & \mathbf{S}([x]X)([x]Y). & \text{(f)}
\end{array}
$$

Here it is to be understood that x does not occur in E, but that it definitely does occur in X and in Y. The variable x may or may not occur in M. Each of the six clauses (a) to (f) specifies a replacement for a component of the form $[x]M$. Given an arbitrary combination involving x we try to apply one of the clauses to it, always trying the clauses in alphabetical order. An example should make this algorithm's operation clear. Consider the combination $xx(\mathbf{B}x)$. The only clause we can apply to this is (f), giving

---

[14]I shall not attempt to fill in all the details of the proof that G^* is combinatorially complete. The reader is referred to Chapter 6 of Curry and Feys (1958) and Section C of Chapter 11 of Curry, Hindley and Seldin (1972) for a more detailed proof.

[15]I will say more about this and other bracket abstraction algorithms in Chapter 7, where this particular algorithm is called algorithm (B).

us $\mathbf{S}([x]xx)([x]\mathbf{B}x)$. We now proceed from left to right. The component $[x]xx$ of the partial result is $\mathbf{S}([x]x)([x]x)$, by clause (f) again, and as $[x]x$ is $\mathbf{I}$, by clause (b), this is equivalent to $\mathbf{SII}$. The component $[x]\mathbf{B}x$ of the partial result is simply $\mathbf{B}$, by clause (c). Putting all this together we have that:

$$[x]xx(\mathbf{B}x) = \mathbf{S}(\mathbf{SII})\mathbf{B}.$$

This can be presented in the following way:

$$
\begin{aligned}
[x]xx(\mathbf{B}x) \quad &= \quad \mathbf{S}([x]xx)([x]\mathbf{B}x), && \text{by (f),} \\
&= \quad \mathbf{S}(\mathbf{S}([x]x)([x]x)([x]\mathbf{B}x), && \text{by (f),} \\
&= \quad \mathbf{S}(\mathbf{SI}([x]x)([x]\mathbf{B}x), && \text{by (b),} \\
&= \quad \mathbf{S}(\mathbf{SII})([x]\mathbf{B}x), && \text{by (b),} \\
&= \quad \mathbf{S}(\mathbf{SII})\mathbf{B}, && \text{by (c).}
\end{aligned}
$$

The analogue of bracket abstraction in the lambda calculus is lambda abstraction. The main difference, however, is that bracket abstraction is *not* a variable-binding operation.[16]

3.6 Combinatory Logic as Machine Code

3.6.1 Fixed-point Combinators

In order to be able to cope with recursion we need to have a fixed-point combinator available in our set of machine code instructions. A function f has a fixed-point at x if $x = fx$ and a fixed-point combinator $\mathbf{Y}$ is one which creates fixed-points for arbitrary functions. Thus $\mathbf{Y}f$ is a fixed-point of f. Following Turing,[17] we define $A \overset{\triangle}{=} \mathbf{B}(\mathbf{SI})(\mathbf{SII})$ and $\mathbf{Y} \overset{\triangle}{=} AA$, then $\mathbf{Y}$ is a fixed-point combinator:

$$
\begin{aligned}
\mathbf{Y}f \quad &\equiv \quad AAf, \\
&\equiv \quad \mathbf{B}(\mathbf{SI})(\mathbf{SII})Af, \\
&\to \quad \mathbf{SI}(\mathbf{SII}A)f, \\
&\to \quad \mathbf{I}f(\mathbf{SII}A)f, \\
&\to \quad f(\mathbf{SII}A)f, \\
&\to \quad f(\mathbf{I}A(\mathbf{I}A)f),
\end{aligned}
$$

---

[16]See Chapter 7 of Barendregt (1984) for a precise statement of the nature of the analogy for various bracket abstraction algorithms.

[17]See Turing (1937) and Barendregt (1984), p. 132.

$$\rightarrow \quad f(A(\mathbf{I}A)f),$$
$$\rightarrow \quad f(AAf),$$
$$\equiv \quad f(\mathbf{Y}f).$$

Although it is possible to define $\mathbf{Y}$ in terms of other combinators, it is usual in a reducer to treat $\mathbf{Y}$ as primitive and governed by the property $\mathbf{Y}f \rightarrow f(\mathbf{Y}f)$. Furthermore, as explained in Chapter 5, this is most efficiently carried out in a graph-reducer by creating a cyclic graph.

There are many possible definitions of fixed-point combinators and the first formal system in which such operators could be constructed was Frege's formal system, the Begriffsschrift.[18]

3.6.2   Defining the Natural Numbers

It is possible to define an iterative sequence of combinators which model the properties of the natural numbers.[19] These combinators are known as *iterators* and they are defined as follows:

$$\mathbf{Z}_0 \quad \overset{\wedge}{=} \quad \mathbf{KI},$$
$$\mathbf{Z}_{n+1} \quad \overset{\wedge}{=} \quad \mathbf{SBZ}_n, \text{for } n \geq 0.$$

The combinator $\mathbf{Z}_0$ corresponds to 0 and $\mathbf{Z}_n$ corresponds to n. It is also possible to define operations in combinatory logic that model the operations of addition, multiplication and exponentiation. The following suffice:

$$\mathbf{Z}_{m+n} \quad = \quad \mathbf{S'BZ}_m\mathbf{Z}_n,$$
$$\mathbf{Z}_{mn} \quad = \quad \mathbf{BZ}_m\mathbf{Z}_n,$$
$$\mathbf{Z}_{m^n} \quad = \quad \mathbf{Z}_m\mathbf{Z}_n.$$

It is also possible to define the predecessor of a number, but it is fairly complicated:

$$\pi \overset{\wedge}{=} \mathbf{C}(\mathbf{C}(\mathbf{CI}(\mathbf{S}(\mathbf{BC}(\mathbf{CI}))(\mathbf{SB})(\mathbf{CI})(\mathbf{KI})))(\mathbf{C}(\mathbf{CI}(\mathbf{KI}))(\mathbf{KI})))\mathbf{K}.$$

π has the property that:

$$\pi\mathbf{Z}_n = \begin{cases} \mathbf{Z}_0, & \text{if } n = 0, \\ \mathbf{Z}_{n-1}, & \text{if } n > 0. \end{cases}$$

---

[18]Defined in Frege (1983). For the definability of fixed-point operators there see Geach (1963), p. 150.

[19]See Curry and Feys (1958), pp. 174–175.

This is not the only way in which it is possible to define analogues of the natural numbers in combinatory logic. Another definition is the following:

$$\mathbf{Z}_0' \;\triangleq\; \mathbf{KI},$$
$$\mathbf{Z}_n' \;\triangleq\; (\mathbf{BW(BB)})^n\mathbf{Z}_0', \text{for } n > 0.$$

The $\mathbf{Z}_n'$ satisfy Peano's axioms just as the $\mathbf{Z}_n$ do. In some contexts the $\mathbf{Z}_n'$ are preferable, because they have the property that $\mathbf{Z}_n'fM$ reduces to

$$f(f(\ldots(fM)\ldots)),$$

where f occurs n times, by head reductions only, as pointed out by Curry, Hindley and Seldin (1972), p. 213, footnote 6. Other numeral systems are discussed in Barendregt (1984), pp. 134 and 150.

3.6.3 Defining List Operators

Just as it is possible to define analogues of the natural numbers in combinatory logic so we can define the fundamental list operators *CONS*, *HEAD* and *TAIL*, and there are several ways of doing this. Clearly, we require the following relations to hold:

$$\begin{aligned} HEAD\,(CONS\,x\,y) \;&=\; x, \\ TAIL\,(CONS\,x\,y) \;&=\; y. \end{aligned}$$

Church's definition of these operators is:

$$\begin{aligned} CONS \;&\triangleq\; \mathbf{BC(CI)}, \\ HEAD \;&\triangleq\; \mathbf{CIK}, \\ TAIL \;&\triangleq\; \mathbf{CI(KI)}, \end{aligned}$$

and Bernay's definition is:

$$\begin{aligned} CONS \;&\triangleq\; \mathbf{C(BC(B(CI)K))}, \\ HEAD \;&\triangleq\; \mathbf{CIZ}_0, \\ TAIL \;&\triangleq\; \mathbf{CIZ}_1. \end{aligned}$$

These definitions are found in Curry, Hindley and Seldin (1972), pp. 218–219.

3.6.4 Defining Booleans and the Conditional

The truth-values *TRUE* and *FALSE* can be modelled in combinatory logic by the CL-terms **K** and **KI**, respectively, and the conditional

$$\text{if } b \text{ then } p \text{ else } q,$$

is then simply bpq, since if $b \rightarrow TRUE$, then $bpq \rightarrow p$ and if $b \rightarrow FALSE$, then $bpq \rightarrow q$.

In order to define the truth-functions *NOT*, *AND* and *OR* we make use of the identities:

$$
\begin{aligned}
NOT\ p &= \text{ if } p \text{ then } FALSE \text{ else } TRUE,\\
AND\ p\ q &= \text{ if } p \text{ then } q \text{ else } FALSE,\\
OR\ p\ q &= \text{ if } p \text{ then } TRUE \text{ else } q.
\end{aligned}
$$

From these it is straightforward to obtain the following:

$$
\begin{aligned}
NOT &= [p]p\ FALSE\ TRUE,\\
AND &= [p][q]p\ q\ FALSE,\\
OR &= [p][q]p\ TRUE\ q,
\end{aligned}
$$

and these give rise to explicit definitions, for example:

$$NOT \triangleq \mathbf{C}(\mathbf{CI}(\mathbf{KI}))\mathbf{K}.$$

The other two are left as exercises for the reader, as is the task of defining a predicate *ZERO*, which is such that $ZERO\ \mathbf{Z_0} \rightarrow TRUE$ and $ZERO\ \mathbf{Z_{n+1}} \rightarrow FALSE$.

3.6.5 Illative Atoms and Delta Reduction

Although it is possible to define analogues of the natural numbers, the primitive list manipulating functions, the truth-values, the conditional and the test for zero in combinatory logic, it is very inefficient to do so from a computational point of view. So far I have been considering a version of combinatory logic that only contains two constants, namely the combinators **S** and **K**, but because of this system's computational inefficiency when considered as the machine code for a reduction machine it is necessary to use a version of combinatory logic that contains far more primitive constants. In the first place, all the combinators that we are going to need are added to the set

63

Con of constants. This is entirely straightforward, but it is also useful to add the numbers as extra constants along with various functions, such as addition and multiplication, for manipulating them and also the primitive list operations and other constants to taste. Such additional constants are known as *illative* atoms.

As well as adding illative atoms to the set *Con* we also have to extend the relation of reduction so that these new atoms can be manipulated in some way. Such reductions are known as *delta* reductions and the ideas involved are easily illustrated. For example, if we add all the numbers of the set *int* of integers to *Con* and also the basic mathematical operators $+, -, \times, \div$ and %, then we will also need lots of delta reductions of the form:

$$
\begin{aligned}
3 + 4 &\rightarrow 7, \\
100 - 11 &\rightarrow 89, \\
8 \times 13 &\rightarrow 104, \\
39 \div 3 &\rightarrow 13, \\
7 \% 3 &\rightarrow 1.
\end{aligned}
$$

Similarly, if we add the constants *CONS*, *HEAD* and *TAIL* as primitive illative atoms, then we will also need to add the delta reductions

$$
\begin{aligned}
HEAD\,(CONS\ x\ y) &\rightarrow x, \\
TAIL\,(CONS\ x\ y) &\rightarrow y.
\end{aligned}
$$

The addition of illative atoms and delta reductions to a system of combinatory logic must be handled carefully, because we want to ensure that the resulting system has the Church–Rosser property. Therefore, we must ensure that we do not include atoms governed by delta reductions which create a system that lacks the Church–Rosser property. In particular, we must be careful with our list-manipulating operators. Adding operators which have the consequence that

$$
CONS\,(HEAD\ x)\,(TAIL\ x) \rightarrow x, \tag{3.4}
$$

for all x, and not just for non-atomic x, to our logic will result in a system that lacks the Church–Rosser property, as Barendregt (1984), pp. 403ff., points out. (The property (3.4) is known as *surjective pairing*.)

I will now describe the machine language of the reduction machine that I will use to compile the non-interactive version of Lispkit described in the previous Chapter and used in the program contained in the Appendix. We require the set *Con* of constants to contain **S, K, I, B, C, S′, B′, C′, Y,** *ADD, SUB, MUL, DIV, REM, SQ, ODD, EVEN, LEQ, EQ, HEAD, TAIL, ATOM, NULL,* **U,** *IF, NOT, AND, OR* and *CHR*; and also *CONS, NIL, TRUE* and *FALSE*. The reduction properties of the first nine of these have already been given. I will mention only the delta reductions that we require here:

$$ADD\ x\ y \quad \rightarrow \quad x' + y',$$
$$SUB\ x\ y \quad \rightarrow \quad x' - y',$$
$$MUL\ x\ y \quad \rightarrow \quad x' \times y',$$
$$DIV\ x\ y \quad \rightarrow \quad x' \div y', \text{ where } \div \text{ is integer division,}$$
$$REM\ x\ y \quad \rightarrow \quad x'\%y', \text{ where } \% \text{ is the remainder operation,}$$
$$SQ\ x \quad \rightarrow \quad x'^2,$$
$$ODD\ x \quad \rightarrow \quad TRUE, \text{ if } x' \text{ is odd,}$$
$$\rightarrow \quad FALSE, \text{ otherwise,}$$
$$EVEN\ x \quad \rightarrow \quad TRUE, \text{ if } x' \text{ is even,}$$
$$\rightarrow \quad FALSE, \text{ otherwise,}$$
$$LEQ\ x\ y \quad \rightarrow \quad TRUE, \text{ if } x' \leq y',$$
$$\rightarrow \quad FALSE, \text{ otherwise,}$$
$$EQ\ x\ y \quad \rightarrow \quad TRUE, \text{ if } x' = y',$$
$$\rightarrow \quad FALSE, \text{ otherwise,}$$
$$HEAD\ x \quad \rightarrow \quad i, \text{ if } x \rightarrow CONS\ i\ j,$$
$$TAIL\ x \quad \rightarrow \quad j, \text{ if } x \rightarrow CONS\ i\ j,$$
$$ATOM\ x \quad \rightarrow \quad TRUE, \text{ if } x' \text{ is atomic,}$$
$$\rightarrow \quad FALSE, \text{ otherwise,}$$
$$NULL\ x \quad \rightarrow \quad TRUE, \text{ if } x \rightarrow NIL,$$
$$\rightarrow \quad FALSE, \text{ otherwise,}$$
$$U\ f\ i \quad \rightarrow \quad f(HEAD\ i)(TAIL\ i),$$
$$IF\ p\ x\ y \quad \rightarrow \quad x', \text{ if } p \rightarrow TRUE,$$
$$\rightarrow \quad y', \text{ if } p \rightarrow FALSE,$$
$$NOT\ p \quad \rightarrow \quad TRUE, \text{ if } p \rightarrow FALSE,$$
$$\rightarrow \quad FALSE, \text{ if } p \rightarrow TRUE,$$
$$AND\ p\ q \quad \rightarrow \quad TRUE, \text{ if } p \rightarrow TRUE \text{ and } q \rightarrow TRUE,$$

$$\rightarrow \quad FALSE, \text{ otherwise,}$$
$$OR \ p \ q \quad \rightarrow \quad FALSE, \text{ if } p \rightarrow FALSE \text{ and } q \rightarrow FALSE,$$
$$\rightarrow \quad TRUE, \text{ otherwise,}$$

where x' means the evaluated version of x. *CHR* x reduces to *ch*, where *ch* is the character whose ASCII value is x. The constants *CONS*, *NIL*, *TRUE* and *FALSE* have no reduction properties associated with them.

Chapter 4

Translating Lispkit into Combinators

4.1 Introduction

In the previous two Chapters I discussed the functional language Lispkit and various systems of combinatory logic. The version presented at the end of Chapter 3 is going to function as the machine code of the reducer that will be described in Chapter 5, and here I explain how it is possible to translate all the different constructs of Lispkit into the terms of this combinatory logic.

4.2 Translating Constants

In Lispkit a constant is distinguished by being the second component of a two-list whose first component is the literal atom *quote*. Constants thus come in the following form:

```
(quote <constant>),
```

where *<constant>* can be either a numeric atom, a literal atom or an arbitrary S-expression. Numeric constants are translated into their numeric values. Thus *(quote 7)*, for example, is simply translated into the constant 7. Literal constants are translated into character strings. Therefore *(quote seven)* is translated into the constant literal *seven*. A quoted S-expression

67

is translated into its combinatory equivalent. Some examples should make this clear. Consider this constant:

    (quote (alpha . beta)).

This is translated into the CL-term:

$$CONS \; alpha' \; beta',$$

where $CONS$ is the combinatory pairing operator and x' indicates the translation into combinatory logic of the Lispkit item x. The constant list:

    (quote (alpha beta)),

is translated into the CL-term:

$$CONS \; alpha' \; (CONS \; beta' \; NIL),$$

where NIL is the combinatory representation of the empty list. As a final example, I shall consider the following quoted expression:

    (quote (alpha (beta gamma) delta)).

This is translated into:

$$CONS \; alpha' \; (CONS \; (CONS \; beta' \; (CONS \; gamma' \; NIL))(CONS \; (delta' \; NIL)).$$

4.3   Translating Function Applications

The general form of a function application in the abstract syntax of Lispkit is:

$$f(e_1, e_2, \ldots, e_n),$$

and this is translated into the CL-term:

$$f'e_1'e_2' \ldots e_n',$$

where e' indicates the CL-term corresponding to the Lispkit item e.

68

4.4 Translating Built-in Functions

Every built-in Lispkit function is translated into a combinatory illative atom. Thus, add is translated into *ADD* and *leq* into *LEQ*. A complete list of translations follows:

Abstract syntax	Concrete syntax	CL-term
$x + y$	(add x y)	$ADD\ x'\ y'$
$x - y$	(sub x y)	$SUB\ x'\ y'$
$x \times y$	(mul x y)	$MUL\ x'\ y'$
$x \div y$	(div x y)	$DIV\ x'\ y'$
$x \% y$	(rem x y)	$REM\ x'\ y'$
$sq\ (x)$	(sq x)	$SQ\ x'$
$odd\ (x)$	(odd x)	$ODD\ x'$
$even\ (x)$	(even x)	$EVEN\ x'$
$x \leq y$	(leq x y)	$LEQ\ x'\ y'$
$x = y$	(eq x y)	$EQ\ x'\ y'$
$head\ (x)$	(head x)	$HEAD\ x'$
$tail\ (x)$	(tail x)	$TAIL\ x'$
$atom\ (x)$	(atom x)	$ATOM\ x'$
$null\ (x)$	(null x)	$NULL\ x'$
$not\ (x)$	(not x)	$NOT\ x'$
x and y	(and x y)	$AND\ x'\ y'$
x or y	(or x y)	$OR\ x'\ y'$
$chr\ (x)$	(chr x)	$CHR\ x'$
$cons\ (x, y)$	(cons x y)	$CONS\ x'\ (CONS\ y'\ NIL)$

4.5 Translating Let-clauses

The abstract syntax of a **let**-clause in Lispkit is:

$$\text{let } x_1 = e_1 \text{ and } x_2 = e_2 \text{ and } \dots \text{ and } x_n = e_n \text{ in } e.$$

It is possible here for n to be 0. In that case the CL-term is simply e', where the prime indicates that we are dealing with the translation of e.

If $n = 1$, then the translation is $[e'_1/x_1]e'$ and in the general case we have the translation:

$$[e'_1/x_1, e'_2/x_2, \dots, e'_n/x_n]e',$$

where the substitutions are to be understood as taking place simultaneously. Because of the connection that exists between substitution and bracket abstraction in combinatory logic, this is equivalent to:

$$([x_1]([x_2]\ldots([x_n]e')\ldots))e_1'e_2'\ldots e_n'.$$

4.6   Translating Letrec-clauses

Translating **letrec**-clauses is more difficult that translating **let**-clauses. The following method comes from that used by Scott and Strachey (1971), pp. 15–19 and 27–28.

The syntax of **letrec**-clauses in Lispkit is the same as that of **let**-clauses, except that the keyword *letrec* takes the place of *let*. It is therefore:

$$\textbf{letrec } x_1 = e_1 \textbf{ and } x_2 = e_2 \textbf{ and } \ldots \textbf{ and } x_n = e_n \textbf{ in } e. \qquad (4.1)$$

If $n = 0$, then (4.1) is translated into e'. If $n = 1$, then (4.1) is translated into:

$$([x_1]e')(\mathbf{Y}([x_1]e_1')).$$

When $n > 1$ the translation is more complicated. I shall, therefore, first discuss the case when $n = 2$ and then I will state the general case. The idea underlying the translation of mutually recursive definitions is to turn them into a single recursive definition—by forming a list of all the left-hand sides—and then using the translation of (4.1) in the case when $n = 1$. When $n = 2$ we have:

$$\textbf{letrec } x_1 = e_1 \textbf{ and } x_2 = e_2 \textbf{ in } e.$$

This is first translated into:

$$\textbf{letrec } < x_1, x_2 >=< e_1, e_2 > \textbf{ in } e,$$

where $< x, y >$ represents a list of two elements, namely x and y, with x being the first element and y the second. We now have a **letrec**-clause with only a single declaration, so it is translated into:

$$([< x_1, x_2 >]e')(\mathbf{Y}([< x_1, x_2 >] < e_1', e_2' >)),$$

and in general the expression:

$$\textbf{letrec } x_1 = e_1 \textbf{ and } x_2 = e_2 \textbf{ and } \ldots \textbf{ and } x_n = e_n \textbf{ in } e,$$

70

is translated into:

$$\textbf{letrec} \ < x_1, x_2, \ldots, x_n > = < e_1, e_2, \ldots, e_n > \textbf{in} \ e,$$

which becomes:

$$([< x_1, \ldots, x_n >]e')(\mathbf{Y}([< x_1, \ldots, x_n >] < e_1', \ldots, e_n' >)).$$

The only thing left to explain in this translation is bracket abstraction with respect to a structured object, namely a list. This involves the uncurrying operator $\mathbf{U}$, which has the reduction property

$$\mathbf{U} f x \to f(HEAD \ x)(TAIL \ x).$$

The general rule is that

$$
\begin{aligned}
[< x_1, x_2, \ldots, x_n >]e &= \mathbf{U}([x_1]([< x_2, \ldots, x_n >]e)), \\
[< >]e &= \mathbf{K}e.
\end{aligned}
$$

4.7 Translating Lambda Clauses

The syntax of a lambda expression in the abstract syntax of Lispkit is:

$$\lambda(x_1, x_2, \ldots, x_n).e,$$

which is represented in the concrete syntax as:

$$(lambda \ (x_1 \ x_2 \ \ldots \ x_n) \ e).$$

This is simply translated into:

$$[x_1]([x_2] \ldots ([x_n]e') \ldots).$$

4.8 Conclusion

The compilation of a Lispkit program into a CL-term is very easy. The only complication is the translation of mutually recursive function definitions. The main reason why this compilation is so straightforward is that Lispkit is such a simple language. In later Chapters I will discuss other constructs that might occur in a functional language and there I will explain how they can be translated into the terms of combinatory logic. The translations described in this Chapter are all based on those contained in Turner (1979b).

Chapter 5

Graph-reduction

5.1   Introduction

In the previous Chapter I showed how a program written in Lispkit could be
translated into a term of combinatory logic. In this one I look at the way in
which this term is evaluated by the method of graph-reduction. That this—
in general—is more efficient than ordinary reduction can be illustrated by
a simple example. Consider the arithmetical expression $(2 + 3) \times (2 + 3)$.
Using ordinary delta reductions this can be evaluated as follows:

$$(2 + 3) \times (2 + 3) \quad \rightarrow \quad 5 \times (2 + 3),$$
$$\rightarrow \quad 5 \times 5,$$
$$\rightarrow \quad 25.$$

But the expression $(2 + 3) \times (2 + 3)$ can also be represented as a graph, like
the one on the extreme left of Fig. 5.1. Here, the sub-graph representing
$2 + 3$ is shared in that it occupies both argument-places of the multiplication
operation. If we replace the occurrence of $2 + 3$ by 5, this corresponds to
performing two reductions in the ordinary evaluation process.

The idea of graph-reduction was introduced by Wadsworth (1971) for the
λ-calculus. Graph-reduction for combinatory logic is more straightforward,
since there is no need to worry about variable capture.

In this Chapter I discuss the way in which a CL-term is represented as a
program graph in a reduction machine and how the process of reduction can
be turned into a series of graph-transformations. I show how the program
graph can be efficiently manipulated if we maintain an auxiliary data structure known as the left ancestors' stack and I mention the desirability of using

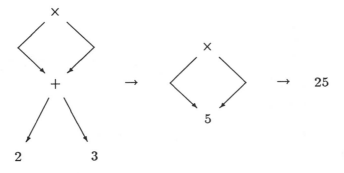

Figure 5.1: An example of graph-reduction.

indirection nodes in order to avoid re-evaluating the same expression in certain circumstances. To conclude I say something about how the interactive Lispkit system, mentioned at the end of Chapter 2, can be implemented.

One thing about which I do not say anything is how the individual nodes of the program graph should be represented. This topic is very well treated in Chapter 10 of Peyton Jones (1987), "Program Representation", pp. 185–192.

5.2 The Abstract Syntax Graph

Let X be the CL-term produced by the translation process described in the previous Chapter. Recall that in Chapter 3 I said that every CL-term X can be expressed in the form $aX_1 \ldots X_n$, where a is an atom—possibly a combinator—and $n \geq 0$. To begin with, the term X is stored in the reducer in the form of its abstract syntax tree, as shown in Fig. 5.2. The commercial at sign @ is used to indicate an application node. Also shown in Fig. 5.2, on the left, is the *left ancestors' stack* or *spine*. The top of the stack is nearest the bottom of the page. The presence of this stack allows for efficient manipulation of the program graph.

Although the representation of the CL-term starts as a tree, many of the graph-transformations introduce shared nodes and the transformation corresponding to the **Y** combinator introduces cycles into the graph. In order to see how the tree becomes a graph let us first consider the graph-transformation corresponding to the reduction of the **S** combinator. This is shown in Fig. 5.3. The sign $\rightarrow_\gamma$ means graph-reduction. Transformations of

73

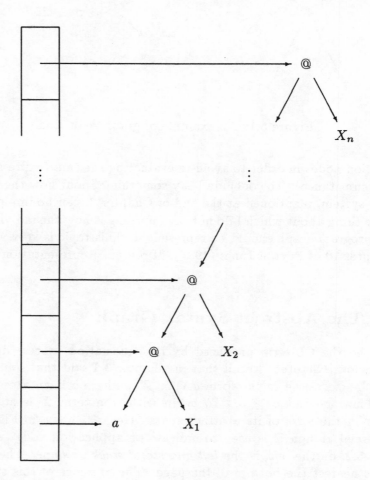

Figure 5.2: The program graph and its spine.

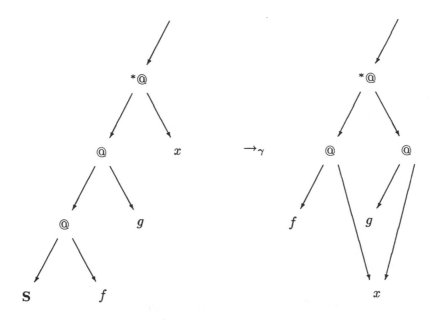

Figure 5.3: Graph-reduction of **S**.

the graph are performed *in situ* and it is important to realize that the node marked with a star $*$ is the very same node in both graphs. This node is *overwritten* with new pointers as shown.

The graph-transformation corresponding to the contraction of the combinator **K** illustrates the need for a garbage collector in a reduction machine and also the desirability of making use of indirection nodes. **K**cx reduces to c and by analogy with the transformation of the **S** combinator we would expect the graph-reduction of **K** to be as shown in Fig. 5.4, that is to say, we overwrite the starred node on the left with a copy of the node representing c. This is all right as far as it goes, but because the original c node might have pointers pointing at it from other parts of the program graph we cannot dispose of it. Similarly, we cannot dispose of the node representing x, since that may have been shared before the transformation took place. In the case of the x node there is nothing else that can be done, but after this transformation we have *two* copies of the node representing c and if both are eventually required in order to evaluate our original CL-term then we have lost the advantages of the graph-structure, that is to say, our reducer

75

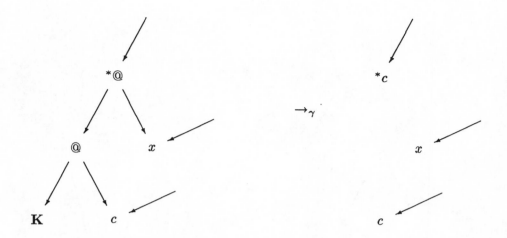

Figure 5.4: Graph-reduction of **K**cx without indirection nodes.

is no longer fully lazy. The way out of this problem is not to overwrite the starred node with a copy of c, but instead to put an indirection node there which points to c.[1] Thus, the preferable graph-transformation corresponding to the **K** combinator is as shown in Fig. 5.5, where the indirection node is indicated by the Greek letter iota ι.

The most interesting graph-transformation is that corresponding to the **Y** combinator, since this introduces cycles into the program graph. **Y**h reduces to $h(\mathbf{Y}h)$, but the graph-transformation corresponding to this is shown in Fig. 5.6. This is discussed more fully in the next Chapter.

These examples of graph-transformations should enable you to devise the appropriate transformations corresponding to each of the combinators—both pure and illative—introduced in Chapter 3.

5.3   Deciding which Contraction to Perform Next

So far I have described the method by which the program graph is transformed by performing graph-reductions on it, but I have said nothing about

---

[1] For a very good discussion of the desirability of using indirection nodes as described see the Appendix, "A Problem in Implementing Noncopying Reduction", of O'Donnell (1977), pp. 105–108.

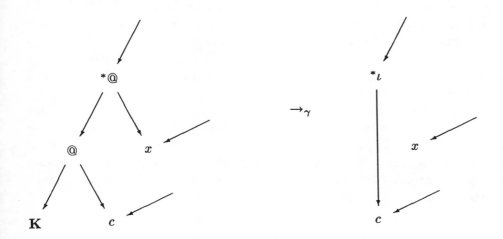

Figure 5.5: Graph-reduction of **K**cx using an indirection node.

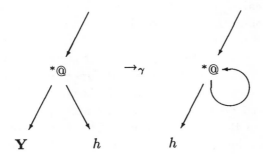

Figure 5.6: Graph-reduction of **Y**h.

which graph-transformations we ought to perform. The growing concensus amongst experienced functional programmers is that lazy evaluation is a very desirable feature to have in an applicative language.[2] The graph-reduction strategy corresponding to lazy evaluation is that of repeatedly contracting the *head* redex of the program graph. Evaluation stops when either the head of the CL-term being reduced is not a combinator with an associated reduction property or it is such a combinator, but it is followed by too few arguments for a contraction to take place. In this latter circumstance it is likely that a programming error has occurred. The only time that internal reductions are carried out is when the head redex is shared or when we are reducing a strict operator, like addition, that requires both of its arguments. The head of the program graph is very easy to locate because it is represented by the node at which the top of the left ancestors' stack points.

5.4 Compiling Interactive Lispkit

In a compiler for the interactive version of Lispkit described towards the end of Chapter 2 each function definition (*def x e*) is translated into a CL-term as it is entered. The resulting CL-term will, in general, contain a number of free variables. This will happen if the function being defined is involved in recursive definitions or if its definition depends on other functions, not necessarily recursively. If x occurs in e, then the CL-term produced will contain one or more occurrences of x. (Examples of such CL-terms will be found in Chapter 7.) This can be represented graphically with a cyclic graph, by replacing each occurrence of x in e with a pointer to the top or root of the graphical representation of that CL-term.

The result of compiling a function definition (*def x e*) is the establishment of a universal binding between x and the CL-translation of e. When the user asks for an expression to be evaluated it is first necessary to assemble the program graph from all the relevant function definitions that are in effect. This is done by replacing each occurrence of a function name f in the expression to be evaluated by a pointer to (a copy of) the graph associated with f in the global bindings. This is repeated recursively until no free variables are left in the expression to be evaluated. Evaluation then proceeds as in the non-interactive case.

---

[2]See, for example, Turner (1981b).

Chapter 6

The Lambda Calculus

6.1 Introduction

The λ-calculus is very similar to combinatory logic and as I dealt with that fully in Chapter 3 I am brief in my account of it here. After explaining the basic ideas of *substitution*, *reduction* and *conversion* I give a succinct account of the semantics of the λ-calculus—which I use to justify the graph-transformation corresponding to the fixed-point combinator $\mathbf{Y}$—and I conclude by saying something about the relationship that exists between combinatory logic and the λ-calculus.

6.2 Reduction

The syntactic categories that the λ-calculus makes use of are those of variables, constants and terms. The category *Var* of variables is to be understood as being ordered in some definite way, so that we can meaningfully talk, for example, about the first unused variable—in the given ordering—that occurs in a particular expression, and so on. Given these syntactic classes, we can define a *term of the λ-calculus*, or simply a *λ-term* or *term*, by the following abstract syntax:

$$\epsilon ::= \kappa \mid \xi \mid \epsilon\epsilon' \mid \lambda\xi.\epsilon,$$

where $\epsilon, \epsilon' \in$ *Ter*, the category of terms, $\kappa \in$ *Con*, the category of constants, and $\xi \in$ *Var*. This abstract syntax states that a λ-term is either a constant or a variable or a combination $\epsilon\epsilon'$, where both ϵ and ϵ' are lambda terms, or an abstraction $\lambda\xi.\epsilon$, where ξ is a variable and ϵ is a lambda term. In what follows—unless otherwise stated—lower-case letters are variables and capital letters are arbitrary λ-terms.

Certain notational conventions are used in writing λ-terms to remove ambiguity. In a combination $xyzuvw$, say, function application associates to the left $((((xy)z)u)v)w$ and an abstraction $\lambda x.\lambda y.P$ can be abbreviated to $\lambda xy.P$. Furthermore, by convention, $\lambda x.PQ$ means $\lambda x.(PQ)$ and not $(\lambda x.P)Q$.

The set of free variables occurring in a λ-term M is denoted by $FV(M)$ and is defined as follows:

$$
\begin{aligned}
FV(k) &= \{\ \}, \text{if } k \text{ is a constant,} \\
FV(x) &= \{x\}, \text{if } x \text{ is a variable,} \\
FV(MN) &= FV(M) \cup FV(N), \\
FV(\lambda x.M) &= FV(M) - \{x\}.
\end{aligned}
$$

A λ-term M is said to be *closed* if it contains no free variables, that is to say, if $FV(M) = \{\ \}$.

The bag of subexpressions of a λ-term M is denoted by $Sub\ (M)$ and is defined as:

$$
\begin{aligned}
Sub(k) &= [\![k]\!], \text{if } k \text{ is a constant,} \\
Sub(x) &= [\![x]\!], \text{if } x \text{ is a variable,} \\
Sub(MN) &= Sub(M) \sqcup Sub(N) \sqcup [\![MN]\!] \\
Sub(\lambda x.M) &= Sub(M) \sqcup [\![\lambda x.M]\!],
\end{aligned}
$$

where $\sqcup$ denotes the union of bags and the brackets $[\![\ ]\!]$ show that we are dealing with a bag. (This is analogous to the use of curly brackets $\{\ \}$ to show that we are dealing with sets and should not be confused with the use of these Strachey brackets to represent quasi-quotation.)

In order to explain reduction in the λ-calculus we have to make use of the notion of substitution. This is more complicated to define here than in the case of combinatory logic, because we have to avoid the capture of free and bound variables. Let x be a variable and let M and X both be λ-terms, then $[M/x]X$ denotes that term which is obtained by replacing all free occurrences of x in X by M:

$$
\begin{aligned}
[M/x]X &\equiv M, \text{if } X \in Var \text{ and } X \equiv x, \\
[M/x]X &\equiv X, \text{if } X \in Var \text{ and } X \not\equiv x, \\
[M/x]YZ &\equiv ([M/x]Y)([M/x]Z),
\end{aligned}
$$

$$[M/x]\lambda y.Y \equiv \lambda y.Y, \text{if } y \equiv x,$$
$$\equiv \lambda y.[M/x]Y, \text{if } y \not\equiv x \text{ and } (x \notin FV(Y) \text{ or } y \notin FV(M)),$$
$$\equiv \lambda z.[M/x]([z/y]Y),$$
$$\text{if } y \not\equiv x \text{ and } x \in FV(Y) \text{ and } y \in FV(M).$$

In the last clause it is to be understood that z is the first variable in Var which does not occur free in either M or Y. The notation $M \equiv N$ means that M and N are syntactically the same.

Sometimes we require the simultaneous substitution of the n λ-terms $N_1, \ldots, N_n$ for $x_1, \ldots, x_n$ in an arbitrary term X. This is represented by the λ-term $X' \equiv [N_1/x_1, \ldots, N_n/x_n]X$ and is defined as:

$$[N_1/x_1, \ldots, N_n/x_n]y \equiv N_i, \text{if } y \equiv x_i,$$
$$\equiv y, \text{if } y \not\equiv x_i,$$
$$[N_1/x_1, \ldots, N_n/x_n]MN \equiv [N_1/x_1, \ldots, N_n/x_n]M[N_1/x_1, \ldots, N_n/x_n]N,$$
$$[N_1/x_1, \ldots, N_n/x_n](\lambda y.M) \equiv$$

$$\lambda y.[N_1/x_1, \ldots, N_{i-1}/x_{i-1}, N_{i+1}/x_{i+1}, \ldots, N_n/x_n]M, \text{if } y \equiv x_i \text{ for some } i.$$

The situation when $y \not\equiv x_i$ in the case $[N_1/x_1, \ldots, N_n/x_n](\lambda y.M)$ is more difficult to deal with. If $y \not\equiv x_i$ for any i, then (i) if no x_i occurs free in M or if $y \notin FV(N_i)$, then $X' \equiv \lambda y.[N_1/x_1, \ldots, N_n/x_n]M$; (ii) if some of the x_i occur free in M and $y \in FV(N_i)$, then $X' \equiv \lambda z.[N_1/x_1, \ldots, N_n/x_n][z/y]M$.

Now—having defined the category of λ-terms and substitution—it is possible to state the reduction rules for performing transformations on λ-terms. I shall write $M \to N$ to mean that the term M *reduces to* N. The reduction rules are as follows. The rule of α-reduction states that:

$$\lambda y.[y/x]X \to \lambda x.X, \text{ if } y \notin FV(X),$$

that of β-reduction that:

$$(\lambda x.M)N \to [N/x]M,$$

and that of η-reduction that:

$$(\lambda x.M)x \to M, \text{ if } x \notin FV(M).$$

Any term of the form $(\lambda x.M)N$ is known as a β-redex and any term of the form $(\lambda x.M)x$, where $x \notin FV(M)$, is known as an η-redex. The right-hand side of each of these reductions is known as a *contractum* and the replacement of a redex by its contractum as a *contraction*. (The converse transformation to reduction is known as an *expansion*.) Thus, $M \rightarrow N$ means that there exists a sequence of λ-terms $M_0, M_1, \ldots, M_n$, such that $M_0 \equiv M$, $M_n \equiv N$ and for all i such that $0 \leq i < n$, M_{i+1} has been obtained from M_i by replacing a single redex by its corresponding contractum.

A term M is *in normal form* if it contains no β-redexes or η-redexes. If $M \rightarrow N$ and N is in normal form, then N is *a normal form* of M.

Two λ-terms M and N are said to be *convertible* if it is possible to transform M into N by means of a finite number of contractions or expansions. (In general there will be some contractions and some expansions.) To signify that M and N are convertible we write $M = N$.

6.3   Reduction Strategies

Given the above definitions, a λ-term may have several redexes in it. For example, the term:

$$(\lambda xy.z(yyx))w((\lambda v.v(uz))w),$$

contains the two redexes $(\lambda xy.z(yyx))w((\lambda v.v(uz))w)$ and $(\lambda v.v(uz))w$. We can choose to contract either of the β-redexes in this first. If we decide to always contract the leftmost redex first—a reduction strategy known as *normal order reduction*—then we get the following reduction path:

$$
\begin{aligned}
(\lambda xy.z(yyx))w((\lambda v.v(uz))w) \quad &\rightarrow \quad (\lambda y.z(yyw))((\lambda v.v(uz))w), \\
&\rightarrow \quad z(((\lambda v.v(uz))w)((\lambda v.v(uz))w)w), \\
&\rightarrow \quad z((w(uz))((\lambda v.v(uz))w)w), \\
&\rightarrow \quad z((w(uz))(w(uz))w).
\end{aligned}
$$

If, on the other hand, we decide to always contract a function's arguments before the function body itself—a reduction strategy known as *applicative order reduction*—then we get the following reduction path:

$$
\begin{aligned}
(\lambda xy.z(yyx))w((\lambda v.v(uz))w) \quad &\rightarrow \quad (\lambda xy.z(yyx))w(w(uz)), \\
&\rightarrow \quad (\lambda y.z(yyw))(w(uz)), \\
&\rightarrow \quad z((w(uz))(w(uz))w).
\end{aligned}
$$

The reduction path produced by choosing normal order reduction is longer than that obtained by using applicative order reduction. This is almost always the case. In fact, for the λI-calculus—a restricted version of the calculus we are considering, in which it is required that $x \in FV(X)$ for $\lambda x.X$ to be a λI-term—it can be proved that the length of the normal reduction path of a λ-term is an *upper bound* for the length of all its reduction paths. For the calculus we are considering the situation is not much better, according to Wadsworth (1971), p. 136, who says that in almost all of the situations in which a λ-term has a normal form there exists a shorter reduction path than the one produced by normal order reduction.

Just as not all CL-terms have a normal form, so not all λ-terms have a normal form. Consider, for example, the term $\Delta = \lambda x.xx$. Then we have:

$$\Delta\Delta \to \Delta\Delta \to \Delta\Delta \to \dots$$

Some λ-terms have a normal form, but not all reduction strategies find it. For example, consider $(\lambda x.3)(\Delta\Delta)$. Normal order reduction gives the following reduction sequence:

$$(\lambda x.3)(\Delta\Delta) \to 3,$$

whereas applicative order reduction gives rise to the following infinite reduction path:

$$(\lambda x.3)(\Delta\Delta) \to (\lambda x.3)(\Delta\Delta) \to (\lambda x.3)(\Delta\Delta) \to \dots$$

A fundamental result in the λ-calculus—as in combinatory logic—is the *(Second) Church–Rosser Theorem*, which states that if a λ-term M has a normal form then it can always be reduced to normal form by normal order reduction. This is the reduction strategy in which the leftmost redex is always contracted first. The *leftmost* redex is the one whose left-hand end is furthest to the left. So, in the λ-term $(\lambda x.x((\lambda y.yzz)x)z)w$ the leftmost redex is the entire term, although part of it extends to the right of the redex $(\lambda y.yzz)x$. See Wadsworth (1976), p. 493, for more details.

6.4 Head Normal Forms

A λ-term M is in *head normal form* if it is of the form:

$$\lambda x_1 x_2 \dots x_n.x M_1 M_2 \dots M_m,$$

where $n, m \geq 0$. The phrase 'head normal form' is often abbreviated to 'hnf'. The *head variable* of this term is x.

If M is of the form:

$$\lambda x_1 x_2 \ldots x_n.(\lambda x.M_0)M_1 M_2 \ldots M_m,$$

where $n \geq 0$ and $m \geq 1$, then $(\lambda x.M_0)M_1$ is called the *head redex* of M.

These definitions are based on the provable fact that every λ-term must have one of the following two forms:

$$\lambda x_1 x_2 \ldots x_n.x M_1 M_2 \ldots M_m,$$

$$\lambda x_1 x_2 \ldots x_n.(\lambda x.M_0)M_1 M_2 \ldots M_m,$$

A term may have several distinct head normal forms. For example, the λ-term:

$$\lambda x.(\lambda x.x)x((\lambda x.x)(\lambda x.x)),$$

has the head normal forms $\lambda x.x((\lambda x.x)(\lambda x.x))$, and $\lambda x.x(\lambda x.x)$. But there is a way of defining a unique head normal form which is often useful. If M has a head normal form, then the last term of the terminating head-reduction sequence of M is called the *principal head normal form* of M. Here a head-reduction sequence of M is a reduction sequence in which the head redex of M is always contracted, so long as this is possible. Contrast this with normal order reduction of M in which the *leftmost* redex of M is always contracted, whether or not it occurs as the head redex of M.

An important corollary of Curry's Standardization Theorem—first proved by Wadsworth—states that a λ-term M has a head normal form iff the head-reduction path of M terminates.

6.5 Justifying the Graph-reduction of Y

In Chapter 5 we saw how the transformation corresponding to the contraction of the **Y** combinator involved the introduction of cycles into the program graph. One of the ways in which this can be justified is semantically, and so I will begin by saying something about the model theory of the λ-calculus.

To give the formal semantics of any logical system involves the definition of an evaluation function—also known as a valuation function or a semantic function—from the terms of the logical system that we are considering to entities in an appropriate mathematical structure. In the case of the λ-calculus the mathematical structures necessary are quite complicated, but it is profitable to consider the nature of the valuation function involved without going into details of those structures. Such a mathematical structure is also known as a model; hence an alternative name for formal semantics is model theory.

The semantic function defined on the λ-calculus is *Eval*:

$$Eval : Ter \rightarrow U \rightarrow E,$$

$$U = Id \rightarrow E,$$

where *Ter* is the category of λ-terms, U is the set of environments, that is to say, the set of functions from variables or identifiers *Var* to values in the model, and E is the set of values that λ-terms can take in this model. The environment is necessary because a λ-term may contain free variables.

The semantic function *Eval* is defined in the following way. For constants k:

$$Eval\ [\![k]\!]\rho = \underline{k},$$

where $\underline{k}$ is the value of k in E. Usually, the underlining is omitted when there is no danger of confusing the constant with its value. The Strachey brackets $[\![\ ]\!]$ are used to combine the functions of quasi-quotation—for an account of which see Stoy (1977), pp. 28–29—and ordinary brackets. For variables x, we have:

$$Eval\ [\![x]\!]\rho = \rho[\![x]\!].$$

Abstractions are a little more interesting:

$$Eval\ [\![\lambda x.E]\!]\rho\epsilon = Eval\ [\![E]\!](\rho \oplus \{x \mapsto \epsilon\}).$$

The operator $\oplus$ makes an environment out of two environments. If x is in the domain of σ, then $(\rho \oplus \sigma)[\![x]\!] = \sigma[\![x]\!]$, otherwise $(\rho \oplus \sigma)[\![x]\!] = \rho[\![x]\!]$. For combinations we have this semantic equation:

$$Eval\ [\![EE']\!]\rho = (Eval\ [\![E]\!]\rho)(Eval\ [\![E']\!]\rho).$$

In the λ-calculus the **Y** combinator can be defined as the λ-term:

$$\lambda h.(\lambda x.h(xx))(\lambda x.h(xx)).$$

When it is important to distinguish this λ-term from the CL-term **Y**, I shall write $\mathbf{Y}_\lambda$ for the λ-term.

Now I can begin to give a justification of the graph-transformation of **Y**, but first I will say something about a common attempt to justify this transformation. Let *Wfe* be the function which when given an arbitrary graph G as argument returns the λ-term that is that graph's linearization.

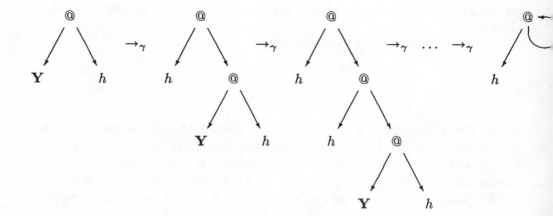

Figure 6.1: A common justification of the graph-reduction of **Y**h.

(This use of *Wfe* is due to Wadsworth (1971).) What Wadsworth (1971) showed was that if we define the notion of graph-reduction appropriately, then if $G_1 \to_\gamma G_2$, then $Wfe(G_1) \to Wfe(G_2)$, where $\to_\gamma$ is graph-reduction and $\to$ is reduction in the λ-calculus. Wadsworth did all this only for *acyclic* graphs. In the case when we allow *cyclic* graphs things are much more complicated. A fairly typical approach to this problem is provided by Glaser, Hankin and Till (1984) who, on p. 102, write:

> The rule for **Y** is slightly less straightforward than the others since the λ-calculus definition would imply an infinite graph. Instead the infinite graph is represented by a finite graph and the reduction rule is shown [in Fig.6.1[1]].

Surely this cannot be correct. It looks as if they are saying that

$$Wfe\,(G_1) \to Wfe\,(G_2), \tag{6.1}$$

where G_1 and G_2 are, respectively, the graphs on the extreme left and the extreme right of Fig. 6.1. To begin with, $Wfe\,(G_2)$ cannot be expressed in the *set* of λ-terms. Rather, $Wfe\,(G_2)$ is a point in the *syntactic domain*:

$$Exp = Kon + Id + (Exp \times Exp) + (Id \times Exp),$$

---

[1]I have made inessential alterations to this figure in order to make it conform to the conventions I am using to represent λ-terms graphically.

where *Kon* is the syntactic domain of all constants, *Id* is the syntactic domain of identifiers and *Exp* is the syntactic domain of all λ-terms.[2] In fact, we have:

$$Wfe\,(G_2) = Fix_{Exp}\,(\lambda y : Exp.`h(y)`). \tag{6.2}$$

(Here the quotation marks have to be understood as quasi-quotation marks.) And *Wfe* (G_1) is just $\mathbf{Y}h$. The sentence (6.1) above cannot be correct because one can easily see that $\mathbf{Y}h$ has no normal form—if h has no associated reduction rule—but *Wfe* (G_2) is in normal form. Therefore, *Wfe* (G_2) cannot occur in any reduction path starting from *Wfe* (G_1).

The transition from G_1 to G_2 is no step of graph-reduction. Rather, its justification is semantic. Let *Eval* be a semantic function with E being a value domain:

$$Eval : Exp \to U \to E,$$

$$\rho \in U = Id \to E.$$

The semantic equations are analogous to those given above. So, making use of the semantic equation for function application, we have the following:

$$Eval\,[\![\mathbf{Y}h]\!]\rho = (Eval\,[\![\mathbf{Y}]\!]\rho)(Eval\,[\![h]\!]\rho). \tag{6.3}$$

Theorem 7.19 of Stoy (1977), p. 127, gives us:

$$Eval\,[\![\mathbf{Y}]\!]\rho = Fix_E, \tag{6.4}$$

where *Fix* is an operator that given a function g as argument returns the least fixed-point of g as its value. (See Chapter 12 for more information about *Fix*.) From which follows:

$$Eval\,[\![\mathbf{Y}h]\!]\rho = Fix_E(Eval\,[\![h]\!]\rho). \tag{6.5}$$

By Theorem 8.29 of Stoy (1977), p. 188, we have that

$$Eval\,[\![Fix_{Exp}\,(\lambda y : Exp.`h(y)`)]\!]\rho = Fix_E(Eval\,[\![h]\!]\rho). \tag{6.6}$$

From (6.5) and (6.6) we get:

$$Eval\,[\![\mathbf{Y}h]\!]\rho = Eval\,[\![Fix_{Exp}\,(\lambda y : Exp.`h(y)`)]\!]\rho. \tag{6.7}$$

---

[2]Here, $+$ is the separated sum of two domains and $\times$ is their product. See Chapter 12 for more information about domains and their sums and products. In this context it is not important that Stoy defines domains to be complete *lattices* whereas the fashion nowadays is to think of them just as being complete posets. For more details about syntactic domains see Stoy (1977), p. 184.

From (6.2) and (6.7) we obtain

$$Eval\ [\![\mathbf{Y}h]\!]\rho = Eval\ [\![Wfe\ (G_2)]\!]\rho, \tag{6.8}$$

and recall that $Wfe\ (G_1) = \mathbf{Y}h$. Therefore we have

$$Eval\ [\![Wfe\ (G_1)]\!]\rho = Eval\ [\![Wfe\ (G_2)]\!]\rho. \tag{6.9}$$

The sentence (6.9) is surprising, because $Wfe\ (G_1)$ has no normal form, but $Wfe\ (G_2)$ is in normal form. Yet, although not reducible to one another, they have the same value, and it is (6.9) which allows us to transform the graph G_1 into the graph G_2.

6.6 Combinatory Logic and the λ-calculus

Let LAM be the set of all λ-terms and CMB the set of all CL-terms. Then there exist standard translations between LAM and CMB, which here will be denoted by ( )$_l$ and ( )$_c$. ( )$_l$ has type CMB $\rightarrow$ LAM and is defined as follows:

$$
\begin{aligned}
(x)_l &= x, \\
(\mathbf{K})_l &= \lambda xy.x, \\
(\mathbf{S})_l &= \lambda xyz.xz(yz), \\
(PQ)_l &= (P)_l(Q)_l,
\end{aligned}
$$

and ( )$_c$ has type LAM $\rightarrow$ CMB and is defined thus:

$$
\begin{aligned}
(x)_c &= x, \\
(MN)_c &= (M)_c(N)_c, \\
(\lambda x.M)_c &= [x](M)_c,
\end{aligned}
$$

where $[x]P$ is bracket abstraction, and for the sake of being definite I shall assume that it is defined by—what in Chapter 7 I call—algorithm (A):

$$
\begin{aligned}
[x]x &= \mathbf{I}, \\
[x]P &= \mathbf{K}P, \text{if } x \notin FV(P), \\
[x](PQ) &= \mathbf{S}([x]P)([x]Q).
\end{aligned}
$$

These definitions of the standard translations are based on those given by Barendregt (1981), pp. 152 and 148.

88

Let $\rightarrow$ denote reduction in combinatory logic and $\rightarrow_\lambda$ reduction in the λ-calculus. Then although there exist standard translations between LAM and CMB the relations $\rightarrow$ and $\rightarrow_\lambda$ are distinct. It is possible to define λ-calculus analogues of $\mathbf{K}$, $\mathbf{S}$ and $\mathbf{I}$, namely $\mathbf{K}_\lambda$, $\mathbf{S}_\lambda$ and $\mathbf{I}_\lambda$, as follows:

$$\mathbf{K}_\lambda \stackrel{\wedge}{=} \lambda xy.x,$$
$$\mathbf{S}_\lambda \stackrel{\wedge}{=} \lambda xyz.xz(yz),$$
$$\mathbf{I}_\lambda \stackrel{\wedge}{=} \lambda x.x,$$

but the defined versions should be kept distinct from the similar, but primitive, operators in combinatory logic.

One of the differences is brought out by the fact that $\mathbf{SK}$ is in normal form, but its corresponding λ-term $(\lambda xyz.xz(yz))(\lambda xy.x)$ is not in normal form because it does reduce to $(\lambda xy.x)(\lambda x.x)$. That is to say, the following does hold:

$$(\lambda xyz.xz(yz))(\lambda xy.x) \rightarrow_\lambda (\lambda xy.x)(\lambda x.x),$$

which can also be written in the form:

$$\mathbf{S}_\lambda \mathbf{K}_\lambda \rightarrow_\lambda \mathbf{K}_\lambda \mathbf{I}_\lambda.$$

But $\mathbf{SK} \not\rightarrow \mathbf{KI}$, that is to say, the CL-term $\mathbf{SK}$ does not reduce to $\mathbf{KI}$. Thus, we have found M and N in CMB such that:

$$M \not\rightarrow N \wedge (M)_l \rightarrow_\lambda (N)_l.$$

There are ways of defining a relation $\rightarrow$ over CMB such that:

$$M \rightarrow N \Leftrightarrow (M)_l \rightarrow_\lambda (N)_l.$$

See Barendregt (1981), Chapter 7 for details, but they are counter-intuitive.

This discussion shows that the notion of a normal form is not invariant between the lambda calculus and combinatory logic. Head normal forms are, however, invariant. That is to say, M is a head normal form in combinatory logic iff $(M)_l$ is a head normal form in the λ-calculus and N is a head normal form in the λ-calculus iff $(N)_c$ is a head normal form in combinatory logic.

Chapter 7

Bracket Abstraction Algorithms

7.1 Introduction

In this Chapter I discuss several bracket abstraction algorithms. Following the precedent set in Curry and Feys (1958), pp. 190ff., these are usually presented in the guise of Markov algorithms. I therefore begin by introducing the fundamental ideas of such algorithms and then go on to discuss abstraction methods that use only a finite number of primitive combinators. This is followed by a number of algorithms which use infinitely many combinators. Such algorithms can be divided into two distinct types. On the one hand, there are those proposed by Abdali and Piperno, for example, which use a *fixed* set of combinators, because they are generated from a finite base. On the other, there are algorithms based on Hughes's notion of a supercombinator. The class of supercombinators needed in a particular abstraction is not given in advance; it is rather determined by the structure of the term on which the abstraction is being carried out. Supercombinator algorithms are discussed in the next Chapter.

7.2 Markov Algorithms

This Section is included for the sake of completeness. The reader who is not mathematically inclined can safely ignore it and go on to the next.[1]

---

[1] The account of Markov algorithms contained here is based on those to be found in Mendelson (1964), pp. 207-228, and Curry (1963), pp. 70-82. Yet another account of

The fundamental operation out of which Markov algorithms are constructed is that of *substitution*, where this is to be understood as the replacement of an occurrence of one expression in another by a different one. In order to see how we can build an algorithm out of substitution we need to introduce some technical ideas.

An *alphabet* is a finite non-empty set of symbols. In this context the space character counts as a symbol, but not every alphabet will contain it. If the alphabet Δ is a subset of Γ, then we say that Γ is an *extension* of Δ.

A *word* in the alphabet Δ is a finite sequence of symbols drawn from Δ. Although the sequence must be finite, it can have zero length. Such a sequence is the unique *empty word* in Δ and is represented as ε.

If A is the word $S_1 S_2 \ldots S_n$ and B is the word $T_1 T_2 \ldots T_m$, where the S_i and the T_j are symbols drawn from Δ, then AB represents the concatenation of these words, namely:

$$S_1 S_2 \ldots S_n T_1 T_2 \ldots T_m.$$

Concatenation is an associative operation, with ε as its identity element.

The word T *occurs* in A if there exist words S and U such that $A \equiv STU$. Either S or U or both can be the empty word. It follows from this definition that the empty word occurs in every word in Δ.

A *Markov algorithm in* an alphabet Δ is an ordered sequence of commands, where a *command* is a specification of how a substitution is to be carried out. Commands are also sometimes known as *productions*. There are two forms that commands can take. A command of the form $A \to B$ is called *simple* and one of the form $A \to \cdot B$ is known as a *terminal* command. I will use the notation:

$$A \to (\cdot)B,$$

to mean a command which is either simple or terminal. (The dot enclosed within parentheses means that it is optional.) Either A or B can be the empty word ε and the signs $\to$ and $\cdot$ are assumed not to be members of Δ. If A is the empty word, then the command is said to be an *initial* command. The command $\epsilon \to B$, which can also be written as $\to B$, is called an initial command because it can be applied to any input word E, since $E = \varepsilon E$.

Given a word E and a command $A \to (\cdot)B$, the command is said to be *applicable* to E if A occurs in E.

Markov algorithms is to be found in Chapter 4 of Monk (1976), pp. 69–75. All these expositions are based on Markov's original work. See, for example, Markov (1961).

Consider the following algorithm:

$$A_1 \rightarrow (\cdot)B_1$$
$$A_2 \rightarrow (\cdot)B_2$$
$$\vdots$$
$$A_n \rightarrow (\cdot)B_n$$

The operation of this algorithm on an input word E proceeds in the following way. Starting from the top, we look for the first command applicable to E. One of two things must happen. Either no command can be applied to E or there is at least one applicable command. In the first case, the algorithm is said to be *blocked* and it terminates with the result E. In the second case—assuming that the applicable command is $A_i \rightarrow (\cdot)B_i$—we replace the leftmost occurrence of A_i in E with B_i, producing E'. In this case the *algorithm* is said to be *applicable* to E. There are now two possibilities to consider. Either the applicable command is a terminal one or it is a simple one. If the command is a terminal one, then it terminates with the result E'; otherwise it must be simple. In this case, we start from the top again, looking for the first command that can be applied to E' and proceed as just described. There is, of course, no guarantee that a particular algorithm will terminate.

There are, therefore, three possible outcomes when we give the word E to an algorithm. (1) The algorithm halts because a terminal command is encountered which is applicable either to E itself or to a word which has been obtained from E by the operation of this algorithm already. (2) The algorithm halts because it becomes blocked. (3) It carries on forever.

The algorithms just discussed are examples of Markov algorithms *in* an alphabet Δ, but there are some procedures that cannot be specified in this way. In order to carry out such operations we need the notion of an algorithm *over* an alphabet Δ. This is defined to be an algorithm in an alphabet Γ, where Γ is an extension of Δ.

To illustrate the operation of a Markov algorithm I shall give as an example the specification of a Markov algorithm that duplicates its input.[2] For definiteness I shall assume that the set Δ consists of just the two symbols a and b; and the set $\Gamma = \Delta \cup \{\alpha, \beta\}$. This algorithm is, therefore, *in* Γ but *over* Δ and it can be specified as follows:

$$\alpha a \rightarrow a\beta a\alpha \tag{7.1}$$

[2]This is a corrected version of that found in Curry (1963), p. 72.

$$\alpha b \;\to\; b\beta b\alpha \tag{7.2}$$

$$\beta aa \;\to\; a\beta a \tag{7.3}$$

$$\beta ab \;\to\; b\beta a \tag{7.4}$$

$$\beta ba \;\to\; a\beta b \tag{7.5}$$

$$\beta bb \;\to\; b\beta b \tag{7.6}$$

$$\beta \;\to\; \tag{7.7}$$

$$\alpha \;\to\; \cdot \tag{7.8}$$

$$\;\to\; \alpha \tag{7.9}$$

Here, the numbers on the right are only for reference purposes. If we give this algorithm the input word *abaa* it proceeds as follows, where the word that is being substituted at each stage is underlined.

abaa	$\to$	$\underline{\alpha}abaa$,	by (7.9),
	$\to$	$a\beta a\underline{\alpha}baa$,	by (7.1),
	$\to$	$a\beta ab\beta b\underline{\alpha aa}$,	by (7.2),
	$\to$	$a\beta ab\beta ba\beta a\underline{\alpha a}$,	by (7.1),
	$\to$	$a\beta ab\beta ba\underline{\beta aa}\beta a\alpha$,	by (7.1),
	$\to$	$a\underline{\beta ab}\beta baa\beta a\beta a\alpha$,	by (7.3),
	$\to$	$ab\beta a\underline{\beta ba}a\beta a\beta a\alpha$,	by (7.4),
	$\to$	$ab\underline{\beta aa}\beta ba\beta a\beta a\alpha$,	by (7.5),
	$\to$	$aba\beta a\underline{\beta ba}\beta a\beta a\alpha$,	by (7.3),
	$\to$	$aba\underline{\beta aa}\beta b\beta a\beta a\alpha$,	by (7.5),
	$\to$	$abaa\beta a\underline{\beta b}\beta a\beta a\alpha$,	by (7.3),
	$\to$	$abaaa\beta b\underline{\beta a}\beta a\alpha$,	by (7.7),
	$\to$	$abaaab\underline{\beta a}\beta a\alpha$,	by (7.7),
	$\to$	$abaaaba\underline{\beta a}\alpha$,	by (7.7),
	$\to$	$abaaabaa\underline{\alpha}$,	by (7.7),
	$\to$	$abaaabaa$,	by (7.8).

7.3 Finite Abstraction Algorithms

In this Section I will consider some of the finite abstraction algorithms that have been discussed in connection with the implementation of applicative programming languages. The simplest is probably the following, which I will refer to as algorithm (A):

$$[x]x \;=\; \mathbf{I},$$

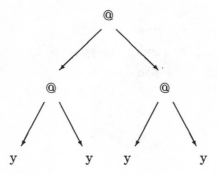

Figure 7.1: Tree-representation of $yy(yy)$.

$$[x]y = \mathbf{K}y, \text{if } y \not\equiv x,$$
$$[x]MN = \mathbf{S}([x]M)([x]N).$$

Here, x and y are variables and M and N are arbitrary CL-terms which may or may not contain x. It should be noted that the order of the clauses in the above algorithm is completely irrelevant, as they are mutually exclusive.

This is a simple algorithm, but it is completely useless for implementation purposes because it generates very large code. If you abstract on n variables, then the size of the output is in the order of 2^n. It is not very difficult to analyze the space complexity of this abstraction algorithm. One of the things that we are interested in is knowing the upper bound for the length of code produced for an input term of known length. For this particular algorithm, the shape of the abstract tree of the input term is irrelevant. Such terms can be represented as binary trees in which every non-leaf node has exactly two subtrees and if the length of the term is m, for $m \geq 1$, then the tree has m terminal nodes and $m - 1$ internal nodes, that is to say, $2m - 1$ nodes altogether. In what follows I shall assume that the variable being abstracted does not occur in the body of the term.

Consider, as an example, the term $yy(yy)$. This can be represented by means of a binary tree as in Fig. 7.1. The result of applying algorithm (A) to this—abstracting, say, the variable x—results in the term $\mathbf{S}(\mathbf{S}(\mathbf{K}y)(\mathbf{K}y))(\mathbf{S}(\mathbf{K}y)(\mathbf{K}y))$,which can be represented by the binary tree in Fig. 7.2. It should be clear that the number of atoms added is the same as the total number of nodes in the parse tree. Thus if we start with a term of length m and abstract a variable that does not occur in it, the resulting term has length $3m - 1$. This is because the term produced contains all

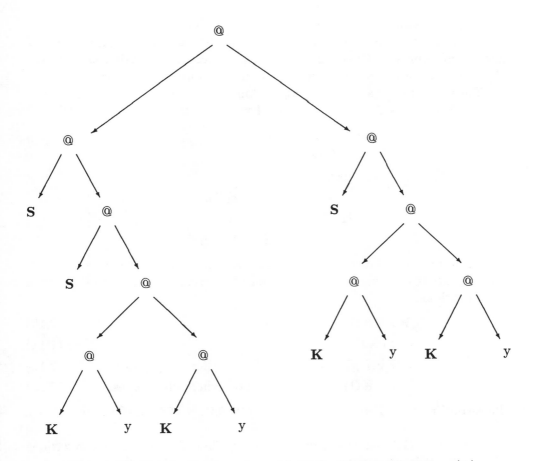

Figure 7.2: Tree-representation of $[x]yy(yy)$ using algorithm (A).

the original atoms, namely m of them, as well as those produced by the abstraction process, which is a further $2m - 1$. If the algorithm is applied n times—each time abstracting on a variable that does not occur in the term—then the resulting code has size:

$$\frac{1}{2}[(2m - 1)3^n + 1].$$

In the remainder of this Section I will use the following conventions: E and F shall stand for CL-terms which definitely do not contain x; M, N and P will represent CL-terms which may or may not contain x and X and Y will stand for CL-terms which definitely do contain the variable x.

The next bracket abstraction algorithm is much discussed in Curry, Hindley and Seldin (1972), pp. 42–67, and I will refer to it as algorithm (B):

$$
\begin{aligned}
[x]E &= \mathbf{K}E, \\
[x]x &= \mathbf{I}, \\
[x]Ex &= E, \\
[x]EX &= \mathbf{B}E([x]X), \\
[x]XE &= \mathbf{C}([x]X)E, \\
[x]XY &= \mathbf{S}([x]X)([x]Y).
\end{aligned}
$$

Although Turner discusses this algorithm his formulation of it is different. He presents it as being the combination of algorithm (A) and the following optimizations:

$$
\begin{aligned}
\mathbf{S}(\mathbf{K}P)(\mathbf{K}Q) &= \mathbf{K}(PQ), & (7.10) \\
\mathbf{S}(\mathbf{K}P)\mathbf{I} &= P, & (7.11) \\
\mathbf{S}(\mathbf{K}P)Q &= \mathbf{B}PQ, \text{if no earlier rule applies,} & (7.12) \\
\mathbf{S}P(\mathbf{K}Q) &= \mathbf{C}PQ, \text{if no earlier rule applies.} & (7.13)
\end{aligned}
$$

These optimizations are found in Turner (1979a), p. 268, and Turner (1979b), p. 35.

Algorithm (B) can be derived from algorithm (A) and the optimizations (7.10)–(7.13) in a straightforward way. In order to justify the production:

$$[x]E = \mathbf{K}E, \qquad (7.14)$$

we begin by assuming that y and z are both atoms distinct from x. Then we have, by algorithm (A):

$$
\begin{aligned}
[x]yz &= \mathbf{S}([x]y)([x]z), \\
&= \mathbf{S}(\mathbf{K}y)(\mathbf{K}z).
\end{aligned}
$$

Making use of Turner's optimization (7.10) this can be rewritten as $\mathbf{K}(yz)$, giving us:

$$[x]yz = \mathbf{K}(yz).$$

Clearly, a similar argument will work in the case when we abstract x from a CL-term E of arbitrary complexity, as required.

In order to justify the production:

$$[x]Ex = E,$$

we first apply algorithm (A) to Ex. This gives us $\mathbf{S}([x]E)([x]x)$. By production (7.14) the expression $[x]E$ can be replaced by $\mathbf{K}E$. We also have that $[x]x$ is $\mathbf{I}$. Therefore, $\mathbf{S}([x]E)([x]x)$ can be replaced by $\mathbf{S}(\mathbf{K}E)\mathbf{I}$, which by Turner's optimization (7.11) becomes E. Thus, we have justified the production $[x]Ex = E$, as required.

In order to justify:

$$[x]EX = \mathbf{B}E([x]X),$$

we begin by applying algorithm (A) to EX. This gives us $\mathbf{S}([x]E)([x]X)$, which is equivalent to $\mathbf{S}(\mathbf{K}E)([x]X)$, by the production (7.14). Making use of Turner's optimization (7.12) we see that this is the same as $\mathbf{B}E([x]X)$, thus justifying the production under discussion, as required.

To justify the production:

$$[x]XE = \mathbf{C}([x]X)E,$$

we first apply algorithm (A) to XE. This results in $\mathbf{S}([x]X)([x]E)$, which can be replaced by $\mathbf{S}([x]X)(\mathbf{K}E)$ as a result of using (7.14). Applying Turner's optimization (7.13) to this yields the term $\mathbf{C}([x]X)E$. This argument justifies the production being discussed, as required.

Turner found that the code produced by algorithm (B) was still too large for it to be of practical use in implementing a functional language. If a CL-term has length m and we abstract n variables from it using algorithm (B), then the upper bound on the size of the resulting term is $mn^2/2 + 2mn - 21m/8$.[3] In order to make the abstraction algorithm more efficient Turner introduced a number of further optimizations. These make use of the extra combinators $\mathbf{B}'$, $\mathbf{C}'$ and $\mathbf{S}'$, which have the following reduction properties:

$$\begin{aligned}
\mathbf{B}'PQRS &\rightarrow PQ(RS), \\
\mathbf{C}'PQRS &\rightarrow P(QS)R, \\
\mathbf{S}'PQRS &\rightarrow P(QS)(RS).
\end{aligned}$$

---

[3] See Joy, Rayward-Smith and Burton (1985), p. 216, for this and other results relating to the complexity of abstraction algorithms.

The resulting algorithm—which I will call (C)—can be written in the following form:

$$
\begin{aligned}
[x]E &= \mathbf{K}E, \\
[x]x &= \mathbf{I}, \\
[x]Ex &= E, \\
[x]EFX &= \mathbf{B'}EF([x]X), \\
[x]EXF &= \mathbf{C'}E([x]X)F, \\
[x]EXY &= \mathbf{S'}E([x]X)([x]Y), \\
[x]EX &= \mathbf{B}E([x]X), \\
[x]XE &= \mathbf{C}([x]X)E, \\
[x]XY &= \mathbf{S}([x]X)([x]Y).
\end{aligned}
$$

This way of writing the rules for $\mathbf{B'}$, $\mathbf{C'}$ and $\mathbf{S'}$ is due to Kennaway (1984), p. 2. Turner (1979a), p. 270, expresses this algorithm as being the result of combining algorithm (B) with the following three optimization rules:

$$
\begin{aligned}
\mathbf{S}(\mathbf{B}PQ)R &= \mathbf{S'}PQR, & (7.15) \\
\mathbf{B}(PQ)R &= \mathbf{B'}PQR, & (7.16) \\
\mathbf{C}(\mathbf{B}PQ)R &= \mathbf{C'}PQR. & (7.17)
\end{aligned}
$$

In order to justify the production:

$$[x]EFX = \mathbf{B'}EF([x]X),$$

we begin by noticing that the result of determining $[x]EFX$, by means of algorithm (B) is $\mathbf{B}(EF)([x]X)$ and employing the optimization (7.16) this is equivalent to $\mathbf{B'}EF([x]X)$, as required.

In order to justify the production:

$$[x]EXF = \mathbf{C'}E([x]X)F,$$

we start by observing that the result of determining $[x]EXF$, by algorithm (B) is $\mathbf{C}([x](EX))F$. Applying the same algorithm again results in $\mathbf{C}(\mathbf{B}E([x]X)F$ and by means of Turner's optimization (7.17) this is equivalent to $\mathbf{C'}E([x]X)F$, as required.

In order to justify the production:

$$[x]EXY = \mathbf{S'}E([x]X)([x]Y),$$

we begin by noticing that the result of determining $[x]EXY$, by means of algorithm (B) is $\mathbf{S}([x](EX))([x]Y)$. Applying the same algorithm again results in $\mathbf{S}(\mathbf{B}E([x]X))([x]Y)$ and employing the optimization (7.15) this is equivalent to $\mathbf{S}'E([x]X)([x]Y)$, as required.

According to Joy, Rayward-Smith and Burton (1985), p. 216, given a CL-term of length m on which n abstractions are performed by algorithm (C), then the length of the output is $\theta(nm)$.

7.3.1 Motivation for Introducing S', C' and B'

In giving the abstraction algorithm (C) it may have appeared as if the combinators $\mathbf{S}'$, $\mathbf{C}'$ and $\mathbf{B}'$ were just pulled out of the hat. It is likely, however, that Turner made use of them after a close inspection of the structure of CL-terms produced by algorithm (B). In order to appreciate this let us consider the abstraction:

$$[x_n][x_{n-1}]\ldots[x_1]MN,$$

where, for $n \geq i \geq 1$, $x_i \in FV(M)$ and $x_i \in FV(N)$. To make the following discussion succinct I shall use the following notation:[4]

$$P_0 \; \triangleq \; P,$$
$$P_i \; \triangleq \; [x_i]P_{i-1}, \text{for } 1 \leq i \leq n.$$

Thus we have that:

$$P_n = [x_n][x_{n-1}]\ldots[x_1]P,$$

and that:

$$(MN)_n = [x_n][x_{n-1}]\ldots[x_1]MN,$$

Using algorithm (B) we have that:

$$(MN)_1 \; = \; \mathbf{S}M_1N_1,$$
$$(MN)_2 \; = \; \mathbf{S}(\mathbf{BS}M_2)N_2,$$
$$(MN)_3 \; = \; \mathbf{S}(\mathbf{BS}(\mathbf{B}(\mathbf{BS})M_3))N_3,$$
$$(MN)_4 \; = \; \mathbf{S}(\mathbf{BS}(\mathbf{B}(\mathbf{BS})(\mathbf{B}(\mathbf{B}(\mathbf{BS}))M_4)))N_4.$$

The length of the CL-terms produced in this progression grows quadratically with the number of times that the abstraction algorithm is applied. The pattern of how the $\mathbf{B}$ and $\mathbf{S}$ combinators are successively added is not

---

[4]This notation was suggested by Peyton Jones's use of ^1p, ^2p, etc., in Peyton Jones (1987), p. 270. The discussion of the $\mathbf{S}'$ combinator is based on his.

immediately apparent and, thus great credit must go to Turner for seeing that a combinator $\mathbf{S}'$, with the property that $\mathbf{S}'PQR$ is equivalent to $\mathbf{S}(\mathbf{B}PQ)R$, significantly reduces the length of the CL-term. This becomes clear as soon as we apply algorithm (C) to the term MN:

$$
\begin{aligned}
(MN)_1 &= \mathbf{S}M_1N_1, \\
(MN)_2 &= \mathbf{S}'\mathbf{S}M_2N_2, \\
(MN)_3 &= \mathbf{S}'(\mathbf{S}'\mathbf{S})M_3N_3, \\
(MN)_4 &= \mathbf{S}'(\mathbf{S}'(\mathbf{S}'\mathbf{S}))M_4N_4.
\end{aligned}
$$

Here, the length of the CL-term only grows linearly with the number of times that the abstraction algorithm is applied.

In order to motivate the introduction of the $\mathbf{C}'$ combinator I shall consider the abstraction:

$$[x_n][x_{n-1}]\ldots[x_1]MN,$$

where, for $n \geq i \geq 1$, $x_i \in FV(M)$ and $x_i \notin FV(N)$. Using algorithm (B) the successive abstractions are:

$$
\begin{aligned}
(MN)_1 &= \mathbf{C}M_1N, \\
(MN)_2 &= \mathbf{C}(\mathbf{BC}M_2)N, \\
(MN)_3 &= \mathbf{C}(\mathbf{BC}(\mathbf{B}(\mathbf{BC})M_3))N, \\
(MN)_4 &= \mathbf{C}(\mathbf{BC}(\mathbf{B}(\mathbf{BC})(\mathbf{B}(\mathbf{B}(\mathbf{BC}))M_4)))N.
\end{aligned}
$$

If you compare this with the case when the x_i also occur in N you will notice that the pattern of the combinators is the same. The only difference is that in this case a $\mathbf{C}$ combinator occurs where an $\mathbf{S}$ combinator occurs in the other example. Not surprisingly, therefore, a combinator $\mathbf{C}'$—which is such that $\mathbf{C}'PQR$ is equivalent to $\mathbf{C}(\mathbf{B}PQ)R$—produces a significant reduction in the length of the CL-term produced, as the following sequence of abstractions shows (using algorithm (C)):

$$
\begin{aligned}
(MN)_1 &= \mathbf{C}M_1N, \\
(MN)_2 &= \mathbf{C}'\mathbf{C}M_2N, \\
(MN)_3 &= \mathbf{C}'(\mathbf{C}'\mathbf{C})M_3N, \\
(MN)_4 &= \mathbf{C}'(\mathbf{C}'(\mathbf{C}'\mathbf{C}))M_4N.
\end{aligned}
$$

In order to motivate the introduction of the $\mathbf{B}'$ combinator I shall consider the abstraction:

$$[x_n][x_{n-1}]\ldots[x_1]MN,$$

where, for $n \geq i \geq 1$, $x_i \notin FV(M)$ and $x_i \in FV(N)$. Using algorithm (B) the successive abstractions are:

$$
\begin{aligned}
(MN)_1 &= \mathbf{B}MN_1, \\
(MN)_2 &= \mathbf{B}(\mathbf{B}M)N_2, \\
(MN)_3 &= \mathbf{B}(\mathbf{B}(\mathbf{B}M))N_3, \\
(MN)_4 &= \mathbf{B}(\mathbf{B}(\mathbf{B}(\mathbf{B}M)))N_4.
\end{aligned}
$$

This case is different from that obtained in the previous two cases. The growth of the CL-term is linear and not quadratic as before. Thus there does not appear to be a need to introduce a $\mathbf{B}'$ combinator, but if we do, then using algorithm (C) we get:

$$
\begin{aligned}
(MN)_1 &= \mathbf{B}MN_1, \\
(MN)_2 &= \mathbf{B}'\mathbf{B}MN_2, \\
(MN)_3 &= \mathbf{B}'(\mathbf{B}'\mathbf{B})MN_3, \\
(MN)_4 &= \mathbf{B}'(\mathbf{B}'(\mathbf{B}'\mathbf{B}))MN_4.
\end{aligned}
$$

The number of combinators needed in each successive abstraction is the same, but the term M does not get nested deeply in the term produced, as it does in the case of the (B) version. That this is an advantage can be seen if we assume that $x_5 \in FV(M)$. With algorithm (B) we get:

$$(MN)_5 = \mathbf{S}(\mathbf{BB}(\mathbf{BB}(\mathbf{BB}(\mathbf{BB}[x_5]M))))N_5,$$

whereas with algorithm (C) this result is:

$$(MN)_5 = \mathbf{S}'(\mathbf{B}'(\mathbf{B}'(\mathbf{B}'\mathbf{B})))([x_5]M)N_5,$$

and $[x_5]M$ is still deeply nested in the first version, but not in the second.

Another reason—no doubt—why Turner included $\mathbf{B}'$ along with $\mathbf{S}'$ and $\mathbf{C}'$ in the improved version of his abstraction algorithm is that the relation of its reduction property to that of $\mathbf{B}$ is analogous to those of $\mathbf{S}'$ to $\mathbf{S}$ and $\mathbf{C}'$ to $\mathbf{C}$. Although that is true, it results in an optimization that works differently. Peyton Jones (1987), p. 272, claims that experiments have shown that the presence of the $\mathbf{B}'$ optimization in an abstraction algorithm actually degrades its performance. This is because—he claims—the $\mathbf{B}'$ optimization does not reduce the size of the CL-term and it might destroy the possibility of an optimization involving either the $\mathbf{C}'$ or the $\mathbf{S}'$ combinators. As an illustration of this he considers the CL-term $\mathbf{C}(\mathbf{B}(cf)g)h$, which becomes

$\mathbf{C}(\mathbf{B}'cfg)h$, if the $\mathbf{B}'$ optimization is applied, but $\mathbf{C}'(cf)gh$ if it is not. Because of this possibility, Sheevel has suggested replacing the $\mathbf{B}'$ combinator with a $\mathbf{B}^*$ one, which has the reduction property:[5]

$$\mathbf{B}^*PQRS \to P(Q(RS)),$$

and the optimization rule:

$$\mathbf{B}P(\mathbf{B}QR) = \mathbf{B}^*PQR.$$

The resulting algorithm is like (C) except that the clause involving $\mathbf{B}'$ has to be replaced with:

$$[x]E(FX) = \mathbf{B}^*EF([x]X),$$

where it is to be understood that $x \notin FV(E)$, $x \notin FV(F)$, but $x \in FV(X)$. I shall call the resulting algorithm (CS).

I do not think that the advantage of $\mathbf{B}^*$ over $\mathbf{B}'$ has yet been conclusively proved. For example, applying the $\mathbf{B}^*$ algorithm to MN, where $x_i \in N$ for $1 \le i \le 5$ and $x_5 \in FV(M)$ but $x_1, x_2, x_3, x_4 \notin FV(M)$ results in the CL-term:

$$\mathbf{S}(\mathbf{BB}(\mathbf{BB}(\mathbf{B}^*\mathbf{BB}[x_5]M)))N_5,$$

which is more complicated than that produced by algorithm (C). Furthermore, experimenting with algorithms (C) and (CS) I have found that (CS) is usually worse, though only slightly so.

7.3.2   An Example of Abstraction

In order to illustrate some of the algorithms mentioned so far in this Chapter I shall display the results of applying algorithms (A), (B), (C) and (CS) to the function *update*. This is a function that occurs in the standard KRC prelude—see Turner (1982b), p. 27—and its definition in the interactive Lispkit system described in Chapter 1 would be:

```
(def update (lambda (f x y z) (if (eq z x) y (f z)))).
```

---

[5]This information comes from Peyton Jones (1987), pp. 272–273, and Turner (1984), p. 5.30.

The result of applying algorithm (A) to this yields a CL-term of length 466:

$$((S((S(KS))((S((S(KS))((S(KK))(KS))))((S((S(KS))((S((S(KS))$$
$$((S(KK))(KS))))((S((S(KS))((S(KK))(KK))))((S(KK))(KS))))))$$
$$((S((S(KS))((S((S(KS))((S(KK))(KS))))((S((S(KS))((S((S(KS))$$
$$((S(KK))(KS))))((S((S(KS))((S(KK))(KK))))((S(KK))(KS))))))$$
$$((S((S(KS))((S((S(KS))((S(KK))(KS))))((S((S(KS))((S((S(KS))$$
$$((S(KK))(KS))))((S((S(KS))((S(KK))(KK))))((S(KK))(KS))))))$$
$$((S((S(KS))((S((S(KS))((S(KK))(KS))))((S((S(KS))((S(KK))(KK))))$$
$$((S(KK))(KK))))))((S((S(KS))((S(KK))(KK))))((S(KK))(K\ IF))))))))$$
$$((S((S(KS))((S((S(KS))((S(KK))(KS))))((S((S(KS))((S((S(KS))$$
$$((S(KK))(KS))))((S((S(KS))((S(KK))(KK))))((S(KK))(KS))))))$$
$$((S((S(KS))((S((S(KS))((S(KK))(KS))))((S((S(KS))((S((S(KS))$$
$$((S(KK))(KS))))((S((S(KS))((S(KK))(KK))))((S(KK))(KS))))))$$
$$((S((S(KS))((S((S(KS))((S(KK))(KS))))((S((S(KS))((S(KK))(KK))))$$
$$((S(KK))(KK))))))((S((S(KS))((S(KK))(KK))))((S(KK))(K\ EQ))))))))$$
$$((S((S(KS))((S(KK))(KK))))((S(KK))(KI))))))))$$
$$((S((S(KS))((S((S(KS))((S(KK))(KS))))((S((S(KS))((S(KK))(KK))))$$
$$((S(KK))(KK))))))((S((S(KS))((S(KK))(KK))))(KI)))))))))$$
$$((S((S(KS))((S((S(KS))((S(KK))(KS))))$$
$$((S((S(KS))((S(KK))(KK))))((S(KK))(KK))))))((S(KK))(KI)))))))))$$
$$((S((S(KS))((S((S(KS))((S(KK))(KS))))((S((S(KS))((S((S(KS))$$
$$((S(KK))(KS))))((S((S(KS))((S(KK))(KK))))((S(KK))(KS))))))$$
$$((S((S(KS))((S((S(KS))((S(KK))(KS))))((S((S(KS))((S(KK))(KK))))$$
$$((S(KK))(KK))))))((S((S(KS))((S(KK))(KK))))((S(KK))I)))))))$$
$$((S((S(KS))((S(KK))(KK))))((S(KK))(KI))))).$$

Applying algorithm (B) to the function *update* results in the following CL-term of length 13:

$$(C((BC)((B(BS))((BC)((B(B\ IF))(C\ EQ))))))).$$

The result of applying algorithm (C) to *update* gives the following CL-term of length 9:

$$((C'(C'S))(((B'C'\ IF)((C'\ EQ)I))),$$

and if we make use of algorithm (CS) the resulting CL-term has length 10:

$$((\mathbf{C}'(\mathbf{C}'\mathbf{S}))(((\mathbf{B}^*(\mathbf{C}' \ IF))((\mathbf{C}' \ EQ)\mathbf{I}))\mathbf{I})).$$

7.3.3 Algorithms Involving J and J′

Joy, Rayward-Smith and Burton (1985) discuss several abstraction algorithms which make use of the following set of combinators: $\mathbf{I}$, $\mathbf{S}$, $\mathbf{B}$, $\mathbf{C}$, $\mathbf{S}'$, $\mathbf{B}'$, $\mathbf{C}'$, $\mathbf{J}$ and $\mathbf{J}'$. The combinators $\mathbf{J}$ and $\mathbf{J}'$ have the following properties:

$$
\begin{aligned}
\mathbf{J}PQR &\rightarrow PQ, \\
\mathbf{J}'PQRS &\rightarrow PQR.
\end{aligned}
$$

It should be noted that the cancellating combinator $\mathbf{K}$ is not in the above set. It can, in fact, be defined in terms of $\mathbf{J}$ and $\mathbf{I}$ as $\mathbf{JI}$, since we have:

$$\mathbf{J}IPQ \rightarrow IP \rightarrow P.$$

Note that the letter $\mathbf{J}$ is also used for a different combinator in the literature, for example, in Barendregt (1984), p.163, where we see that

$$\mathbf{J}PQRS \rightarrow PQ(PSR).$$

This combinator will not be used here and $\mathbf{J}$ will always refer to Joy's combinator.

One algorithm using these combinators that Joy, Rayward-Smith and Burton (1985) consider is:

$$
\begin{aligned}
[x]x &= \mathbf{I}, \\
[x]y &= \mathbf{J}Iy, \text{if } x \not\equiv y, \\
[x]Ex &= E, \\
[x]EXY &= \mathbf{S}'E([x]X)([x]Y), \\
[x]EXF &= \mathbf{C}'E([x]X)F, \\
[x]EFX &= \mathbf{B}'EF([x]X), \\
[x]EFG &= \mathbf{J}'EFG, \\
[x]XY &= \mathbf{S}([x]X)([x]Y), \\
[x]XE &= \mathbf{C}([x]X)E, \\
[x]EX &= \mathbf{B}E([x]X), \\
[x]EF &= \mathbf{J}EF.
\end{aligned}
$$

Here it is to be understood that x does not occur in either E, F or G, but x definitely does in X and Y. On p. 216 they call this algorithm Abs/J/2, and they say that if the length of the term to which it is applied is m and the algorithm is applied with n different variables, then the upper bound for the length of the resulting code is $m(2n + 1)$. Another algorithm that they consider which makes use of this set of combinators is like the first, except that it does not contain the clause $[x]Ex = E$. The complexity of this algorithm is again $m(2n + 1)$.

7.3.4 Including W

Turner (1981a), p. 150, introduces the following optimization rule for the combinator **W**:

$$\mathbf{S}PI = \mathbf{W}P.$$

This results in the production

$$[x]Xx = \mathbf{W}([x]X), \text{ if } x \in FV(X). \tag{7.18}$$

This can be justified as follows, assuming that $x \in FV(X)$:

$$
\begin{aligned}
[x]Xx &= \mathbf{S}([x]X)([x]x), \\
&= \mathbf{S}([x]X)\mathbf{I}, \\
&= \mathbf{W}([x]X).
\end{aligned}
$$

The production (7.18) can straightforwardly be incorporated into any of the algorithms discussed so far.

7.3.5 Another Representation for Abstraction Algorithms

Some writers—for example, Peyton Jones (1987), pp. 270 and 273, and Glaser, Hankin and Till (1984), p. 98—use a different representation for algorithms (B) and (C) which makes use of an auxiliary function *opt*. In this representation algorithm (C) becomes:[6]

$$
\begin{aligned}
[x]MN &= opt([x]M, [x]N), \\
[x]x &= \mathbf{I}, \\
[x]y &= \mathbf{K}y, \text{ if } x \not\equiv y.
\end{aligned}
$$

---

[6]This follows the account to be found in Glaser, Hankin and Till (1984) in that it uses a two-place *opt* function, whereas Peyton Jones (1987) uses only a one-place version of it. Nothing of substance hangs on this.

where the optimization function *opt* is defined as follows:

$$
\begin{aligned}
opt(\mathbf{K}P, \mathbf{K}Q) &= \mathbf{K}(PQ), \\
opt(\mathbf{K}P, \mathbf{I}) &= P, \\
opt(\mathbf{K}(PQ), R) &= \mathbf{B}'PQR, \\
opt(\mathbf{K}P, Q) &= \mathbf{B}PQ, \\
opt(\mathbf{B}PQ, \mathbf{K}R) &= \mathbf{C}'PQR, \\
opt(P, \mathbf{K}Q) &= \mathbf{C}PQ, \\
opt(\mathbf{B}PQ, R) &= \mathbf{S}'PQR.
\end{aligned}
$$

To get the $\mathbf{B}^*$ version replace the $\mathbf{B}'$ clause with:

$$ opt(\mathbf{K}P, \mathbf{B}QR) = \mathbf{B}^*PQR. $$

And if we want to include $\mathbf{W}$ in our algorithm, then we add the clause:

$$ opt(P, \mathbf{I}) = \mathbf{W}P. $$

7.4 Infinite Abstraction Algorithms

7.4.1 Abdali's Algorithm

The algorithm that Abdali (1976) develops is a one-sweep algorithm that makes use of an infinite—but finitely generated—set of combinators. In order to explain what a one-sweep algorithm is, consider the problem of abstracting the n variables $x_1, x_2, \ldots, x_n$ from M. A *one-sweep* abstraction algorithm is one which abstracts all these variables simultaneously, whereas a *multi-sweep* algorithm is one which abstracts only one variable at a time. The length of the output of Abdali's algorithm is proportional to the length of its input and it makes use of the following sequences of combinators:

$$
\begin{aligned}
\mathbf{K}_n P Q_1 \ldots Q_n &\;\rightarrow\; P, \text{for } n \geq 1 \\
\mathbf{I}_n^m P_1 \ldots P_n &\;\rightarrow\; P_m, \text{for } n \geq m \geq 1 \\
\mathbf{B}_n^m P Q_1 \ldots Q_m R_1 \ldots R_n &\;\rightarrow\; P(Q_1 R_1 \ldots R_n) \ldots (Q_m R_1 \ldots R_n), \text{for } m, n \geq 1.
\end{aligned}
$$

Here, the Ps, Qs, etc., are arbitrary CL-terms. In order to present Abdali's algorithm we need to define some terms. Let E be a CL-term. If E is not atomic, then $E \equiv E_1 E_2$, for some CL-terms E_1 and E_2. The term E_1 is the *left immediate component* of E and E_2 is the *right immediate component* of

106

E. Both E_1 and E_2 are *immediate components* of E. A CL-term F is a *component* of E if either $F \equiv E$ or if F is a component of an immediate component of E. Recall that every combinatory term E can be represented in the form $hG_1G_2\ldots G_n$, where h is an atom. The *primal components* of E are just $h, G_1, G_2, \ldots, G_n$. The *initial components* are:

$$h, \quad hG_1, \quad hG_1G_2, \quad \ldots, \quad hG_1G_2\ldots G_n.$$

As an example, consider the term [7]

$$IF\ (EQ\ i\ 1)(HD\ s)(f(SUB\ i\ 1)(TL\ s)).$$

This has primal components IF, $EQ\ i\ 1$, $HD\ s$ and $f(SUB\ i\ 1)(TL\ s))$. And its initial components are IF, $IF(EQ\ i\ 1)$, $IF\ (EQ\ i\ 1)(HD\ s)$ and

$$IF\ (EQ\ i\ 1)(HD\ s)(f(SUB\ i\ 1)(TL\ s)).$$

The actual algorithm is as follows. In this it is to be understood that E is a CL-term and that $x_1, x_2, \ldots, x_n$ are variables. $[x_1, x_2, \ldots, x_n]E$ is the first of the following:

1. If $x_i \notin FV(E)$ for all i such that $1 \leq i \leq n$, then $\mathbf{K}_n E$.

2. If $E \equiv x_1 x_2 \ldots x_n$, then $\mathbf{I}$.

3. If $E \equiv x_i$ for some i such that $1 \leq i \leq n$, then $\mathbf{I}_n^i$.

4. If $E \equiv Gx_1 x_2 \ldots x_n$ and $x_i \notin FV(G)$ for all i such that $1 \leq i \leq n$, then G.

5. If $E \equiv Gx_m \ldots x_n$ for some m such that $1 < m \leq n$ and $x_i \notin FV(G)$ for all i such that $m \leq i \leq n$, then $[x_1, \ldots, x_{m-1}]G$.

6. If $E \equiv F_1 F_2 \ldots F_m$, where $F_1, F_2, \ldots, F_m$ are the primal components of E and $F_1 \equiv x_i$ for some i such that $1 \leq i \leq n$, then

$$\mathbf{B}_n^m \mathbf{I}\, \mathbf{I}_n^i([x_1, x_2, \ldots, x_n]F_2)\ldots([x_1, x_2, \ldots, x_n]F_m).$$

7. If $E \equiv F_1 F_2 \ldots F_m$, where F_1 is the longest initial component of E such that $x_i \notin FV(F_1)$ for all i such that $1 \leq i \leq n$ and $F_2, \ldots, F_m$ are primal components of E, then

$$\mathbf{B}_n^{m-1} F_1([x_1, x_2, \ldots, x_n]F_2)\ldots([x_1, x_2, \ldots, x_n]F_m).$$

---

[7] This term corresponds to that Lispkit function which selects the i-th element from a list s.

As an example I shall consider

$$[f, i, s].IF\ (EQ\ i\ 1)(HD\ s)(f(SUB\ i\ 1)(TL\ s)).$$

This is transformed into the CL-term

$$\mathbf{B}_3^3\ IF(\mathbf{B}_3^2(\mathbf{K}_3\ EQ)\mathbf{I}_3^2(\mathbf{K}_3\ 1))(\mathbf{B}_3^1\ HD\ \mathbf{I}_3^3)$$
$$(\mathbf{B}_3^3\mathbf{I}\,\mathbf{I}_3^1(\mathbf{B}_3^2(\mathbf{K}_3\ SUB)\mathbf{I}_3^2(\mathbf{K}_3\ 1))(\mathbf{B}_3^1\ TL\ \mathbf{I}_3^3).$$

Abdali's algorithm is actually much easier to use than at first appears. Unlike the other algorithms in this Section, its motivation was not the efficient compilation of functional programs, but rather to play a role in the use of combinatory logic to provide a theory of computing. Unfortunately, it is outside the scope of this book to discuss this approach here. The interested reader is referred to Orgass and Fitch (1969a, 1969b).

One of the two reasons that Turner (1979a), p. 270, gives against using Abdali's algorithm rather than algorithm (C) is that it 'uses an infinite number of combinators ... which would give the proposed target computer an undesirably complicated instruction set', although he acknowledges that it can produce more compact code than his own algorithm.

7.4.2 Noshita's Algorithm

The fundamental observation underlying Noshita's algorithm is that any finite sequence of identical combinators can be represented by a single symbol. Thus $\mathbf{S}^i$, for example, in Noshita's system has the same effect as the combination $\mathbf{SS}\ldots\mathbf{S}$, where $\mathbf{S}$ occurs i times, but the storage required for $\mathbf{S}^i$ is much less than that required for the combination of $i\ \mathbf{S}$ combinators. In fact, if the length of the input is n and we abstract a variable from this by Noshita's method, then the length of the output will be $O(n \log n)$.

Noshita (1985) makes use of the combinators $\mathbf{I}$, $\mathbf{K}$, $\mathbf{S}^i$, $\overline{\mathbf{S}}^i$, $\mathbf{B}^i$, $\overline{\mathbf{B}}^i$, $\mathbf{C}^i$ and $\overline{\mathbf{C}}^i$, where $i \geq 1$. (I follow his notational conventions in this Subsection.) The connection between the last six of these and the combinators that we have already met is that $\overline{\mathbf{S}}^1 = \mathbf{S}$, $\mathbf{S}^1 = \mathbf{S}'$, $\overline{\mathbf{B}}^1 = \mathbf{B}$, $\mathbf{B}^1 = \mathbf{B}'$, $\overline{\mathbf{C}}^1 = \mathbf{C}$ and $\mathbf{C}^1 = \mathbf{C}'$. Thus, the following relations hold:

$$\begin{aligned}
\mathbf{S}^i PQRS &= \mathbf{S}^{i-1} P(QS)(RS), \\
\mathbf{B}^i PQRS &= \mathbf{B}^{i-1} PQ(RS), \\
\mathbf{C}^i PQRS &= \mathbf{C}^{i-1} P(QS)R, \\
\overline{\mathbf{S}}^i PQR &= \overline{\mathbf{S}}^{i-1} PR(QR),
\end{aligned}$$

$$\overline{\mathbf{B}}^i PQR = \overline{\mathbf{B}}^{i-1} P(QR),$$
$$\overline{\mathbf{C}}^i PQR = \overline{\mathbf{C}}^{i-1} (PR)Q.$$

The algorithm can now be stated in the following way:

$$[x]x = \mathbf{I},$$
$$[x]E = \mathbf{K}E,$$
$$[x]ExX = \overline{\mathbf{S}}^1 E([x]X),$$
$$[x]ExF = \overline{\mathbf{C}}^1 EF,$$
$$[x]\mathbf{S}^i EXY = \mathbf{S}^{i+1} E([x]X)([x]Y),$$
$$[x]\overline{\mathbf{S}}^i XY = \overline{\mathbf{S}}^{i+1} ([x]X)([x]Y),$$
$$[x]\mathbf{B}^i EFX = \mathbf{B}^{i+1} EF([x]X),$$
$$[x]\overline{\mathbf{B}}^i FX = \overline{\mathbf{B}}^{i+1} F([x]X),$$
$$[x]\mathbf{C}^i EXF = \mathbf{C}^{i+1} E([x]X)F,$$
$$[x]\overline{\mathbf{C}}^i XE = \overline{\mathbf{C}}^{i+1} ([x]X)E,$$
$$[x]EXY = \mathbf{S}^1 E([x]X)([x]Y),$$
$$[x]EFX = \mathbf{B}^1 EF([x]X),$$
$$[x]EXF = \mathbf{C}^1 E([x]X)F,$$
$$[x]Ex = E,$$
$$[x]XY = \overline{\mathbf{S}}^1 ([x]X)([x]Y),$$
$$[x]EX = \overline{\mathbf{B}}^1 E([x]X),$$
$$[x]XE = \overline{\mathbf{C}}^1 ([x]X)E.$$

Here, it is to be understood that the variable x does not occur in either E or F, but it definitely does in X and Y.

7.4.3   Piperno's Algorithm

The algorithm that Piperno (1987) considers is a linear one which involves the use of regular combinators. Intuitively, a regular combinator $\mathbf{R}$ is one which has no effect on its first argument. Thus the general form of a regular combinator's reduction property is

$$\mathbf{R}xy_1y_2\ldots y_n \to xY_1Y_2\ldots Y_n,$$

where each of the Y_i can be any combination, permutation or multiplication of some or all of the y_i. The actual regular combinators that Piperno uses are based on those devised by Curry (1930, 1932) over 50 years ago, and Piperno's algorithm is a modification of one of Curry's early algorithms, which is given in Curry (1933). Before presenting the algorithm I shall define what a regular combinator is and then I shall introduce the particular regular combinators used by Piperno.

A term E is *pure* if it is a combination of variables. Thus, a pure term contains no constants. A *combinator* E is a closed λ-term and it is *proper* only when $E \equiv \lambda y_1 y_2 \ldots y_n.F$, where F is a pure combination of the y_i. A *regular* combinator E is a proper combinator such that $E \equiv \lambda x y_1 y_2 \ldots y_n.x Y_1 Y_2 \ldots Y_m$, where the Y_i are pure combinations of the y_j.

Piperno makes use of five sequences of combinators, namely the identificators, the compositors, the permutators, the multiplicators and the cancellators.

For $n \geq 0$, the *identificators* $\mathbf{I}_n$ have the reduction property:

$$\mathbf{I}_n x_0 x_1 \ldots x_n \rightarrow x_0 x_1 \ldots x_n.$$

They can be defined inductively by means of the equations:

$$\mathbf{I}_0 = \mathbf{I},$$
$$\mathbf{I}_{t+1} = \mathbf{B}\mathbf{I}_t, \text{ for } t \geq 0.$$

For $n \geq 1$ and $r \geq 0$ the *multiplicators* $\mathbf{W}_{n,r}$ have the reduction properties:

$$\mathbf{W}_{n,r} x_0 x_1 \ldots x_n \rightarrow x_0 x_1 \ldots x_{n-1} \underbrace{x_n x_n \ldots x_n}_{r+1 \text{times}}.$$

They can also be defined inductively by means of the equations:

$$\mathbf{W}_1 = \mathbf{W},$$
$$\mathbf{W}_{t+1} = \mathbf{B}\mathbf{W}_t, \text{ for } t \geq 1,$$
$$\mathbf{W}_{n,0} = \mathbf{I}_n,$$
$$\mathbf{W}_{n,1} = \mathbf{W}_n,$$
$$\mathbf{W}_{n,s+1} = \mathbf{W}_n \circ \mathbf{W}_{n,s},$$

where $M \circ N$ is an alternative way of writing $\mathbf{B}MN$.

The *permutators* $\mathbf{C}_{m+n,m}$, for $m \geq 1$ and $n \geq 0$, have the following reduction property:

$$\mathbf{C}_{m+n,n} x_0 x_1 \ldots x_{m+n} \rightarrow x_0 x_1 \ldots x_{m-1} x_{m+n} x_m x_{m+1} \ldots x_{m+n-1}.$$

110

The permutators can be defined inductively by means of the following three sets of equations.[8] The first set is:

$$C_1 = C,$$
$$C_{t+1} = BC_t, \text{ for } t \geq 1;$$

the second set of equations is:

$$C_{m+1,m} = C_m,$$
$$C_{m+k+1,m} = C_{m+k+1,m+k} \circ C_{m+k,m}, \text{ for } k \geq 1;$$

and the third set is:

$$C_{m,m} = I_m, \text{ for } m \geq 1.$$

The *compositors* $B_n B_m$, for $m \geq 0$ and $n \geq 1$, have the reduction property:

$$B_n B_m x_0 x_1 \ldots x_{m+n+1} \rightarrow x_0 x_1 \ldots x_m (x_{m+1} \ldots x_{m+n+1}).$$

They can also be defined inductively by means of the equations:

$$B_0 = I,$$
$$B_{t+1} = B \circ B_t,$$
$$B_0 B_t = B_t,$$
$$B_{s+1} B_t = B(B_s B_t).$$

For $n \geq 1$ the *cancellators* K_n have the reduction properties:

$$K_n x_0 x_1 \ldots x_n \rightarrow x_0 x_1 \ldots x_{n-1}.$$

They can also be defined inductively by means of the equations:

$$K_1 = K,$$
$$K_{t+1} = BK_t, \text{ for } t \geq 1.$$

Piperno distinguishes—as does Abdali—between a *one-sweep* and a *multi-sweep* version of the algorithm. The one-sweep version abstracts on several variables simultaneously, whereas the multi-sweep version abstracts only one variable at a time. I shall only consider the multi-sweep version here. The

---

[8]I am grateful to Dr Piperno for supplying me with the correct versions of these definitions. The versions given in his article suffer from typographical errors.

algorithm works in several phases. In the description of the algorithm I will make use of the notation $MCC(E)$, where E is a CL-term. This is to be understood as the multiset or bag $[\![k_1, k_2, \ldots, k_n]\!]$ of all the maximal constant components of E. $\mathbf{H}$ represents a combination of combinators.

The problem is to abstract the variable x from the term E. The algorithm begins from the *initial position* $[x]\mathbf{I}E$—note the insertion of the combinator $\mathbf{I}$—and it terminates with the following transformation:

$$[x]\mathbf{H}v_1 \ldots v_s x = \mathbf{H}v_1 \ldots v_s,$$

if x does not occur in v_j for $1 \le j \le s$.

The first phase of the algorithm involves the removal of parentheses which enclose combinations involving x. The following transformation is repeated until all such parentheses have been eliminated:

$$[x]\mathbf{H}E \equiv [x]\mathbf{H}h_{0,1} \ldots h_{0,j_0}(h_{1,1}M_{1,2} \ldots M_{1,j_1}) \ldots (h_{p,1}M_{p,2} \ldots M_{p,j_p})$$

$$= [x]\mathbf{B}_{j_0}\mathbf{B}_{j_1-1}\mathbf{H}h_{0,1} \ldots h_{0,j_0}h_{1,1}M_{1,2} \ldots M_{1,j_1} \ldots (h_{p,1}M_{p,2} \ldots M_{p,j_p}),$$

where $h_{i,1} \in MCC(E) \cup \{x\}$ for $0 \le i \le p$ and for $2 \le j \le j_0$, $h_{0,j} \equiv x$ or x does not occur in $h_{0,j}$ and there is at least one occurrence of x in $h_{1,1}M_{1,2} \ldots M_{1,j_1}$.

The second phase of the algorithm permutes the arguments of $\mathbf{H}$ until all occurrences of x are at the extreme right:

$$[x]\mathbf{H}h_1 \ldots h_{r-1}h_r h_{r+1} \ldots h_j h_{j+1} \ldots h_p$$

$$= [x]\mathbf{C}_{j,r}\mathbf{H}h_1 \ldots h_{r-1}h_{r+1} \ldots h_j h_r h_{j+1} \ldots h_p,$$

where for $1 \le k \le r-1, h_k \equiv x$ or x does not occur in h_k; and $h_r \equiv x$; and for $r+1 \le k \le j, x$ does not occur in h_k; and for $j+1 \le k \le p, h_k \equiv x$.

The third phase replaces several occurrences of x with a single one:

$$[x]\mathbf{H}v_1 \ldots v_s \underbrace{x \ldots x}_{r \text{ times}} = [x]\mathbf{W}_{s+1,r}\mathbf{H}v_1 \ldots v_s x,$$

where x does not occur in v_k for $1 \le k \le s$.

The final phase of the algorithm—before termination—inserts an occurrence of x if there was not one before:

$$[x]\mathbf{H}v_1 \ldots v_s = [x]\mathbf{K}_{s+1}\mathbf{H}v_1 \ldots v_s x,$$

where x does not occur in v_k for $1 \le k \le s$.

To illustrate the operation of Piperno's algorithm I shall consider the problem of abstracting s from the term

$$IF\ (EQ\ i\ 1)(HD\ s)(f(SUB\ i\ 1)(TL\ s)).$$

Let $M_1 \equiv IF\ (EQ\ i\ 1)$ and $M_2 \equiv f(SUB\ i\ 1)$. As neither M_1 nor M_2 depend for their meaning on s they can be treated as units. The initial position of the algorithm is obtained by putting **I** at the front of the term from which we are abstracting s:

$$\begin{aligned}
& [s]\mathbf{I}\ M_1\ (HD\ s)(M_2\ (TL\ s)) \\
=\ & [s](\mathbf{B}_1\mathbf{B}_1)\mathbf{I}\ M_1\ HD\ s\ (M_2\ (TL\ s)), \\
=\ & [s](\mathbf{B}_3\mathbf{B}_1 \circ \mathbf{B}_1\mathbf{B}_1)\mathbf{I}\ M_1\ HD\ s\ M_2\ (TL\ s), \\
=\ & [s](\mathbf{B}_4\mathbf{B}_1 \circ \mathbf{B}_3\mathbf{B}_1 \circ \mathbf{B}_1\mathbf{B}_1)\mathbf{I}\ M_1\ HD\ s\ M_2\ TL\ s, \\
=\ & [s](\mathbf{C}_{5,3} \circ \mathbf{B}_4\mathbf{B}_1 \circ \mathbf{B}_3\mathbf{B}_1 \circ \mathbf{B}_1\mathbf{B}_1)\mathbf{I}\ M_1\ HD\ M_2\ TL\ s\ s, \\
=\ & [s](\mathbf{W}_{5,2} \circ \mathbf{C}_{5,3} \circ \mathbf{B}_4\mathbf{B}_1 \circ \mathbf{B}_3\mathbf{B}_1 \circ \mathbf{B}_1\mathbf{B}_1)\mathbf{I}\ M_1\ HD\ M_2\ TL\ s, \\
=\ & (\mathbf{W}_{5,2} \circ \mathbf{C}_{5,3} \circ \mathbf{B}_4\mathbf{B}_1 \circ \mathbf{B}_3\mathbf{B}_1 \circ \mathbf{B}_1\mathbf{B}_1)\mathbf{I}\ M_1\ HD\ M_2\ TL.
\end{aligned}$$

Piperno's algorithm is further discussed in the next Chapter, where it is compared with Hughes's supercombinator abstraction algorithm.

Chapter 8

Supercombinators

8.1 Introduction

In this Chapter I look at algorithms that make use of supercombinators. To begin with, I describe Burton's balancing transformation which is applied to a term before that term is subjected to bracket abstraction. Burton introduced the notion of a supercombinator—under the name of autonomous function—but his algorithm leaves a lot to be desired. Then I discuss Hughes's work which has led to the most efficient implementations of purely functional languages, namely those based on the G-machine. To conclude, I compare Hughes's supercombinator abstraction algorithm with the multi-sweep version of Piperno's compositive abstraction algorithm discussed in the previous Chapter.

8.2 Burton's Balancing Operation

Finding the complexity of Turner's algorithm (C) unacceptable and being interested in the evaluation of functional programs on parallel machines, Burton suggested that the λ-term translation of a functional program be subjected to a balancing transformation before being compiled into combinators.[1] The balancing transformation can only be applied to certain λ-terms, namely those which are autonomous expressions, but—fortunately—every λ-term is equivalent to some autonomous expression. In order to define what an autonomous expression is we first have to define

---

[1] The following account is based on Burton (1982), Joy, Rayward-Smith and Burton (1985), pp.21ff., and Kennaway and Sleep (1987a).

a simple function. A *simple function* is a closed λ-term $\lambda x_1 x_2 \ldots x_n.E$, where E contains no subexpressions which are λ-abstractions. Because a simple function is a closed λ-term a variable can only occur in E if it is one of the x_i. Examples of simple functions are: $\lambda xyz.xy(xz)$, $\lambda xyz.xxyyzz$, $\lambda xyz.zy$, $\lambda xy.x$, $\lambda xy.y$ and $\lambda x.x$. An *autonomous function* F is either a simple function or it is the result of replacing zero or more atoms in an autonomous function by simple functions. Examples of autonomous functions are: $\lambda yz.(\lambda xy.x)y((\lambda xy.x)z)$, $\lambda yz.(\lambda xyz.zy)(\lambda xyz.zy)yyzz$ and $\lambda yz.zy$. It is now possible to define an *autonomous expression* as a combination $B_1 B_2 \ldots B_n$, where each B_i is either a constant or an autonomous function or an autonomous expression.

In order to explain how an arbitrary λ-term can be transformed into an autonomous expression, let F be a λ-term $\lambda x_1 x_2 \ldots x_n.E$, where E is not a λ-abstraction and where F contains free variables $y_1, y_2, \ldots, y_m$, then F is equivalent to the autonomous expression

$$(\lambda y_1 y_2 \ldots y_m x_1 x_2 \ldots x_n.E)y_1 y_2 \ldots y_m.$$

Performing the above transformation throughout an arbitrary λ-term yields an equivalent autonomous expression. In the worst case, however, this transformation causes a quadratic expansion in the sizes of the λ-term. One of the advantages of evaluating autonomous expressions—as opposed to arbitrary λ-terms—on a parallel machine is that autonomous expressions do not contain what Burton calls global variables, that is to say, variables bound by an enclosing λ-abstraction, and such global variables are—according to Burton (1982), p. 202—those which are likely to involve high communication costs. The class of autonomous functions is exactly the same as the class of functional programs without a global variable reference.

The balancing operation *balance* (E), where E is an autonomous expression is defined as follows:

$$
\begin{aligned}
balance(E) \quad &= \quad E, \text{if } \#E \leq 3, \\
&= \quad balance(E_1)balance(E_2), \text{if } 3\#E_1 \leq 2\#E \text{ and } 3\#E_2 \leq 2\#E, \\
&= \quad ([x].balance([x/F]E))balance(F).
\end{aligned}
$$

Here, $\#E$ signifies the number of non-constant atoms in E and if E is non-atomic, then we have that $E \equiv E_1 E_2$. Furthermore, $F = select\ (E)$, where $select\ (E)$ is any subexpression G of E for which $|\ \#E - 2\#G\ |$ is a minimum. In Burton's original article the bracket abstraction algorithm used is (C). Note that in the third clause of the definition there occurs the notation

$[x/F]E$. For this to be meaningful F must be a subexpression of E and x must be a variable that is not free in E. In that case it yields a term E' which is the same as E except that the expression F has been replaced by the variable x. Only one occurrence of F is replaced, even if there is more than one in E.

If in the course of this balancing operation we come across an autonomous expression, then that is to be balanced independently. Such internal transformations are assumed to be completed before their containing expression. Some examples of the effect of the function $balance(F)$ are as follows:

$$balance\ (a(b(cd))) \ = \ (\lambda x.a(bx))(cd),$$
$$balance\ (abcd) \ = \ (\lambda x.xcd)(ab).$$

The length of code produced by this balancing transformation is—according to Joy, Rayward-Smith and Burton (1985), p. 218—$O(m\log n)$, where m is the size of the original autonomous expression and n is the number of variables abstracted from E.

In order to make the ideas involved in Burton's balancing operation clearer I shall work through an example. A program to calculate 5^2 can be written in Lispkit as:

```
(letrec ((power (quote 2)) (quote 5))
   (power lambda (x) (lambda (y)
      (if (eq x (quote 0))
          (quote 1)
          (if (even x)
              (sq ((power (div x (quote 2))) y))
              (mul y ((power (sub x (quote 1))) y)))))))).
```

The declaration involved in this program is translated into the following term $\mathbf{Y}([p,x,y]E)$, where E is the CL-term

$IF\ (EQ\ x\ 0)1(IF\ (EVEN\ x)(SQ\ (p(DIV\ x\ 2)y))(MUL\ y(p(SUB\ x\ 1)y)))$,

but before we perform the abstraction of y, x and p we have to apply the function $balance$ to the subexpression E from which those variables are to be abstracted. Here, $\#E = 9$, $\#E_1 = 1$ and $\#E_2 = 8$, therefore we need to use the third clause of the definition of the function $balance$ in order to calculate

116

$balance(E)$. This involves locating $select(E)$. There are two subexpressions for which $|\,\#E - 2\#G\,|$ is minimal in E, namely

$$IF\ (EVEN\ x)(SQ\ (p\ (DIV\ x\ 2)\ y)),$$

and the expression
$$MUL\ y(p(SUB\ x\ 1)y).$$

Let us choose the second of these as $select(E)$. Then E becomes

$$([a].balance(E'))balance(E''),$$

where

$$E' \equiv IF\ (EQ\ x\ 0)1(IF\ (EVEN\ x)(SQ\ (p(DIV\ x\ 2)y))a),$$
$$E'' \equiv MUL\ y(p(SUB\ x\ 1)y).$$

Now, let us consider $balance(E')$. Here, again we need to apply the third clause of the definition of the function $balance$. There is only one choice for $select(E')$ and that is $SQ\ (p(DIV\ x\ 2)y)$. Therefore $balance(E')$ is

$$([b]balance(IF\ (EQ\ x\ 0)1(IF\ (EVEN\ x)b\ a)))balance(SQ\ (p(DIV\ x\ 2)y)).$$

The term $SQ\ (p(DIV\ x\ 2)y)$ only contains three variables, so applying $balance$ to it leaves it unchanged, but applying the function $balance$ to the expression

$$E''' \equiv IF\ (EQ\ x\ 0)1(IF\ (EVEN\ x)b\ a))$$

involves the use of the third clause of the definition of that function. In this case we have

$$select(E''') \equiv IF\ (EVEN\ x)b,$$
$$balance(E''') \equiv ([c](IF\ (EQ\ x\ 0)1(c\ a)))(IF\ (EVEN\ x)b).$$

Putting all this together we have that $balance(E')$ is the expression

$$([b](([c](IF\ (EQ\ x\ 0)1(c\ a)))(IF\ (EVEN\ x)b)))(SQ\ (p(DIV\ x\ 2)y)).$$

Now, we consider the expression E''. To evaluate $balance(E'')$ we again have to use the third clause of the definition of $balance$. Doing this yields:

$$select(E'') \equiv p(SUB\ x\ 1),$$
$$balance(E'') \equiv ([d](MUL\ y\ (d\ y)))(p(SUB\ x\ 1)).$$

Finally, we can bring all these results together and reveal $balance(E)$ to be

$$([a](([b](([c](IF\ (EQ\ x\ 0)1(c\ a)))(IF\ (EVEN\ x)b)))(SQ\ (p(DIV\ x\ 2)y))))$$
$$([d](MUL\ y\ (d\ y)))(p(SUB\ x\ 1)).$$

If we actually perform all the abstractions in this term using algorithm (C), then we obtain the CL-term:

$$((((\mathbf{S'S})(((\mathbf{B'(S'S'((BC)((S(((C'C'((BB'(((C'B}1)$$
$$((\mathbf{B}\ IF)(((\mathbf{C'}\ EQ)\mathbf{I})0)))1)))(\mathbf{CI})))$$
$$((\mathbf{B}\ IF)\ EVEN)))) (((\mathbf{B'(B'B))}\ SQ)(((\mathbf{C'B)I}(((\mathbf{C'}\ DIV)\mathbf{I})2)))))$$
$$(((\mathbf{B'(B'C))}(((\mathbf{S'(B'}\ MUL))\mathbf{I})(\mathbf{CI})))(((\mathbf{C'B)I}(((\mathbf{C'}\ SUB)\mathbf{I})1))))$$

This has length 56. However, if we calculate $[p][x][y]E$ directly, without performing the balancing operation, then we obtain a term whose length is only 44. The actual term is:

$$(((\mathbf{B'S})(((\mathbf{C'B'((B}\ IF)(((\mathbf{C'}\ EQ)\mathbf{I})0)))1))(((\mathbf{S'S})$$
$$(((\mathbf{B'(S'S'((B}\ IF)\ EVEN))(((\mathbf{B'(B'B))}\ SQ)$$
$$(((\mathbf{C'B)I}(((\mathbf{C'}\ DIV)\mathbf{I})2)))))(((\mathbf{B'(B'(S'}\ MUL)))\mathbf{I})$$
$$(((\mathbf{C'B)I}(((\mathbf{C'}\ SUB)\mathbf{I})1)))))$$

According to Joy, Rayward-Smith and Burton (1985), pp. 217ff., there are circumstances in which balancing does improve the performance of an abstraction algorithm.

8.3   Hughes's Contribution

Hughes (1982, 1984a) introduced the term 'supercombinator' with the same meaning as *autonomous function*, but the really significant contribution that he made to the implementation of functional languages was the algorithm that he devised for locating supercombinators in a λ-term. All the most efficient implementations of lazy functional languages at present are based on Hughes's work. Before presenting the algorithm I shall define certain phrases relating to supercombinators.[2]

A *supercombinator* α of *arity* n, where $n \geq 0$, is a closed λ-term:

$$\lambda x_1 x_2 \ldots x_n . E,$$

---

[2]These are based on definitions given by Peyton Jones (1986), p. 182.

where E is not a λ-abstraction and—furthermore—if E contains any sub-expressions which are themselves λ-abstractions, then they must be super-combinators as well.

A *supercombinator redex* is a combination:

$$\alpha M_1 M_2 \ldots M_n,$$

where α is a supercombinator of arity n and the M_i are its n arguments. A *supercombinator contraction* is the replacement of supercombinator redex by its corresponding contractum and a *supercombinator expansion* is the converse transformation.

An example should make these ideas clearer. This is an example of a supercombinator:

$$\alpha \equiv \lambda pqs.(ADD\ s\ (MUL\ p\ q)),$$

and a supercombinator redex can be illustrated by $\alpha\ 3\ 67\ 5$, which has the contractum $(ADD\ 5\ (MUL\ 3\ 67))$.

In order to explain how we transform an arbitrary λ-term into super-combinators it is first necessary to introduce the concept of a free expression. This is best done by considering a simple example, and for this purpose I will use that which Hughes (1982), p. 16, uses. This is the function which selects the i-th element of a list s. In the following Lispkit program this function f is used to select the second element from a list of vowels.

```
(letrec
   (f (quote 2) (quote (a e i o u)))
   (f lambda (i) (lambda (s)
         (if (eq i 1)
             (head s)
             (f (sub i 1) (tail s)))))))
```

Note that here f is a higher-order function of type $int \rightarrow list\ \alpha \rightarrow \alpha$, rather than a two-place first-order function of type $(int \times list\ \alpha) \rightarrow \alpha$. A function of this type could just as easily be defined in the same Lispkit system. The Lispkit function f is equivalent to the λ-term:

$$F \equiv \mathbf{Y}(\lambda fis.(IF\ (EQ\ i\ 1)(HD\ s)(f(SUB\ i\ 1)(TL\ s)))).$$

If we wanted to translate this into combinators, then we would repeatedly replace the current innermost λ-abstraction by bracket abstraction and apply a suitable abstraction algorithm. In the case of the term F this would have to be done three times. The resulting CL-term would then be made up entirely out of constants. One problem with this approach is that when we came to evaluate an expression containing this term each combinator reduction would only involve a small manipulation of the program graph. These are relatively small grain operations. By contrast, supercombinators involve larger grain operations. Another of the differences between combinators and supercombinators is that the class of supercombinators that we are going to need in any particular application is not known in advance. To illustrate how a supercombinator is obtained from a λ-term I will first consider the innermost abstraction of the term F, namely:

$$M \equiv \lambda s.IF\ (EQ\ i\ 1)(HD\ s)(f(SUB\ i\ 1)(TL\ s)).$$

The notion of a free variable is well-understood and in M the free variables are i and f. The *free expressions* of a λ-term which is an abstraction are all its subexpressions that do not depend for their meaning on the binding variable. It is thus possible for constants to be constituents of free expressions. M has a large number of free expressions; some of them are: $EQ, EQ\ i, EQ\ i\ 1$ and $IF\ (EQ\ i\ 1)$. Out of all the free expressions of a λ-term it is possible to single out the *maximal free expressions* or *mfes*. These are only those free expressions which are not proper subexpressions of a free expression. Thus, $EQ\ i$ is not a maximal free expression of M, because it is a proper subexpression of the free expression $EQ\ i\ 1$, but $IF\ (EQ\ i\ 1)$ is a maximal free expression of M. M has only one further maximal free expression and that is $f\ (SUB\ i\ 1)$.

As the maximal free expressions of M do not depend on the binding variable s it is possible to "export" them out of the body of the λ-abstraction by performing expansions on them. In the example under consideration—by performing two expansions—we obtain the term:

$$N \equiv \underbrace{\lambda pqs.p(HD\ s)(q(TL\ s))}_{\alpha}\underbrace{(IF\ (EQ\ i\ 1))}_{M_1}\underbrace{(f\ (SUB\ i\ 1))}_{M_2},$$

where M_1 and M_2 are the two mfes already mentioned. The initial segment of N, namely $\lambda pqs.p(HD\ s)(q(TL\ s))$, contains no free variables, so it is a supercombinator. Let us call it α. Clearly it has the following reduction property:

$$\alpha pqs \rightarrow p(HD\ s)(q(TL\ s)).$$

The definition of the function F can now be transformed into:

$$\mathbf{Y}(\lambda fi.\alpha(IF\ (EQ\ i\ 1))(f(SUB\ i\ 1)),$$

and we can again transform the innermost λ-abstraction into a constant applicative form involving a supercombinator. This time:

$$\lambda i.\alpha(\mathit{IF}\ (\mathit{EQ}\ i\ 1))(f(\mathit{SUB}\ i\ 1)),$$

becomes βf, where:

$$\beta \equiv \lambda fi.\alpha(\mathit{IF}\ (\mathit{EQ}\ i\ 1))(f(\mathit{SUB}\ i\ 1)),$$

and, therefore, has the reduction property:

$$\beta fi \to \alpha(\mathit{IF}\ (\mathit{EQ}\ i\ 1))(f(\mathit{SUB}\ i\ 1)).$$

Thus, we can transform F into $\mathbf{Y}(\lambda f.\beta f)$, which—by making use of η-conversion—is just the same as $\mathbf{Y}\beta$. Putting all these things together, we see that our original Lispkit function definition has been transformed into $\mathbf{Y}\beta$, where:

$$\begin{aligned}
\alpha pqs \quad &\to \quad p(\mathit{HD}\ s)(q(\mathit{TL}\ s)), \\
\beta fi \quad &\to \quad \alpha(\mathit{IF}\ (\mathit{EQ}\ i\ 1))(f(\mathit{SUB}\ i\ 1)).
\end{aligned}$$

8.3.1 Optimal Ordering of Parameters

In the example just discussed we introduced a supercombinator α which satisfied the property that:

$$\alpha pqs \to p(\mathit{HD}\ s)(q(\mathit{TL}\ s)),$$

but it would have been just as "sensible" to introduce a supercombinator α' such that:

$$\alpha' qps \to p(\mathit{HD}\ s)(q(\mathit{TL}\ s)).$$

In this case we would have had to deal with a term $N' \equiv \alpha' M_2 M_1$, rather than $N \equiv \alpha M_1 M_2$. In this example there is no advantage in choosing either α or α', but in the general case the ordering of the parameters that are passed to a supercombinator has a great effect on the number of supercombinators needed and on the efficiency of the evaluation process. Let us consider the supercombinator redex $\alpha M_1 M_2 \ldots M_n$, where α is a supercombinator of arity n and let $x_1, x_2, \ldots, x_p$ be the binding variables of the λ-term in which our redex occurs, with x_1 being the outermost and x_p the innermost. The M_i will contain some—but not necessarily all—of the variables $x_1, x_2, \ldots, x_p$. Consider the variable x_p. In the optimal ordering all of the M_i which contain

x_p should be to the right of all the M_i which do not contain x_p. Let k be the maximum number such that M_k does not contain x_p and now let us consider

$$\alpha M_1 M_2 \ldots M_k.$$

Clearly, we require that each of the M_i which do contain x_{p-1} to occur to the right of all of the M_i which do not contain x_{p-1}, and so on for each of the x_i.

8.3.2 The Supercombinator Algorithm

Starting from an arbitrary Lispkit program the compilation process involving Hughes's supercombinators proceeds as follows. First, the Lispkit program is turned into a λ-term, say E. Then we carry out the following steps:

1. Locate the innermost λ-abstraction in E. If there are several, pick the leftmost. Call this λ-abstraction $\lambda x.F$.

2. Let $M_1, M_2, \ldots, M_n$ be the non-constant maximal free expressions occurring in F, optimally ordered, and let $F' \equiv [x_1/M_1, \ldots, x_n/M_n]F$, where the x_i are variables not occurring in F.

3. Give the term F' a name, say α, and then replace $\lambda x.F$ with the term $\alpha M_1 M_2 \ldots M_n$ in E.

4. Repeat steps 1–3 until all λ-abstractions have been accounted for.

A supercombinator reducer is fully lazy. This means that every term is evaluated at most once after the variables it contains have been bound.

8.3.3 Another Example

In order to compare the result of the supercombinator algorithm with some of the other algorithms I have discussed I will show the result of applying Hughes's algorithm to the λ-term which calculates powers by Pingala's algorithm. The λ-tem in question, p, is

$$\mathbf{Y}(\lambda pxy.IF\ (EQ\ x\ 0)1(IF\ (EVEN\ x)$$
$$(SQ\ (p(DIV\ x\ 2)y))(MUL\ y(p(SUB\ x\ 1)y)))).$$

Considering the innermost λ-abstraction we see that its maximal free expressions are $IF\ (EQ\ x\ 0)1, IF\ (EVEN\ x), p(DIV\ x\ 2)$ and $p(SUB\ x\ 1)$. The required supercombinator is, therefore, α with the reduction property:

$$\alpha tqrsy \rightarrow t(q(SQ\ (ry))(MUL\ y(sy))).$$

Substituting in the original definition transforms it into:

$$\mathbf{Y}(\lambda px.\alpha(IF\ (EQ\ x\ 0)1)(IF\ (EVEN\ x))(p(DIV\ x\ 2))(p(SUB\ x\ 1))).$$

Considering the innermost λ-abstraction we see that the required supercombinator is β, whose reduction property is:

$$\beta px \rightarrow \alpha(IF\ (EQ\ x\ 0)1)(IF\ (EVEN\ x))(p(DIV\ x\ 2))(p(SUB\ x\ 1)).$$

Using this and η-conversion, the definition of p is transformed into $\mathbf{Y}\beta$.

8.3.4   Level Numbers

There is a very nice algorithm for determining all the maximal free expressions of any λ-term. It is described, for example, in Hughes (1984a), pp. 40–41. The algorithm makes use of the notion of an expression's *lexical level*, or *level* for short. In order to calculate this we have to first associate a number with each binding occurrence of a variable in a given λ-term. Using the term:

$$\lambda fis.(IF\ (EQ\ i\ 1)(HD\ s)(f(SUB\ i\ 1)(TL\ s))),$$

for illustrative purposes, we associate the number 1 with the outermost binding variable, which in this case is f. Then, we associate 2 with the next binding variable, namely i, and so on. Thus, s is associated with 3. For convenience, constants are assigned the number 0.

The lexical level of each subexpression that is not a λ-abstraction in the above λ-term can now be calculated. We know the level of each atomic term, the lexical level of a combination PQ is simply the maximum of the levels of P and Q. We do not need to be able to work out the lexical level of a λ-abstraction, because we are going to repeatedly replace the innermost λ-abstraction by a constant applicative form. Thus, in the above term, as the variable f has level 1 and the subexpression $(SUB\ i\ 1)$ has level 2, therefore $(f(SUB\ i\ 1)$ has level 2. The expression $(TL\ s)$ has level 3, therefore $(f(SUB\ i\ 1)(TL\ s))$ also has lexical level 3.

Given that we can calculate each subexpression's level, we can now individuate all the maximal free expressions in a λ-term. An expression is a maximal free expression if its level number is strictly less than that of its immediately enclosing application. Note that this locates all the maximal free expressions in a λ-term and not just those of the innermost λ-abstraction.

The level number associated with each expression in a term also enables us to order the parameters of a supercombinator optimally. Let $\alpha M_1 M_2 \ldots M_n$, be a redex. Then the terms $M_1, M_2, \ldots, M_n$, are ordered optimally if they are in the order of increasing level numbers. That is to say, M_i comes before M_j iff the level of M_i is less than or equal to that of M_j.

8.4 Piperno's Algorithm and Supercombinators

In discussing Piperno's algorithm I used as an example the abstraction of the variable s from the term

$$IF\ (EQ\ i\ 1)(HD\ s)(f(SUB\ i\ 1)(TL\ s)).$$

This results in the term $\mathbf{H}\ M_1\ HD\ M_2\ TL$, where

$$
\begin{aligned}
\mathbf{H} &\equiv (\mathbf{W}_{5,2} \circ \mathbf{C}_{5,3} \circ \mathbf{B}_4\mathbf{B}_1 \circ \mathbf{B}_3\mathbf{B}_1 \circ \mathbf{B}_1\mathbf{B}_1)\mathbf{I}, \\
M_1 &\equiv IF\ (EQ\ i\ 1), \\
M_2 &\equiv f(SUB\ i\ 1).
\end{aligned}
$$

The terms M_1 and M_2 are maximal free expressions and, if we amend Piperno's algorithm to include the permutation and optimal ordering of maximal free expressions, we can then establish the connection between it and Hughes's supercombinator algorithm. In this case, the result of the amended algorithm would be

$$\mathbf{C}_{3,1}(\mathbf{C}_{4,3}\mathbf{H})HD\ TL\ M_1\ M_2.$$

The supercombinator α—where $\alpha pqs \rightarrow p(HD\ s)(q(TL\ s))$—corresponds to the combinator $\mathbf{C}_{3,1}(\mathbf{C}_{4,3}\mathbf{H})HD\ TL$, which, when expanded, is

$$(\mathbf{C}_{3,1} \circ \mathbf{C}_{4,3} \circ \mathbf{W}_{5,2} \circ \mathbf{C}_{5,3} \circ \mathbf{B}_4\mathbf{B}_1 \circ \mathbf{B}_3\mathbf{B}_1 \circ \mathbf{B}_1\mathbf{B}_1)\mathbf{I}\ HD\ TL.$$

In the general case, the amended version of Piperno's algorithm, when applied to an abstraction $[x]E$, results in a CL-term of the following form: $\mathbf{R}\mathbf{I}K_1 \ldots K_i M_1 \ldots M_j$, where $\mathbf{R}$ is a regular combinator, $K_1, \ldots, K_i$ are constant subexpressions of E and $M_1, \ldots, M_j$ are the maximal free expressions of $\lambda x.E$. The result of applying the supercombinator algorithm to E

124

would be a term $\alpha M_1 \ldots M_j$ such that $\alpha M_1 \ldots M_j \to E$, where $M_1, \ldots, M_j$ are as above. Thus, the supercombinator α corresponds to the CL-term $\mathbf{R}\mathbf{I}K_1 \ldots K_i$.

As already mentioned, Piperno's algorithm is linear, but its advantage over Hughes's algorithm—or so Piperno claims—is that it uses a *fixed* set of combinators, whereas supercombinators are generated in a way that depends on the term being analysed. Thus, it is simpler to implement the instruction set of a reducer that employs the combinators that Piperno's algorithm uses. To the best of my knowledge, these claims of Piperno's are only theoretical and have not been tested in practice.

Chapter 9

Pattern-matching

9.1 Introduction

To begin with, in Chapter 4 I considered how to translate a Lispkit program into combinator machine code. A simple example of such a program is the following, which calculates the length of a given list, in this case the list $(a\ b\ c\ d\ e)$:

```
(letrec
   (length (quote (a b c d e)))
      (length lambda (x)
         (if (eq x (quote Nil))
             (quote 0)
             (add (quote 1)
                  (length (tail x)))))).
```

Using the bracket abstraction algorithm (C), this compiles into the following CL-term:

$$(((\mathbf{CI})((CONS\ a)((CONS\ b)((CONS\ c)((CONS\ d)((CONS\ e)\ NIL))))))$$
$$(\mathbf{Y}(((\mathbf{B'S})(((\mathbf{C'}\ IF)(((\mathbf{C'}\ EQ)\mathbf{I})\ NIL))0))$$
$$(((\mathbf{B'}(\mathbf{B'}\ ADD))1)(((\mathbf{C'B})\mathbf{I})\ TAIL))))).$$

Near the end of Chapter 2 I considered how the Lispkit programming environment could be modified so that it might be used interactively. In such a system we would first define the function *length* and then use it to find out

126

the length of various lists. As an example of a sample interactive session we have the following:

```
==>    (define length (lambda (x)
            (if (eq x (quote NIL))
                (quote 0)
                (add (quote 1)
                    (length (tail x))))))

==> (length (quote (a b c d e)))

5

==> (length (quote (a b)))

2
```

Towards the end of Chapter 5 I showed how such an interactive version of Lispkit could be implemented. The definition of the *length* function in such a system would be compiled into the CL-term:

$$((S(((C'\ IF)(((C'\ EQ)I)\ NIL))0))(((B'\ ADD)1)((B\ length)\ TAIL))).$$

Some people—most notably Turner—dislike the traditional Lisp syntax and have departed from it quite significantly. The favourite alternative syntax is modelled on recursion equations and this also allows the use of pattern-matching. KRC is an example of such a language. Here the definition of a function is distinct from its use—as in the examples from the interactive Lispkit system just given—but KRC also supports pattern-matching, so the definition of the *length* function can be split into two parts as follows:

$$length\ [\ ]\ =\ 0,$$
$$length\ (a:x)\ =\ 1+length\ x.$$

By analogy with the compilation of the above Lispkit program, we would assume that the two clauses of the KRC definition of *length* would be transformed into:

$$length\ =\ [NIL]\ 0,$$
$$length\ =\ [CONS\ a\ x]\ ADD\ 1\ (length\ x).$$

127

Here, I have used *NIL* for the empty list in order to avoid such combinations of symbols as $[[\ ]]E$ for abstracting the empty list from an expression E. Several problems still remain with the suggested translation. The first is that we need to give some account of bracket abstraction with respect to a constant like *NIL* and also with respect to a structured object like $(CONS\ a\ x)$. The latter problem was discussed in connection with the way in which mutually recursive definitions in Lispkit are translated into combinatory logic, but further considerations apply here. The second problem concerns how we are to put together the various components of the definition of the *length* function.

Turner solved both of these problems by introducing a number of further combinators. In order to deal with the problem of abstracting the empty list from an arbitrary term he introduced the combinator *MATCH*, to cope with abstracting structured objects the strict uncurrying combinator, namely $\underline{U}$,[1] and to deal with the problem of combining the separately compiled clauses the combinator *TRY*. Once such combinators have been introduced for dealing with pattern-matching involving list operations it is possible to use similar ideas in the compilation of other structured data types.

9.2   Extending the Abstraction Algorithm

Turner (1981a) extends the notion of bracket abstraction to allow the abstraction of constants and structured objects and not just isolated variables. Let *CONS* be the curried pairing operator. Turner allows $[CONS\ x\ y]M$, and he defines it so that

$$[CONS\ x\ y]M = \underline{U}([x]([y]M)),$$

where the strict uncurrying operator $\underline{U}$ has the following reduction properties:

$$\underline{U}f(CONS\ x\ y) \quad \to \quad fxy,$$
$$\underline{U}fz \quad \to \quad FAIL.$$

Here, *FAIL* is an additional constant that cannot occur in a legal program. It has the property that $FAIL\ x \to FAIL$.[2] The combinator $\underline{U}$ is similar to U

---

[1] Turner actually uses the combination of symbols $\underline{U}$, but it looks better—in my opinion—to underline the letter $\underline{U}$.

[2] In the extension of *SASL* proposed by Abramson (1986), which he calls HASL, *FAIL* can be a component of a legal program.

that we met in Chapter 4, except that there it was not necessary to consider what happens when **U** is applied to an unstructured object. The reason that we have to consider this possibility here is that, intuitively, what happens to a multi-clause function definition like that of *length* when we translate it into combinatory logic is that it is transformed into a term in which we "try" to apply it to an argument until a match occurs and this may have to be done as many times as there are clauses in the multi-clause definition. This "trying" is performed—not surprisingly—by the combinator *TRY*, which has the following properties:

$$TRY \ FAIL \ y \ \rightarrow \ y,$$
$$TRY \ x \ y \ z \ \rightarrow \ TRY \ (xz) \ (yz), \text{if } x \text{ is a function,}$$
$$TRY \ x \ y \ \rightarrow \ x.$$

In this context, to say that x is a function means that if x is reduced to head normal form, then it has a combinator for its head. The final case can only occur if x is not a function and does not reduce to *FAIL*.

TRY is the "glue" with which the component abstractions of a multi-clause function definition are combined together. *TRY* does have a rather strange definition. This is because Turner introduced it in order to compile SASL and in that language the number of formal parameters that a function has in each clause of a multi-clause definition does not have to be fixed, like the definition of *TRY* itself.

The only thing remaining to be done is to explain abstraction of a constant k. In this case $[k] \ M = MATCH \ k \ M$, where *MATCH* has the following properties:

$$MATCH \ x \ y \ z \ \rightarrow \ y, \text{ if } x = z,$$
$$MATCH \ x \ y \ z \ \rightarrow \ FAIL, \text{ if } x \neq z,$$

and in this context, $x = z$ means that x and z have the same normal form.

This rather informal discussion will become clearer if we consider some examples.

9.3 Some Examples

In this Section I will consider the compilation of the *length* function into Turner's extended set of combinators. The definition of *length* is:

$$length \ [\ ] \ = \ 0,$$
$$length \ (a : x) \ = \ 1 + length \ x.$$

129

I will consider each part of this definition in turn. The first equation becomes:

$$length = [NIL]\ 0,$$

which is transformed into:

$$length = MATCH\ NIL\ 0.$$

The second equation of the definition of *length* becomes:

$$length = [CONS\ a\ x]ADD\ 1\ (length\ x),$$

which is transformed as follows:

$$
\begin{aligned}
length\ &=\ \underline{U}([a]([x]ADD\ 1\ (length\ x))),\\
&=\ \underline{U}([a](\mathbf{B'}ADD\ 1\ ([x]length\ x))),\\
&=\ \underline{U}([a](\mathbf{B'}ADD\ 1\ length\ )),\\
&=\ \underline{U}(\mathbf{K}(\mathbf{B'}ADD\ 1\ length\ )).
\end{aligned}
$$

Putting these parts of the definition together gives us:

$$length = TRY\ (MATCH\ NIL\ 0)(\underline{U}(\mathbf{K}(\mathbf{B'}ADD\ 1\ length))).$$

In order to see how this works I shall go through the steps necessary to evaluate *length* [7]. This becomes:

$$TRY\ (MATCH\ NIL\ 0)(\underline{U}(\mathbf{K}(\mathbf{B'}ADD\ 1\ length)))(CONS\ 7\ NIL).$$

Because *MATCH NIL* 0 is a function, this is transformed into:

$$
\begin{aligned}
& TRY\ (MATCH\ NIL\ 0\ (CONS\ 7\ NIL))\\
& ((\underline{U}(\mathbf{K}(\mathbf{B'}ADD\ 1\ length)))(CONS\ 7\ NIL)).
\end{aligned}
\tag{9.1}
$$

In order to evaluate this, we have to begin by evaluating the first argument to *TRY*. Since, *NIL* and (*CONS* 7 *NIL*), that is to say, the first and third arguments to the function *MATCH*, do not have the same normal form,

$$MATCH\ NIL\ 0\ (CONS\ 7\ NIL) \rightarrow FAIL.$$

Therefore, (9.1) is transformed into:

$$TRY\ FAIL((\underline{U}(\mathbf{K}(\mathbf{B'}ADD\ 1\ length)))(CONS\ 7\ NIL)).$$

Thus we have:

$$length \ (CONS \ 7 \ NIL) \ \rightarrow \ \underline{U}(K(B'ADD \ 1 \ length))(CONS \ 7 \ NIL),$$
$$\rightarrow \ K(B'ADD \ 1 \ length)1 \ NIL,$$
$$\rightarrow \ B'ADD \ 1 \ length \ NIL,$$
$$\rightarrow \ ADD \ 1 \ (length \ NIL).$$

To evaluate $(length \ NIL)$ we first replace it by its definiens:

$$TRY \ (MATCH \ NIL \ 0)(\underline{U}(K(B'ADD \ 1 \ length)))NIL.$$

This becomes:

$$MATCH \ NIL \ 0 \ NIL \ (\underline{U}(K(B'ADD \ 1 \ length))NIL),$$

which reduces to 0.

Putting all this together, we have

$$length \ (CONS \ 7 \ NIL) \rightarrow ADD \ 1 \ 0 \rightarrow 1.$$

The *length* function illustrates pattern matching in a simple case, but most real-life examples are more complicated. One of the complications derives from the fact that KRC allows guarded expressions to occur on the right-hand side of function definitions and another comes about because more complicated multi-clause definitions than that which occurs in the *length* example are allowed. Both these features are exemplified by Ackermann's function, which can be coded in KRC as follows:

$$ack \ i \ j \ = \ j + 1, \ i = 0,$$
$$= \ ack \ (i - 1) \ 1, \ j = 0,$$
$$= \ ack \ (i - 1) \ (ack \ i \ (j - 1)).$$

This is compiled into a CL-term in the following way:

$$ack \ = \ [i][j](IF \ (EQ \ i \ 0)(ADD \ j \ 1) \ (IF \ (EQ \ j \ 0) \ (ack \ (SUB \ i \ 1) \ 1)$$
$$(ack \ (SUB \ i \ 1) \ (ack \ i \ (SUB \ j \ 1)))))).$$

If we actually perform the bracket abstraction algorithm in this case, we get the term:

$$((S(((C'S'((B \ IF)(((C' \ EQ)I)0)))(((C' \ ADD)I)1)))(((S'S)(((B'(C'IF))$$
$$(((C' \ EQ)I)0))(((C' \ ack)(((C' \ SUB)I)1))1)))(((S'(B' \ ack))$$
$$(((C' \ SUB)I)1))(((C'(B' \ ack))I)(((C' \ SUBI)1)))))).$$

In the general case the definition will contain both pattern-matching and guarded expressions, such as the definition of *insert* in the KRC prelude:[3]

$$insert\ a\ [\ ] \quad = \quad [a],$$
$$insert\ a\ (b:x) \quad = \quad a:b:x, a \leq b,$$
$$= \quad b:insert\ a\ x.$$

The first equation of this becomes:

$$insert = [a][NIL](CONS\ a\ NIL),$$

which is the CL-term:

$$P \equiv \mathbf{B'}MATCH\ NIL\ (\mathbf{C}\ CONS\ \mathbf{I}\ NIL).$$

The second equation is transformed into:

$$insert \quad = \quad [a][CONS\ b\ x](IF\ (LEQ\ a\ b)$$
$$(CONS\ a\ (CONS\ b\ x))(CONS\ b\ (insert\ a\ x))).$$

which becomes:

$$[a](\underline{\mathbf{U}}([b]([x](IF\ (LEQ\ a\ b)(CONS\ a\ (CONS\ b\ x))(CONS\ b\ (insert\ a\ x)))))).$$

This is transformed into the CL-term:

$$Q \equiv ((\mathbf{BU})(((\mathbf{S'S})(((\mathbf{S'(S'S')})(((\mathbf{B'B})\ IF)\ LEQ))$$
$$((((\mathbf{C'(B'(B'}\ CONS)))\mathbf{I})\ CONS)))((((\mathbf{B'(C'(B'}\ CONS)))\mathbf{I})\ insert))).$$

Putting these together results in the term $MATCH\ P\ Q$.

9.4 Translating Pattern-matching in KRC

In order to give the general compilation algorithm for the KRC subset that I have been considering I have to first describe its abstract syntax.[4] ξ will be used to refer to identifiers, δ for definitions, κ for constants, ρ for the right-hand sides of function definitions, π for patterns and ϵ for expressions. The syntax for a single function definition is:

$$\delta \quad ::= \quad \xi\ \pi_1 \ldots \pi_n = \rho$$
$$| \quad \delta\ \xi\ \pi_1 \ldots \pi_n = \rho$$

---

[3]See Turner (1982b), p. 24. The function *insert* is used in the definition of *sort*.
[4]This syntax is based on that for SASL given by Turner (1981a).

The first alternative is the syntax of a simple or single-clause function definition and the second alternative is that of a multi-clause function definition. In a multi-clause definition the separate clauses are to be understood—in the concrete case—as occurring on distinct lines.

The syntax for right-hand sides is very easy:

$$
\begin{aligned}
\rho \quad ::= \quad & \epsilon \\
| \quad & \epsilon_1, \epsilon_1' \\
= \quad & \epsilon_2, \epsilon_2' \\
& \vdots \\
= \quad & \epsilon_{n-1}, \epsilon_{n-1}' \\
= \quad & \epsilon_n, \epsilon_n' \\
| \quad & \epsilon_1, \epsilon_1' \\
= \quad & \epsilon_2, \epsilon_2' \\
& \vdots \\
= \quad & \epsilon_{n-1}, \epsilon_{n-1}' \\
= \quad & \epsilon_n
\end{aligned}
$$

A right-hand side is either an expression or a sequence of guarded expressions, all but the first preceded by an equals sign, or it is a sequence of $n - 1$ guarded expressions followed by a single unguarded expression, all but the first of which is preceded by an equals sign.

The syntax of expressions is:

$$
\begin{aligned}
\epsilon \quad ::= \quad & \alpha\epsilon \\
| \quad & \epsilon\beta\epsilon' \\
| \quad & \epsilon\epsilon' \\
| \quad & \xi \\
| \quad & \kappa
\end{aligned}
$$

Thus, an expression is either a built-in monadic function application or a built-in dyadic infix function application or a user-defined function application or an identifier or a constant.

The syntax of patterns is:

$$
\begin{aligned}
\pi \quad ::= \quad & \xi \\
| \quad & \kappa \\
| \quad & \pi : \pi
\end{aligned}
$$

133

A pattern is either an identifier or a constant or it is formed from two patterns by means of the infix cons operator.

The function *CD*—compile definition or declaration—compiles a single definition producing a global binding between the name of the function and its compiled form. The primitive function *declare* actually performs this association. The functions *CL* and *CR*, respectively, compile the left-hand side of a function declaration and its right-hand side.

I suppose that—like Peyton Jones (1987)—I should write things like $CD[\![\delta]\!]$ in order to stress that *CD* is a function whose arguments—and values—are expressions, but here I think it is clearer to omit the Strachey brackets:

$$
\begin{aligned}
CD\ \delta &= declare\ (CL\ \delta, CR\ \delta), \\
CL\ (\xi\ \pi_1 \ldots \pi_n = \rho) &= \xi, \\
CL\ (\delta\ \xi\ \pi_1 \ldots \pi_n = \rho) &= \xi, \\
CR\ (\xi\ \pi_1 \ldots \pi_n = \rho) &= \lfloor \pi_1 \rfloor (\ldots \lfloor \pi_n \rfloor (CE\ \rho) \ldots), \\
CR\ (\delta\ \xi\ \pi_1 \ldots \pi_n = \rho) &= TRY(CR\ \delta)(CR\ (\xi\ \pi_1 \ldots \pi_n = \rho)).
\end{aligned}
$$

The operation denoted by $\lfloor \pi \rfloor$ is strict abstraction and it is defined as follows:

$$
\begin{aligned}
\lfloor \xi \rfloor \gamma &= [\xi]\gamma, \\
\lfloor \kappa \rfloor \gamma &= \text{MATCH}\ \kappa\ \gamma, \\
\lfloor \pi_1 : \pi_2 \rfloor \gamma &= \underline{\mathbf{U}}(\lfloor \pi_1 \rfloor (\lfloor \pi_2 \rfloor \gamma)).
\end{aligned}
$$

This has been explained previously and is included here for reference.

The only thing that remains to be explained is the function *CE*, which compiles what follows the equals sign in a multi-clause function definition. From the definition of ρ there are three cases to consider, namely the situation in which ρ is just an expression or the circumstance that ρ is a sequence of guarded expressions. In the second possibility, there are two subcases. Either the final expression is a guarded expression or it is not. In the case when ρ is a single expression its translation is entirely straightforward. It can be handled by the methods discussed in Chapter 4. Let us call the function which performs this simple translation *TR*. The translation of sequences of guarded expressions is then handled by the following two definitions:

$$
CE\ \begin{aligned}(\epsilon_1,\epsilon_1'\\=\epsilon_2,\epsilon_2'\\ \vdots \\ =\epsilon_{n-1},\epsilon_{n-1}'\\=\epsilon_n,\epsilon_n')\end{aligned}\ =\ \begin{aligned}(IF(TR\ \epsilon_1')(TR\ \epsilon_1)\\(IF(TR\ \epsilon_2')(TR\ \epsilon_2)\\ \vdots \\ (IF(TR\ \epsilon_{n-1}')(TR\ \epsilon_{n-1})\\(IF(TR\ \epsilon_n')(TR\ \epsilon_n)\\ FAIL))\ldots)),\end{aligned}
$$

$$
CE\ \begin{aligned}(\epsilon_1,\epsilon_1'\\=\epsilon_2,\epsilon_2'\\ \vdots \\ =\epsilon_{n-1},\epsilon_{n-1}'\\=\epsilon_n)\end{aligned}\ =\ \begin{aligned}(IF(TR\ \epsilon_1')(TR\ \epsilon_1)\\(IF(TR\ \epsilon_2')(TR\ \epsilon_2)\\ \vdots \\ (IF(TR\ \epsilon_{n-1}')(TR\ \epsilon_{n-1})\\(TR\ \epsilon_n))\ldots)).\end{aligned}
$$

9.5 Conclusion

The algorithm presented here has certain limitations. It is restricted to patterns made up from numerical and boolean constants, the empty list and the primitive list constructor. It does not support repeated occurrences of the same variable on the left-hand side of a function definition and it cannot handle local **whererec**-clauses. It is possible to extend the algorithm so that it can deal with these things as well as the occurrence of user-defined type primitives and constructors on the right-hand sides of function declarations. See Chapters 4 and 5 of Peyton Jones (1987), written by him and Wadler, for an account of such a more general algorithm.

Chapter 10

Categorical Combinators

10.1 Introduction

Categorical combinatory logics are formal systems—similar to the combinatory logics studied in Chapter 3—which make use of the ideas of category theory. Lambek (1980) showed the equivalence of the typed λ-calculus and the theory of Cartesian closed categories, and this led Curien (1985a, 1985b, 1986) to develop various categorical combinatory logics. Such logics can be used in the implementation of functional programming languages. The phases of this implementation can be conceptualized as follows. (In an actual implementation several of these conceptual phases could be coalesced.) (1) The program is translated into a term of the λ-calculus. (2) This λ-term is expressed in de Bruijn's namefree notation. (3) The namefree term is compiled into a term of a categorical combinatory logic, that is to say, a CCL-term. (4) This CCL-term is then evaluated.

In the work of Curien and his collaborators the evaluation is carried out by what they call a *categorical abstract machine*, which—by their own account—is an amalgam of Landin's SECD machine and Turner's graph-reducer. As such it lies outside the scope of this book, but in a series of papers Lins (1985a, 1985b, 1985c, 1986b) has shown how a CCL-term can be evaluated on a (modified) reduction machine. Because of this possibility I decided to include this Chapter, in which I present the basic ideas of this implementation technique.

To begin with, I briefly explain the ideas of a Cartesian closed category, then I give an account of Curien's system CCL_β and also of Lins's simplified version of this. After that I explain de Bruijn's namefree notation for the λ-calculus and how a namefree λ-term can be compiled into Lins's simplified categorical combinators. The structure of this Chapter is, therefore, the reverse of a compiler based on categorical combinators, since I first show how to evaluate a CCL-term and only then do I show how a λ-term is compiled into a CCL-term. (The translation of a functional program into a λ-term has already been explained in Chapter 4.)

10.2   Cartesian Closed Categories

It is not surprising that the theory of Cartesian closed categories is relevant to the study of functional languages, since that theory can be seen to be a system of types and—as such—is a theory of functions. (See Scott (1980) for an amplification of this point.) In this Section I will define what a Cartesian closed category is, but first I have to define a category.

A *category* consists of a class of *objects*, between every pair of which there exists a set of *morphisms*. Let X and Y be objects. Then we represent the set of morphisms from X to Y as $X \to Y$. If f is a morphism from X to Y, depicted as $f : X \to Y$, then X is called its *domain* and Y its *codomain*.

For something to be a category there must exist an operation called *composition*, which is such that the composition of two morphisms $f : X \to Y$ and $g : Z \to A$ always exists if $Y = Z$ and in that case is written $g \circ f$. Furthermore, composition must be associative. That is to say,

$$(h \circ g) \circ f = h \circ (g \circ f),$$

must hold for all morphisms $f : A \to B$, $g : B \to C$ and $h : C \to D$.

Finally, for every object A of the category, there must exist a morphism Id_A, such that $Id_A : A \to A$, which has the properties that:

$$f \circ Id_A = f,$$
$$Id_A \circ g = g,$$

for all morphisms $f : A \to B$ and $g : B \to A$. Such a morphism is known as an *identity* morphism or a *neutral element*. When the type of the identity morphism can be inferred from the context or if it is of no particular significance, then the subscript will be omitted.

A *Cartesian category* is a category in which every pair of objects A and B has a Cartesian product $A \times B$. An element of $A \times B$ is called a *couple* and is written (a,b). In a Cartesian category there also has to exist a *pairing* operator, depicted using angle brackets $< , >$, which is such that if $f : C \to A$ and $g : C \to B$, then $< f, g >: C \to A \times B$.

Furthermore, there must exist *projection functions* $Fst_{A,B}$ and $Snd_{A,B}$, defined for all objects A and B, which are such that:

$$Fst_{A,B} : A \times B \quad \to \quad A,$$
$$Snd_{A,B} : A \times B \quad \to \quad B,$$

and the following properties must hold of these operators:

$$Fst_{A,B} \circ < f, g > \quad = \quad f,$$
$$Snd_{A,B} \circ < f, g > \quad = \quad g,$$
$$< Fst_{A,B} \circ h, Snd_{A,B} \circ h > \quad = \quad h,$$

for all morphisms $f : C \to A$, $g : C \to B$ and $h : C \to A \times B$. These properties ensure that the pairing and projection functions are well-behaved in the category. When the types of the projection functions can be inferred from the context or if they are not particularly important, then their subscripts will be omitted.

Finally, in a Cartesian category there must exist a terminal object $\top$ and for each object A, a morphism $0_A : A \to \top$, such that $f = 0_A$, for all $f : A \to \top$. That is to say, given an object A, there exists a unique morphism from A to the terminal object $\top$. The significance of the terminal object in a Cartesian category is that one of the things that we want to be able to define is A^n. When $n > 1$ we have that $A^n = A^{n-1} \times A$. The existence of the terminal object allows us to define A^0 as $\top$, for all objects A. The existence of a terminal object in a Cartesian category will not play any rôle in the remainder of this Chapter.

In a *Cartesian closed category* there also occurs an *evaluation* operator $App_{B,C}$ and a *currying* operator $\Lambda_{A,B,C}$. The application operator is such that:

$$App_{B,C} : (B \to C) \times B \to C.$$

Intuitively, $App_{B,C}$ takes a morphism f and a possible argument x and applies f to x or evaluates f at x. Thus, $App_{B,C}(f, x) = fx$. And the currying operator has the property that if $h : A \times B \to C$, then $\Lambda_{A,B,C}h : A \to (B \to C)$. Intuitively, $\Lambda_{A,B,C}h = \lambda xy.h(x, y)$. These two operators must satisfy the following properties:

$$App_{B,C} \circ < (\Lambda_{A,B,C}h) \circ Fst_{A,B}, Snd_{A,B} > \quad = \quad h,$$
$$\Lambda_{A,B,C}(App_{B,C} \circ < k \circ Fst_{A,B}, Snd_{A,B} >) \quad = \quad k,$$

where $h : A \times B \rightarrow C$ and $k : A \rightarrow (B \rightarrow C)$. Usually the subscripts on the evaluation and currying operators will be omitted when they can be inferred from the context or when they are not particularly important.

The existence of the evaluation and currying operators in a Cartesian closed category means that "function" spaces $A \rightarrow B$ are being treated as first-class citizens, that is to say, in such a category domains and codomains can themselves be "function" spaces.

For reference purposes, I will bring together all the axioms which define a Cartesian closed category. They are:

$$(h \circ g) \circ f \;=\; h \circ (g \circ f), \tag{10.1}$$

$$f \circ Id \;=\; f, \tag{10.2}$$

$$Id \circ g \;=\; g, \tag{10.3}$$

$$Fst \circ < f, g > \;=\; f, \tag{10.4}$$

$$Snd \circ < f, g > \;=\; g, \tag{10.5}$$

$$< Fst \circ h, Snd \circ h > \;=\; h, \tag{10.6}$$

$$App \circ < \Lambda h \circ Fst, Snd > \;=\; h, \tag{10.7}$$

$$\Lambda(App \circ < k \circ Fst, Snd >) \;=\; k. \tag{10.8}$$

Sometimes it is more convenient to replace (10.6)–(10.8) by:

$$< x, y > \circ z \;=\; < x \circ z, y \circ z >, \tag{10.9}$$

$$App \circ < \Lambda x, y > \;=\; x \circ < Id, y >, \tag{10.10}$$

$$\Lambda x \circ y \;=\; \Lambda(x \circ < y \circ Fst, Snd >). \tag{10.11}$$

I will not prove the equivalence of (10.1)–(10.8) and (10.1)–(10.5) together with (10.9)–(10.11) here; I will just do some of the derivations for illustrative purposes, leaving the rest as exercises for the interested reader.

Equation (10.9) can be derived from (10.1), (10.4) and (10.5). First, put $< x, y > \circ z$ for h in (10.6):

$$< Fst \; \circ (< x, y > \circ z), Snd \; \circ (< x, y > \circ z) >=< x, y > \circ z. \tag{10.12}$$

Using the fact that functional composition is associative (10.1), together with the axioms (10.4) and (10.5), the left-hand side of (10.12) can be simplified, yielding (10.9).

Equation (10.10) can be derived from (10.1), (10.2), (10.4) and (10.5). First, compose both sides of (10.7) with $< Id, g >$:

$$App \circ < \Lambda h \circ Fst, Snd > \circ < Id, g >= h \circ < Id, g > .$$

By (10.9), the left-hand side of this is

$$App \circ <(\Lambda h \circ Fst) \circ < Id, g >, Snd \circ < Id, g >>,$$

which simplifies to $App \circ < \Lambda h, g >$ by the use of (10.1), (10.2), (10.4) and (10.5) yielding (10.10). Previously I showed how (10.9) could be derived from (10.1), (10.4) and (10.5).

10.3 Categorical Combinatory Logic

In order to make use of the theory of Cartesian closed categories in the implementation of a functional language it has to be phrased as a *rewriting* system. Curien's system CCL_β, expressed as a rewriting system, is made up out of the following rules, which are from Curien (1986), p. 25:

$$
\begin{array}{rcll}
(x \circ y) \circ z & \rightarrow & x \circ (y \circ z), & \text{(ass)} \\
Id \circ x & \rightarrow & x, & \text{(idl)} \\
x \circ Id & \rightarrow & x, & \text{(idr)} \\
Fst \circ < x, y > & \rightarrow & x, & \text{(fst)} \\
Snd \circ < x, y > & \rightarrow & y, & \text{(snd)} \\
< x, y > \circ z & \rightarrow & < x \circ z, y \circ z >, & \text{(dpair)} \\
App \circ < \Lambda x, y > & \rightarrow & x \circ < Id, y >, & \text{(beta)} \\
\Lambda x \circ y & \rightarrow & \Lambda(x \circ < y \circ Fst, Snd >). & \text{(d}\Lambda\text{)}
\end{array}
$$

These are just the axioms (10.1)–(10.5) and (10.9)–(10.11) expressed as rewrite rules. Note that Curien makes no use of any equations involving the terminal object of a Cartesian closed category. It should also be noted that the rewriting system CCL_β is not locally confluent, as pointed out by Lins (1985c), p. 2. The reason for this is the presence of rewrite rules derived from (10.6), that is to say, surjective pairing. The names of these rewrite rules are those used by Curien (1986) and are included here so that the reader can more easily find his way around that book.

In order to evaluate a CCL-term efficiently Curien and his collaborators devised an abstract machine called the *categorical abstract machine*. See Curien (1986), pp. 11–18, and also Cousineau, Curien and Mauny (1985) for further details.

10.4 Simplified Categorical Combinators

On the assumption that we want to implement lazy evaluation, that is to say, we want to "simulate" a leftmost-outermost reduction strategy for the contraction of β-redexes, Lins (1985b) simplifies Curien's rewriting rules to the following:

$$\underline{n} \circ \langle x, y \rangle \quad \rightarrow \quad \underline{(n-1)} \circ x, \text{if } n > 0,$$
$$\underline{0} \circ \langle x, y \rangle \quad \rightarrow \quad y,$$
$$\triangleleft x, y \triangleright \circ z \quad \rightarrow \quad \triangleleft x \circ z, y \circ z \triangleright,$$
$$\triangleleft \Lambda(x), y \triangleright \quad \rightarrow \quad x \circ \triangleleft \text{Id}, y \triangleright,$$
$$\triangleleft \Lambda(x) \circ y, z \triangleright \quad \rightarrow \quad x \circ \triangleleft y, z \triangleright,$$

where the notation $\triangleleft$, $\triangleright$ is an abbreviation for $App \circ \langle \, , \, \rangle$ and $\underline{n}$, for $n \geq 0$, is defined as follows:

$$\underline{0} \quad \overset{\wedge}{=} \quad Snd,$$
$$\underline{n+1} \quad \overset{\wedge}{=} \quad \underline{n} \circ Fst.$$

In order to serve as the machine code of an abstract machine which can be used in the implementation of applicative languages, we need to be able to handle constants (such as numbers and characters), built-in functions (like addition and the various list-manipulating operators) and recursion. To deal with constants Lins adds the rewrite rules

$$c \circ x \rightarrow c, \text{if } c \text{ is a constant.}$$

Built-in functions are handled in Lins (1985c), p. 2, by including many rewrite rules of the form

$$App \circ \langle App \circ \langle ADD, x \rangle, y \rangle \rightarrow x + y,$$

which can also be written as

$$\triangleleft \triangleleft ADD, x \triangleright, y \triangleright \rightarrow x + y.$$

These are similar to the delta reductions which govern the behaviour of illative atoms mentioned in Chapter 3.

To handle recursion we use $\mathbf{Y}$ and Lins has the following rewrite rule to deal with it:

$$\triangleleft \mathbf{Y}, f \triangleright \rightarrow \triangleleft f, \triangleleft \mathbf{Y}, f \triangleright \triangleright.$$

In an actual implementation in a graph-reducer this would—as usual—create a cyclic graph. In order to efficiently evaluate CCL-terms Lins (1986b) has developed a graph-reduction machine, but the details of this are not included here. The interested reader is referred to Lins's excellent paper.

10.5   De Bruijn's Notation for the Lambda Calculus

De Bruijn (1972) presents a way of writing λ-terms which uses neither bound nor binding variables. Bound variables are replaced by numbers and binding variables are simply omitted. The best way in which to understand this nameless notation is by considering a λ-term depicted as a tree. Consider, for example, the combinator $\mathbf{S}_\lambda$, which is $\lambda fgx.fx(gx)$. The tree-representation of this is shown in Fig. 10.1. With each bound variable it is possible to associate a number known as its *reference depth*.[1] The reference depth of a variable is the number of lambdas that occur between it and its binding lambda on the path joining the two.[2] Thus, in Fig. 10.1, the bound variable f has a reference depth of 2, both bound occurrences of the variable x have a reference depth of 0 and the reference depth of the bound variable g of 1. In order to prevent such de Bruijn numbers being confused with genuine numbers I will underline de Bruijn's numbers. To obtain the de Bruijn notation for a λ-term we simply replace each bound variable by its reference depth and we just delete all binding occurrences of variables. In this case we get the term $\lambda\lambda\lambda.\underline{2}\,\underline{0}(\underline{1}\,\underline{0})$. De Bruijn calls such an expression *namefree*. Note that it is not true in general that each bound occurrence of the same variable in a λ-term will be replaced by the same de Bruijn number in its namefree form. For example, the namefree version of $\lambda x.x(\lambda y.xy)$ is $\lambda.\underline{0}(\lambda.\underline{1}\,\underline{0})$. Here, the first bound occurrence of x is replaced by $\underline{0}$ and its second bound occurrence by $\underline{1}$.

If a λ-abstraction $\lambda u.P$ contains any free variables, then we imagine it to be preceded by $\dots \lambda z.\lambda y.\lambda x$, according to some definite ordering of all the variables we allow, and we calculate the de Bruijn form as already mentioned.

Substitution in de Bruijn's notation for the lambda calculus is defined

---

[1] The reference depth of a variable should not be confused with its lexical level as used in Hughes's supercombinator abstraction algorithm. Such a confusion has occurred in the literature.

[2] In De Bruijn's original article the occurrence of the lambda in the binder is included in the count, but it is more usual in the computing literature to leave it out of the count. Nothing of substance hangs on the choice we make here.

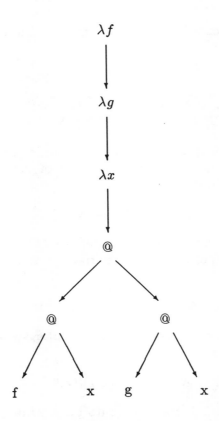

Figure 10.1: Tree-representation of $\lambda fgx.fx(gx)$.

as follows:

$$[N/\underline{m}]n \;=\; \begin{cases} \underline{n}, & \text{if } n < m, \\ U_0^n(N), & \text{if } n = m, \\ \underline{n-1}, & \text{if } n > m, \end{cases}$$

$$[N/\underline{m}]M_1 M_2 \;=\; [N/\underline{m}]M_1[N/\underline{m}]M_2,$$

$$[N/\underline{m}]\lambda.M \;=\; \lambda.([N/\underline{m+1}]M).$$

The operator U_i^m is called the *lifting operator* and it is defined as follows:

$$U_i^m(j) \;=\; \begin{cases} j, & \text{if } j < i, \\ j + m, & \text{if } j \geq i, \end{cases}$$

$$U_i^m(N_1 N_2) \;=\; U_i^m(N_1)U_i^m(N_2),$$

$$U_i^m(\lambda.N) \;=\; \lambda.(U_{i+1}^m(N)).$$

(These definitions are taken from Curien (1986), p. 22.)

Let M' denote the de Bruijn translation of the λ-term M. Then β-reduction can be defined as:

$$((\lambda x.M)N)' \to [N'/\underline{0}]M',$$

that is to say, the de Bruijn translation of $(\lambda x.M)N$ is the result of substituting the translation of N for $\underline{0}$ in the translation of M. As an example, I shall consider the λ-term:

$$N \equiv (\lambda y.(\lambda z.zy)y)((\lambda t.t)z),$$

which, as Curien (1986) says, 'contains all interesting situations' (p. 22). The de Bruijn translation of this is:

$$N' \equiv (\lambda.(\lambda.\underline{0}\,\underline{1})\underline{1})((\lambda.\underline{0})\underline{2}).$$

The free variable y in N is translated into $\underline{1}$ and z into $\underline{2}$ because we imagine N to be preceded by $\lambda z.\lambda y.\lambda x$.

To perform a single β-reduction on N' we proceed as follows:

$$
\begin{aligned}
[(\lambda.\underline{0})\underline{2})/\underline{0}]((\lambda.\underline{0}\,\underline{1})\underline{1}) \quad &\to \quad [(\lambda.\underline{0})\underline{2}/\underline{0}](\lambda.\underline{0}\,\underline{1})[(\lambda.\underline{0})\underline{2})/\underline{0}]\underline{1}, \\
&\equiv \quad (\lambda.([[((\lambda.\underline{0})\underline{2})/\underline{1}](\underline{0}\,\underline{1})))\underline{0}, \\
&\equiv \quad (\lambda.([[((\lambda.\underline{0})\underline{2})/\underline{1}]\underline{0}[((\lambda.\underline{0})\underline{2})/\underline{1}]\underline{1}))\underline{0}, \\
&\equiv \quad (\lambda.(\underline{0}U_0^1((\lambda.\underline{0})\underline{2})))\underline{0}, \\
&\equiv \quad (\lambda.(\underline{0}((\lambda.\underline{0})\underline{3})))\underline{0}.
\end{aligned}
$$

This is because of the following:

$$
\begin{aligned}
U_0^1((\lambda.\underline{0})\underline{2}) &= (U_0^1\lambda.\underline{0})(U_0^1\underline{2}), \\
&= (\lambda.U_1^1\underline{0})\underline{3}, \\
&= (\lambda.\underline{0})\underline{3}.
\end{aligned}
$$

Even this simple example should convince the reader that de Bruijn's notation is not suitable for human manipulation of λ-terms, but it has advantages
for the computer representation of such terms.

10.6   Compiling Namefree Terms

Curien's translation of a λ-term in de Bruijn's notation into CCL_β is given
as follows:

$$
\begin{aligned}
[\![\lambda.M]\!] &= \Lambda([\![M]\!]), \\
[\![MN]\!] &= App \circ < [\![M]\!], [\![N]\!] >, \\
[\![\underline{0}]\!] &= Snd, \\
[\![n+1]\!] &= Snd \circ Fst^{n+1},
\end{aligned}
$$

where Fst^i is defined as follows:

$$
\begin{aligned}
Fst^1 &\triangleq Fst, \\
Fst^{n+1} &\triangleq Fst \circ Fst^n.
\end{aligned}
$$

This translation scheme is from Lins (1985a), p. 4. He presents the following
algorithm for compiling a namefree λ-term into a term of his simplified CCL
logic:

$$
\begin{aligned}
[\![\lambda.M]\!] &= \Lambda([\![M]\!]), \\
[\![MN]\!] &= \lhd[\![M]\!], [\![N]\!] \rhd, \\
[\![\underline{n}]\!] &= \underline{n}, \\
[\![c]\!] &= c, \text{if } c \text{ is a constant.}
\end{aligned}
$$

Strictly, in the rule $[\![\underline{n}]\!] = \underline{n}$ we should distinguish the $\underline{n}$ on the right and on
the left, since on the left we have a de Bruijn number, whereas on the right—
as defined above—we have an abbreviation for a CCL-term, but because the
notation $\underline{n}$ occurs in different contexts no confusion should arise. In an actual
implementation the CCL-term $\underline{n}$ need not be expanded out according to its
definition, since Lins's rewrite rules make no essential use of the "internal"
structure of $\underline{n}$.

145

10.7 An Example

In order to illustrate the ideas presented in this Chapter I shall present the translation of a simple Lispkit program into categorical combinators. Consider the following program:

$$f1 \textbf{ whererec } f = \lambda(i).cons\ (i, (f(i + 1))).$$

This is equivalent to the λ-term:

$$(\lambda f.f1)(\textbf{Y}(\lambda f i.CONS\ i(f(ADD\ i\ 1)))),$$

whose de Bruijn translation is

$$(\lambda.\underline{0}1)(\textbf{Y}(\lambda.\lambda.CONS\ \underline{0}(\underline{1}(ADD\ \underline{0}1)))),$$

and the CCL translation of this—in Lins's scheme—is

$$\triangleleft \Lambda(\triangleleft\underline{0}, 1 \triangleright), \triangleleft \textbf{Y}, \Lambda(\Lambda(\triangleleft \triangleleft CONS, \underline{0} \triangleright, \triangleleft\underline{1}, \triangleleft \triangleleft ADD, \underline{0} \triangleright, 1 \triangleright \triangleright \triangleright \triangleright \triangleright.$$

I shall not attempt to show how this is rewritten as the terms produced are mostly completely unreadable.

Chapter 11

Reduction and Transformation

11.1   Introduction

The method of graph-reduction as a technique of implementation was first applied to the λ-calculus by Wadsworth (1971) and later extended to combinatory logic by Turner (1979b), but it is possible to use the method directly on the abstract syntax graph of the applicative program being evaluated. In this case the implementation technique is referred to as *source reduction*.[1] This is not a particularly efficient way of implementing a functional language; its interest lies in the fact that it can be easily incorporated into a program transformation system and also in the fact that it can be modified to perform *partial evaluation* or *mixed computation*. The phrase 'mixed computation' is particularly apt, because what it refers to is a mixture of program evaluation and program transformation. In this Chapter I begin by describing how source reduction works and then I give a brief introduction to program transformation. This includes an account of Wadler's method of compiling ZF-expressions and also of dependency analysis. After that I explain what partial evaluation is and mention how similar ideas can be incorporated into a combinator-based compiler to give meaningful run-time error messages.

---

[1] For a brief account of the use of this method, see Hughes (1984a), Section 9.3, "Graph Reduction of the Source", pp. 119–121.

11.2   Source Reduction

In order to explain the technique of source reduction I shall work through a simple example, namely that of reversing a list using the function *foldleft*. A KRC program to reverse the list [7,3] is as follows:

$$foldleft\ f\ b\ [\ ] \quad = \quad b, \tag{11.1}$$

$$foldleft\ f\ b\ (a:x) \quad = \quad foldleft\ f\ (f\ a\ b)\ x, \tag{11.2}$$

$$cons\ a\ x \quad = \quad a:x, \tag{11.3}$$

$$reverse \quad = \quad foldleft\ cons\ [\ ], \tag{11.4}$$

$$reverse\ [7,3]? \tag{11.5}$$

A source reducer would store each of the equations (11.1) to (11.4) as a pair of syntax graphs and I shall assume that these are acyclic. Each such pair is regarded as a rewrite rule which allows us to replace an instance of the left-hand side in a graph being evaluated by the corresponding instance of the right-hand side. So, to begin with—in order to evaluate (11.5)—we begin by applying rule (11.4). This gives us

$$foldleft\ cons\ [\ ]\ [7,3],$$

and now rule (11.2) is applicable, yielding

$$foldleft\ cons\ [\ ]\ (cons\ 7\ [\ ])\ [3].$$

Rule (11.2) is again applicable. This time it results in

$$foldleft\ cons\ [\ ]\ (cons\ 3\ (cons\ 7\ [\ ]))\ [\ ].$$

It is now possible to use rule (11.1), which gives us

$$cons\ 3\ (cons\ 7\ [\ ]).$$

This is equivalent to $3:7:[\ ]$, by two applications of (11.3), and this can be rewritten as $[3,7]$.[2]

As already mentioned, source reduction is not a particularly efficient way of implementing a functional programming language. One of its advantages

---

[2] In the unfold/fold type of program transformation system described later in this Chapter the replacement of an occurrence of the left-hand side of a function definition by its corresponding right-hand side is known as *unfolding* the function definition.

is that it is well-suited—after suitable modification—to perform the partial evaluation of a functional program. There are also certain minor advantages, which follow from the fact that there is a close correspondence between the text of the program and its graph. For example, the program text can easily be recreated from the internal graph, very intelligible error messages can be produced which refer to the actual names used in the program text, and a source reducer can easily be combined with a program transformation system.[3]

A very nice way of implementing source reduction for a KRC-like language is by making use of a subtree replacement system. This is not an ideal name for the technique involved, since it involves directed acyclic graphs and not just trees. See O'Donnell (1977, 1985) for further details.

11.3 Program Transformation

Wadler (1984), p. 50, distinguishes between three main types of program transformation system. The first is the unfold/fold system of Burstall and Darlington (1977). The second is the system based on the application of laws like (using a KRC-like notation):

$$(map\ f) \circ (map\ g)\ =\ map\ (f \circ g),$$
$$append\ \circ (map\ (map\ f))\ =\ (map\ f) \circ append,$$
$$append\ \circ (map\ (filter\ p))\ =\ (filter\ p) \circ append,$$

where $append$ is list addition and map and $filter$ are defined thus:

$$map\ f\ [\ ]\ =\ [\ ],$$
$$map\ f\ (a:x)\ =\ f\ a: map\ f\ x,$$

$$filter\ p\ [\ ]\ =\ [\ ],$$
$$filter\ p\ (a:x)\ =\ a: filter\ p\ x,\ p\ a,$$
$$=\ filter\ p\ x.$$

This kind of transformation system is favoured by Backus (1978). See also Chapter 5 of Henson (1987), pp. 212–260; Bird (1986) is useful, though his approach is slightly different.

---

[3]These advantages are discussed in greater detail in Anane and Axford (1986, 1987).

The third type of transformation system that Wadler mentions is his own listless transformer which involves eliminating intermediate lists from certain functional programs. It is not universally applicable, but is very useful when it is. I shall not describe Wadler's listless machine here, but I will illustrate the ideas involved by describing his derivation of the optimal compilation method for ZF-expressions. But before doing that, however, I will describe the unfold/fold transformation system.

11.3.1 Unfold/fold Program Transformations

The unfold/fold system of program transformation is due to the work of Burstall and Darlington (1977), although it has mostly been used by Darlington (1978, 1982, 1987). A program transformation can be thought of as a function whose arguments and values are both programs.[4] Let θ be a transformation and π a program, then the program $\theta\pi$ has the same input–output behaviour as π. In other words, the program $\theta\pi$ calculates the same abstract mathematical function that π calculates. The value of the program transformation method lies in the fact that the original program π might be very inefficient but easily comprehensible, whereas the transformed program $\theta\pi$ is, hopefully, more efficient. In general, it will also be more difficult to understand than π. The motivation of transformation systems is that it allows a programmer to first of all write a program π to solve the problem at hand, without concerning himself with matters of efficiency. Once he has done that, he can then concentrate solely on making his program more efficient. The separation of the tasks of problem-solving and increasing efficiency is beneficial, since they—typically—involve conflicting techniques and make different demands on the programmer.

I will now describe the main types of program transformations in Darlington's unfold/fold system.

Unfolding Let $E = E'$ be the definition that we wish to unfold, where the expression E is defined as E', and let $F = F'$ be the equation that is to be transformed. For this to be possible an instance of E, say E_1, must occur in F'. Let E_1' be the corresponding instance of E'. To unfold the definition $E = E'$ in the equation $F = F'$ we replace the occurrence of E in F', namely E_1, with E_1'. Call the result of this substitution F'', then we can add the equation $F = F''$ to our program.

---

[4] This is a simplified account of program transformation, since some transformations—like instantiation—take additional parameters to the program being transformed.

Folding Let $E = E'$ be the definition that we want to fold, where the expression E is defined as E', and let $G = G'$ be the equation that is to be transformed. For this to be possible an instance of E', say E_1', must occur in G'. Let E_1 be the corresponding instance of E. To fold the definition $E = E'$ in the equation $G = G'$ we replace the occurrence of E' in G', namely E_1', with E_1. Call the result of this substitution G'', then we can add the equation $G = G''$ to our program.

Definition This program transformation allows us to add an equation $E = E'$ to our program if E is not an instance of the left-hand side of any existing equation in the program.

Instantiation Let $E = E'$ be an equation in our program. Then the program transformation *instantiation* allows us to add a substitution instance of $E = E'$ to the program. Instantiation is also known as substitution.

Laws Let $E = E'$ be an equation in our program. Then the program transformation *laws* allows us to add $E = E''$ to our system of equations, where E'' has been obtained from E' by making use of any of the properties of the primitive operators of our language. For example, we might use the fact that addition is commutative and associative to transform E' into E''.

The following example of a program transformation comes from Darlington (1982), but it has been translated into KRC. The definitions of the standard KRC functions *length* and *append* are given as follows:

$$length\ [\,] \quad = \quad 0, \tag{11.6}$$
$$length\ (a:x) \quad = \quad 1 + length\ x, \tag{11.7}$$

$$append\ [\,]\ y \quad = \quad y, \tag{11.8}$$
$$append\ (a:x)\ y \quad = \quad a:append\ x\ y. \tag{11.9}$$

Now let us consider the problem of defining a function to calculate the combined length of two lists l_1 and l_2. A first attempt at this problem might be the following:

$$lot\ l_1\ l_2 = length\ (append\ l_1\ l_2). \tag{11.10}$$

Here, 'lot' stands for 'length of two'. This solution is not very efficient, but it can be transformed to a more efficient version using the techniques of program transformation.

First, substitute $[\,]$ for l_1 in equation (11.10). This results in the equation:

$$lot\ [\,]\ l_2 = length\ (append\ [\,]\ l_2). \qquad (11.11)$$

This is an example of the program transformation known as *instantiation*. We now use unfolding with equation (11.8) as the definition $E = E'$ and equation (11.11) as $F = F'$:

$$\overbrace{append\ [\,]\ y}^{E} = \overbrace{y}^{E'},$$

$$\underbrace{lot\ [\,]\ l_2}_{F} = \underbrace{length\ \overbrace{(append\ [\,]\ l_2)}^{E_1}}_{F'}.$$

This results in the equation:

$$\underbrace{lot\ [\,]\ l_2}_{F} = \underbrace{length\ \overbrace{l_2}^{E_1'}}_{F''}. \qquad (11.12)$$

Now we use instantiation by substituting $(a : x)$ for l_1 in equation (11.10), giving:

$$lot\ (a : x)\ l_2 = length\ (append\ (a : x)\ l_2). \qquad (11.13)$$

We now use the transformation unfold again, taking (11.9) to be $E = E'$ and (11.13) to be $F = F'$:

$$\overbrace{append\ (a : x)\ y}^{E} = \overbrace{a : (append\ x\ y)}^{E'},$$

$$\underbrace{lot\ (a : x)\ l_2}_{F} = \underbrace{length\ \overbrace{(append\ (a : x)\ l_2)}^{E_1}}_{F'}.$$

This transformation gives rise to:

$$\underbrace{lot\ (a : x)\ l_2}_{F} = \underbrace{length\ \overbrace{(a : (append\ x\ l_2))}^{E_1'}}_{F''}.$$

By unfolding definition (11.7) this becomes:

$$lot\ (a : x)\ l_2 = 1 + length\ (append\ x\ l_2). \qquad (11.14)$$

Now we use the transformation fold with definition (11.10) playing the role of $E = E'$ and (11.14) being $G = G'$:

$$\overbrace{lot\ l_1\ l_2}^{E} = \overbrace{length\ (append\ l_1\ l_2)}^{E'},$$

$$\underbrace{lot\ (a:x)\ l_2}_{G} = \underbrace{1 + \overbrace{length\ (append\ x\ l_2)}^{E'_1}}_{G'}.$$

This transformation gives rise to the equation:

$$\underbrace{lot\ (a:x)\ l_2}_{G} = \underbrace{1 + \overbrace{lot\ x\ l_2}^{E_1}}_{G''}. \tag{11.15}$$

Thus, we have arrived at the more efficient definition of lot:

$$
\begin{aligned}
lot\ [\ ]\ y &= length\ y, \\
lot\ (a:x)\ y &= 1 + lot\ x\ y.
\end{aligned}
$$

As another example of a program transformation consider the following definition of the *length* function, which returns the length of a list:[5]

$$length\ y = foldright\ (\mathbf{K}\ (add\ 1))\ 0\ y, \tag{11.16}$$

where $add\ i\ j$ is just $i + j$ and *foldright* is the following higher-order function:

$$foldright\ f\ b\ [\ ] = b, \tag{11.17}$$
$$foldright\ f\ b\ (a:x) = f\ a\ (foldright\ f\ b\ x). \tag{11.18}$$

As Hughes (1984b), p. 4, points out one way to understand *foldright* $f\ b\ x$ is as a higher-order function that replaces all of the occurrences of *cons* in the list x by the function f and all the occurrences of $[\ ]$ in x by b.[6]

To begin the transformation of (11.16) we substitute $[\ ]$ for y in (11.16), giving:

$$length\ [\ ] = foldright\ (\mathbf{K}\ (add\ 1))\ 0\ [\ ]. \tag{11.19}$$

---

[5]The definition of *length* in terms of *foldright* given here is a correction of that found in Hughes (1984b), p. 5.

[6]The higher-order function *foldright* is, in fact, a special case of a more general homomorphism, as explained in the Glossary. Henson (1987), pp. 126–144, contains an excellent account of the utility of various homomorphisms in writing functional programs.

Unfolding equation (11.17) in (11.19) yields:

$$length\ [\ ] = 0. \tag{11.20}$$

Now for the case *length* $(a : x)$. We first substitute $(a : x)$ for y in (11.16). This results in the equation:

$$length\ (a : x) = foldright\ (\mathbf{K}\ (add\ 1))\ 0\ (a : x). \tag{11.21}$$

Unfolding (11.18) in (11.21) yields:

$$length\ (a : x) = \mathbf{K}\ (add\ 1)\ a\ (foldright\ (\mathbf{K}\ (add\ 1))\ 0\ x). \tag{11.22}$$

Folding (11.16) in (11.22) gives rise to the equation:

$$length\ (a : x) = \mathbf{K}\ (add\ 1)\ a\ (length\ x). \tag{11.23}$$

Using the fact that $\mathbf{K}\ P\ Q$ reduces to P—that is to say, using the transformation known as *laws*—yields:

$$length\ (a : x) = add\ 1\ (length\ x). \tag{11.24}$$

Thus, we have transformed the definition (11.16) into the following pair of equations:

$$\begin{aligned} length\ [\ ] &= 0, \\ length\ (a : x) &= add\ 1\ (length\ x). \end{aligned}$$

11.3.2 Compiling ZF-expressions

Wadler has devised an optimal method of compiling ZF-expressions—optimal in the sense that they perform the fewest possible *CONS* operations—which he arrived at by transforming a less efficient version. Because of the use his derivation makes of program transformation techniques I include this Subsection in this Chapter.[7]

The reduction rules for ZF-expressions are as follows:

$$\{e; a \leftarrow [\ ]; \ldots\} \quad \rightarrow \quad [\ ], \tag{11.25}$$

$$\{e; a \leftarrow (b : x); \ldots\} \quad \rightarrow \quad [b/a]\{e; \ldots\} + +\{e; a \leftarrow x; \ldots\}, \tag{11.26}$$

$$\{e; TRUE; \ldots\} \quad \rightarrow \quad \{e; \ldots\}, \tag{11.27}$$

$$\{e; FALSE; \ldots\} \quad \rightarrow \quad [\ ], \tag{11.28}$$

$$\{e\} \quad \rightarrow \quad [e]. \tag{11.29}$$

---

[7]The following discussion is based on Chapter 7 of Peyton Jones (1987), pp. 127–138, written by Wadler, and also on a talk he presented at Aston University on 25 November 1987.

In the case when we are dealing with a finite list in the first generator the reductions (11.25) and (11.26) are equivalent to

$$\{e; a \leftarrow [b_1, \ldots, b_n]; \ldots\} \rightarrow [b_1/a]\{e; \ldots\} + + \ldots + + [b_n/a]\{e; \ldots\}.$$

Recall that $[e/x]f$ is the same as $(\lambda x.f)e$. Therefore this can be expressed as:

$$\{e; a \leftarrow [b_1, \ldots, b_n]; \ldots\} \rightarrow (\lambda a.\{e; \ldots\})b_1 + + \ldots + + (\lambda a.\{e; \ldots\})b_n.$$

The right-hand side of this is equivalent to

$$flatmap\ (\lambda a.\{e; \ldots\})[b_1, \ldots, b_n],$$

where *flatmap* is defined as follows:

$$
\begin{aligned}
flatmap\ f\ [\,] &= [\,], \\
flatmap\ f\ (x:y) &= (f\ x) + + (flatmap\ f\ y).
\end{aligned}
$$

The type of *flatmap* is $(\alpha \rightarrow list\ \beta) \rightarrow list\ \alpha \rightarrow list\ \beta$ and its operation can be illustrated by means of a simple example. Define *lists* $i = [1..i]$. Then

$$flatmap\ lists\ [1..5] = [1, 1, 2, 1, 2, 3, 1, 2, 3, 4, 1, 2, 3, 4, 5].$$

Using *flatmap* the reduction rules (11.25) and (11.26) can be combined to form

$$\{e; a \leftarrow y; \ldots\} \rightarrow flatmap\ (\lambda a.\{e; \ldots\})\ y. \tag{11.30}$$

Equations (11.27) and (11.28) are equivalent to

$$\{e; b; \ldots\} \rightarrow \textbf{if}\ b\ \textbf{then}\ \{e; \ldots\}\ \textbf{else}\ [\,]. \tag{11.31}$$

An alternative way of defining *flatmap* is as follows:

$$
\begin{aligned}
flatmap\ f\ &=\ h, \\
&\textbf{whererec} \\
&h\ [\,] = [\,], \\
&h\ (c:w) = (f\ c) + + (h\ w).
\end{aligned}
$$

This allows us to write (11.30) as

$$
\begin{aligned}
\{e; a \leftarrow y; \ldots\}\ &\rightarrow\ h\ y, \\
&\textbf{whererec} \\
&h\ [\,] = [\,], \\
&h\ (c:w) = (\lambda a.\{e; \ldots\})c + + (h\ w).
\end{aligned}
\tag{11.32}
$$

Now I propose to generalize the reductions considered above by appending an arbitrary list z to each of them. Equation (11.32) becomes in this case:

$$\{e; a \leftarrow y; \ldots\} + + z \quad \rightarrow \quad (h\ y) + + z,$$
$$\mathbf{whererec}$$
$$h\ [\ ] = [\ ],$$
$$h\ (c : w) = (\lambda a.\{e; \ldots\})c + + (h\ w).$$

By means of program transformation this becomes

$$\{e; a \leftarrow y; \ldots\} + + z \quad \rightarrow \quad g\ y, \tag{11.33}$$
$$\mathbf{whererec}$$
$$g\ [\ ] = z,$$
$$g\ (c : w) = (\lambda a.\{e; \ldots\})c + + (g\ w).$$

Generalizing (11.31) results in

$$\{e; b; \ldots\} + + z \rightarrow (\mathbf{if}\ b\ \mathbf{then}\ \{e; \ldots\}\ \mathbf{else}\ [\ ]) + + z,$$

which can be transformed into

$$\{e; b; \ldots\} + + z \rightarrow \mathbf{if}\ b\ \mathbf{then}\ \{e; \ldots\} + + z\ \mathbf{else}\ z. \tag{11.34}$$

The final case straightforwardly becomes

$$\{e\} + + z \rightarrow e : z. \tag{11.35}$$

What is the point of all this? The above equivalences allow us to derive an efficient way of compiling ZF-expressions. In the following translation scheme *comp* is the function which performs the translation. It uses *aux* as an auxiliary function:[8]

$$comp\ [\![\{e; \ldots\}]\!] = aux\ [\![\{e; \ldots\} + + [\ ]\ ]\!]. \tag{11.36}$$

$$aux\ [\![\{e; a \leftarrow y; \ldots\} + + z]\!] \quad \rightarrow \quad g\ comp\ [\![y]\!], \tag{11.37}$$
$$\mathbf{whererec}$$

---

[8]I use Strachey brackets $[\![\ ]\!]$ to enclose syntactic items. This is done for clarity. The situation here is different from that in Section 4 of Chapter 9, where I *omitted* Strachey brackets for clarity. The difference is that there I was dealing with an abstract syntax, whereas here I am applying the translation functions *comp* and *aux* to concrete syntax.

$$g\ [\ ] = comp\ [\![z]\!],$$
$$g\ (x:w) = aux\ [\![(\lambda a.\{e;\ldots\})x + +(g\ w)]\!],$$
$$aux\ [\![\{e;b;\ldots\} + +z]\!]\quad \rightarrow\quad IF\ b\ (aux\ [\![\{e;\ldots\} + +z]\!])$$
$$(comp\ [\![z]\!]),\qquad\qquad (11.38)$$
$$aux\ [\![\{e\} + +z]\!]\quad \rightarrow\quad CONS\ (comp\ [\![e]\!])(comp\ [\![z]\!]).\qquad (11.39)$$

The translation schemes (11.37), (11.38) and (11.39) are obtained from (11.33), (11.34) and (11.35), respectively, by applying the functions *comp* and *aux* and simplifying as much as possible.

11.3.3 Dependency Analysis

The top-level of a Lispkit program is generally a **letrec**-clause, but rarely are all the functions defined in terms of all the others. Dependency analysis is a program transformation that has as its input a **letrec**-clause in which there might occur definitions of functions that are not mutually recursive, but in its output function definitions only occur in the same **letrec**-clause if they are mutually recursive and non-recursive functions are put into **let**-clauses. Thus, typically, the output of the dependency analysis transformation is an expression consisting of nested **let**- and **letrec**-clauses.

There are several reasons for performing the dependency analysis transformation on a functional program. (1) It is possible to implement **let**-clauses more efficiently than **letrec**-clauses. (2) The fewer functions defined in a **letrec**-clause, the more efficient its implementation. (3) Carrying out strictness analysis is more efficient if carried out on a program which has been subjected to the dependency analysis transformation. (4) There are situations in which Milner's type-checking algorithm will not result in a well-typing unless dependency analysis has been performed.[9]

To explain the method I shall consider an example, namely the third definition of Fibonacci numbers given in Chapter 2, which is reproduced in Fig. 11.1. The first thing to do is to construct a *call-structure graph* or *functional dependency graph* corresponding to this **letrec**-clause. Such a graph is a directed one whose vertices are the names of the functions occurring in the top-level **letrec**-clause and the arc $x \mapsto y$, where x and y are function names, is a member of the arc-set iff y is used in the definition of x. In general, a directed graph consists of a vertex-set and an arc-*family*,

---

[9]Strictness analysis is explained in Chapter 12 and type systems are discussed in Chapter 13. This Section is based on section 6.2.8, "Dependency Analysis", of Peyton Jones (1987), pp. 118–121.

```
(letrec (fib (quote 7))
  (fib lambda (n)
    (if (eq n (quote 0))
        (quote 0)
        (if (eq n (quote 1))
            (quote 1)
            (add (select (sub n (quote 1)) fiblist)
                 (select (sub n (quote 2)) fiblist)))))
  (fiblist map fib (from (quote 0)))
  (select lambda (i x)
    (if (eq i (quote 0))
        (head x)
        (select (sub i (quote 1)) (tail x))))
  (map lambda (f x)
    (if (eq x (quote NIL))
        (quote NIL)
        (cons (f (head x))
              (map f (tail x)))))
  (from lambda (p)
    (cons p (from (add p (quote 1))))))
```

Figure 11.1: A program to calculate the seventh Fibonacci number.

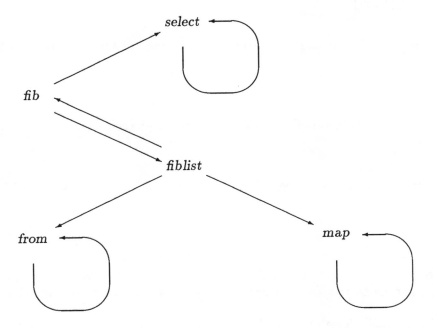

Figure 11.2: The call-structure graph of the program to calculate *fib* 7.

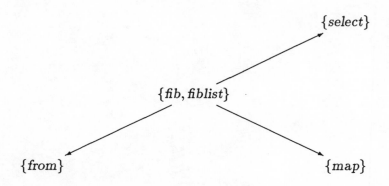

Figure 11.3: The strongly connected components of the program graph.

$$\{\text{fib}, \text{fiblist}\} \rightarrow \{\text{from}\} \rightarrow \{\text{map}\} \rightarrow \{\text{select}\}.$$

Figure 11.4: The topologically sorted version of the program graph.

but in the call-structure graph we only include the arc $x \mapsto y$ *once*, even if y occurs several times in the definition of x. The functional dependency graph corresponding to the above program is, therefore, as shown in Fig. 11.2.

The second phase of dependency analysis is to locate the strongly connected components of the call-structure graph. This results in a reduced or coalesced graph which must be acyclic, as shown in Aho, Hopcroft and Ullman (1983), p. 223. The vertices of the reduced graph are sets of function names and there is an arc from X to Y iff $x \mapsto y$ is an arc in the original graph and $x \in X$ and $y \in Y$. The reduced graph for the example I am considering is given in Fig. 11.3.

The third step is to perform a topological sort on this reduced graph and the result of this is shown in Fig. 11.4. The final step is to generate a Lispkit program based on this information and the resulting program is shown in Fig. 11.5.

```
(letrec
  (letrec
    (letrec
      (letrec (fib (quote 7))
        (fib lambda (n)
          (if (eq n (quote 0))
              (quote 0)
              (if (eq n (quote 1))
                  (quote 1)
                  (add (select (sub n (quote 1)) fiblist)
                       (select (sub n (quote 2)) fiblist)))))
        (fiblist map fib (from (quote 0))))
      (from lambda (p)
              (cons p (from (add p (quote 1)))))))
    (map lambda (f x)
            (if (eq x (quote NIL))
                (quote NIL)
                (cons (f (head x))
                      (map f (tail x))))))
  (select lambda (i x)
    (if (eq i (quote 0))
        (head x)
        (select (sub i (quote 1)) (tail x)))))
```

Figure 11.5: The transformed Lispkit program to calculate *fib* 7.

11.4 Partial Evaluation

11.4.1 The Mathematical Background

Partial evaluation is an interesting idea which combines the methods of program transformation and implementation. It can be seen as an application in computing of the S-m-n Theorem, which comes from recursive function theory. Thus I will begin by giving an account of this theorem. Those who are not mathematically inclined can omit the rest of this Subsection. What follows does not make any essential use of the material presented here.

The S-m-n Theorem states that for all natural numbers $m, n \geq 0$ there exists a primitive recursive function $S_n^m(z, y_1, \ldots, y_m)$ such that, if e is a number which recursively defines $\phi(y_1, \ldots, y_m, x_1, \ldots, x_n)$, then for each fixed sequence $u_1, \ldots, u_m$ of natural numbers, $S_n^m(e, u_1, \ldots, u_m)$ recursively defines $\phi(u_1, \ldots, u_m, x_1, \ldots, x_n)$ as a function of $x_1, \ldots, x_n$.

Using the λ-notation we can restate the S-m-n Theorem as saying that if e recursively defines $\lambda y_1 \ldots y_m x_1 \ldots x_n . \phi(y_1, \ldots, y_m, x_1, \ldots, x_n)$, then for each fixed sequence $u_1, \ldots, u_m$ of natural numbers, $S_n^m(e, u_1, \ldots, u_m)$ recursively defines $\lambda x_1 \ldots x_n . \phi(u_1, \ldots, u_m, x_1, \ldots, x_n)$.[10]

To further explain the significance of this theorem, let $E^i(x_0, x_1, \ldots, x_i)$ be a universal function for all partial recursive functions of i variables.[11] This means that if e recursively defines the partial recursive function $g(x_1, \ldots, x_i)$ then

$$g(x_1, \ldots, x_i) = E^i(e, x_1, \ldots, x_i),$$

for all arguments $x_1, \ldots, x_i$. Thus, E^i can be thought of as a computer or evaluator which executes the "program" e with input data $x_1, \ldots, x_i$. The S-m-n Theorem can, therefore, be reformulated as stating that there exists a recursive function $S_n^m(x_0, x_1, \ldots, x_m)$, such that for every function $f(x_1, \ldots, x_{m+n})$, the following holds:

$$
\begin{aligned}
f(x_1, \ldots, x_{m+n}) &= E^n(S_n^m(e, x_1, \ldots, x_m), x_{m+1}, \ldots, x_{m+n}), \\
&= E^{m+n}(e, x_1, \ldots, x_{m+n}),
\end{aligned}
$$

where e recursively defines $f(x_1, \ldots, x_{m+n})$. Thus what S_n^m does is to create an n-place function from an $(m+n)$-place function by filling up the first m argument-places.

---

[10] For more details see Kleene (1952), pp. 342ff.

[11] This way of explaining the significance of the S-m-n Theorem is due to Ershov (1982), p. 53, where the universal function is called $U^i(x_0, x_1, \ldots, x_i)$.

As a simple example, let us consider the function $p(x, y)$, which is to be understood as y^x, and let e recursively define $p(x, y)$. Thus we have:

$$p(x, y) = E^2(e, x, y),$$
$$= E^1(S_1^1(e, x), y).$$

Here, $S_1^1(e, x)$ is that function of x that when given a number, say 5, as its argument returns that function which calculates fifth powers. Thus in Ershov's terminology, S_1^1—and S_n^m in general—is a *partial evaluator*. In fact, he calls it a *trivial* partial evaluator, for reasons that I hope will become apparent.

11.4.2   Partial Evaluation in Computing

Consider the following KRC program which calculates y to the power of x, that is to say, y^x:

$$power\ [x, y] = 1,\ x = 0,$$
$$= square\ (power\ [x/2, y]),\ even\ x,$$
$$= y * power\ [x - 1, y].$$

The type of *power* is $int \times int \to int$, where I use the notation $int \times int$ for the type of two-lists of non-negative numbers. For simplicity, I am assuming here that *square* and *even* are primitive functions with the obvious meanings. Now, let us consider the expression:

$$power\ [5, z].$$

If we actually submitted this for evaluation to the KRC interpreter, when z had not been previously defined, then we would get an error message pointing this out. However, let us consider what happens if we perform the textual substitution of 5 for x and z for y in the source code of the definition of the *power* function. That results in the program text:

$$power\ [5, z] = 1,\ 5 = 0,$$
$$= square\ (power\ [5/2, z]),\ even\ 5,$$
$$= z * power\ [5 - 1, z].$$

We know that the guards $5 = 0$ and *even* 5 are both false, so the first two lines of the definition cannot hold. Furthermore, we have that $5 - 1 \to 4$; so the above program text can be transformed to give us:

$$power\ [5, z] = z * power\ [4, z].$$

Clearly, we can carry on performing still further substitutions and simplifications on the expression *power* $[4, z]$. Such a procedure eventually gives rise to the program text:

$$power\ [5, z] = z * square\ (square\ z).$$

This is an example of *partial evaluation*. As well as making use of the program transformations substitution and simplification (or laws) it also involves the manipulation of expressions composed of variables and constants which would give rise to errors if submitted to a reducer as usually implemented.

As another example of partial evaluation let us consider the function *select*, which locates the i-th element from a list s:

$$
\begin{aligned}
select\ [i, s] \quad &= \quad hd\ s, \ i = 1, \\
&= \quad select\ [i - 1, tl\ s].
\end{aligned}
$$

Now, I will consider the partial evaluation *select* $[3, s]$. Substituting 3 for i in the above definition gives us:

$$
\begin{aligned}
select\ [3, s] \quad &= \quad hd\ s, \ 3 = 1, \\
&= \quad select\ [3 - 1, tl\ s].
\end{aligned}
$$

The guard $3 = 1$ is false, so the second clause must obtain. Using the fact that $3 - 1 \rightarrow 2$ in the second clause, this can be expanded to give:

$$
\begin{aligned}
select\ [2, tl\ s] \quad &= \quad hd\ (tl\ s), \ 2 = 1, \\
&= \quad select\ [2 - 1, tl\ (tl\ s)].
\end{aligned}
$$

Here, again, the first clause does not obtain, because $2 = 1$ is false. Repeating the substitution and simplification process, we get:

$$
\begin{aligned}
select\ [1, tl\ (tl\ s)] \quad &= \quad hd\ (tl\ (tl\ s)), \ 1 = 1, \\
&= \quad select\ [1 - 1, tl\ (tl\ (tl\ s))].
\end{aligned}
$$

This time the first clause does obtain, because $1 = 1$ is true. Putting all these things together gives us the partial evaluation:

$$select\ [3, s] = hd\ (tl\ (tl\ s)).$$

11.4.3   The Partial Evaluator Mix

In this Subsection I introduce the partial evaluator **mix**. What **mix** does is to automatically perform the transformations given in the previous Subsection. Thus, **mix** applied to the KRC program *power* and to 5 and *z* gives the program:

$$z * square \, (square \, z).$$

We could have defined another program—say *five*—straight off, as follows:

$$five \, z = z * square \, (square \, z).$$

It is easy in all this to get confused between KRC programs and the functions they define, so I will use the letter π for the program which defines the *power* function. You can think of π as a string of characters. Similarly, I will use the letter ϕ for the program which defines the *five* function. We can then symbolize what **mix** does as follows:

$$K \textbf{ mix } [\pi, 5] = \phi, \tag{11.40}$$

where K is the semantic function of the programming language KRC.

Let D be a set which contains both all the programs in all the languages that we are dealing with and also all the possible data objects that might form their input and output. Then, the *semantic function* for a language L is a function of type $D \to D^* \to D$, such that the domain of this function consists of all the syntactically correct programs written in L. Here, D^* is the set of all the finite lists or finite sequences of elements drawn from D and $X \to Y$ means the set of partial functions from X to Y. Following Jones, Sestoft and Søndergaard (1985), p. 126, I will identify a programming language with its semantic function.

In the equation (11.40) we want both sides to compute the same value. Thus, for all x we require

$$\begin{aligned} K \, (K \textbf{ mix } [\pi, 5]) \, [x] &= K \, \phi \, [x], \\ &= K \, \pi \, [5, x]. \end{aligned}$$

It might be easier to understand what K does if you realize that $K \, \pi \, [5, 2] = 8$ and $K \, \phi \, [2] = 8$. The general property of **mix**, for any language L, is the following:

$$L \, (L \textbf{ mix } [\pi, w]) \, [x] = L \, \pi \, [w, x],$$

where π is a program that expects two arguments in the form of a list. This can be explained as follows. If **mix** is applied to π and the first argument it requires, say w, then the result is a program which when applied to something which is suitable as a second argument to π, say x, has exactly the same result as if π was applied directly to w and x. Thus, we "factor" the operation performed by π into two separate programs.

11.4.4 Compilers and Interpreters

Now I would like to apply **mix** to the area of compilers and interpreters. This Subsection is based on Jones, Sestoft and Søndergaard (1985), pp. 127–129, and Sestoft (1986), pp. 237–238. We can think of a compiler *comp* as a program which takes a program in one language and returns one in another. For definiteness, let us assume that *comp* is written in L and that the programs it compiles are written in S. For simplicity, I shall also assume that the code the compiler produces is also written in language L. Thus we have

$$L \; comp \; [\pi] = ob,$$

where π is the source code in the language S and ob is the object code in the language L. In order to simplify the following discussion I shall assume that ob takes a single argument, so we have:

$$
\begin{aligned}
L \; ob \; [d] \;\; &= \;\; a, \\
&= \;\; S \; \pi \; [d].
\end{aligned}
$$

An interpreter *int*, on the other hand, is a program which takes two arguments, a program and its input data, and returns the result of running that program on those data:

$$L \; int \; [\pi, d] = a.$$

Now, let us consider the result of applying **mix** to an interpreter and a program, and applying the result to some data:

$$
\begin{aligned}
L \; (L \; \mathbf{mix} \; [int, \pi]) \; [d] \;\; &= \;\; L \; int \; [\pi, d], \\
&= \;\; a.
\end{aligned}
$$

But we also have:

$$L \; (L \; comp \; [\pi]) \; [d] = L \; ob \; [d] = a.$$

Putting these things together gives us:

$$L \; (L \; \mathbf{mix} \; [int, \pi]) \; [d] = L \; (L \; comp \; [\pi]) \; [d].$$

166

So—removing the argument from both sides—we have

$$L \text{ mix } [int, \pi] = L \text{ comp } [\pi].$$

What this means is that if you apply **mix** to an interpreter and a program, you get the same as compiling that program.

Now let us apply **mix** to itself and an interpreter, that is to say, let us consider L **mix** $[\textbf{mix}, int]$. Making the substitutions in the definition of **mix** we have:

$$
\begin{aligned}
L\ (L \text{ mix } [\textbf{mix}, int])\ [\pi] \ &= \ L \text{ mix } [int, \pi], \\
&= \ L \text{ comp } \pi, \\
&= \ ob.
\end{aligned}
$$

Thus, L **mix** $[\textbf{mix}, int]$ is a compiler, since it produces object code for an arbitrary program π.

By a similar argument a compiler generator can be obtained. Define,

$$cocom \triangleq L \text{ mix } [\textbf{mix}, \textbf{mix}].$$

This transforms interpreters into compilers:

$$
\begin{aligned}
L \text{ cocom } [int] \ &= \ L\ (L \text{ mix } [\textbf{mix}, \textbf{mix}])\ [int], \\
&= \ L \text{ mix } [\textbf{mix}, int],
\end{aligned}
$$

which is what we had previously.

11.4.5 Other Uses of Partial Evaluation

Another application of partial evaluation or mixed computation is in the area of universal parsers. As is well known, a universal parser for a class of grammars is a two-place function which takes a grammar and an input string as its arguments and yields a parse tree. If we partially evaluate such a universal parser with a particular grammar as its first argument then we get a language-specific parser.

As another example, consider the case of a theorem-prover P which takes a set of axioms A and a theorem to be proved T as its arguments and returns either yes, no or eternal silence, as its answer. We must allow for eternal silence as most interesting logical systems are undecidable. We might be interested in proving a number of theorems of, say, Euclidean geometry. In that case, it would make sense to partially evaluate P with A taken to be the set of Euclid's axioms.

11.4.6 Discussion

What, then, is the point of all this? In the area of language implementation it is usually easier to implement a new language by writing an interpreter for it than by writing a compiler for it. This is largely because you do not have to worry about the different things that happen at compile time and at run time. Interpreters do everything at once, but they are usually too inefficient for practical use. The above method for generating compilers from interpreters is not particularly efficient, but it does produce compilers that are very efficient. This has been borne out by the work of Neil Jones and his associates in Copenhagen. See, for example, Jones, Sestoft and Søndergaard (1985).

Concerning *cocom*, Jones, Sestoft and Søndergaard (1985), p. 129, say that it is more general than a compiler generator, being—in fact—a general currying operation. As such, it transforms a program representing a function which expects a two-list as its argument, say $f[x, y]$, into a program which when given some data, say d, as argument yields one representing the function $\lambda y.f[d, y]$. Thus, the type of *cocom* is given by

$$cocom : rep\ (\alpha \times \beta \to \gamma) \to rep\ (\alpha \to rep\ (\beta \to \gamma)),$$

where *rep* $(\alpha \to \beta)$ means the collection of programs representing functions from α to β and where I have written $\alpha \times \beta$ to indicate the set of two-lists.

It is instructive to compare *cocom* with the function *uncurry* defined by Turner (1976), p. 30, which in KRC is

$$curry\ f\ x\ y = f\ [x, y].$$

The type of *curry* is

$$curry : (\alpha \times \beta \to \gamma) \to \alpha \to \beta \to \gamma.$$

The difference is that *cocom* is a *meta*-program whose input and data are themselves programs, whereas *curry* is not a meta-program. Its input and output are not, in general, programs.

The method of partial evaluation is not restricted to functional programming languages. Ershov (1982) and Futamura (1983) both give examples of its application to programs written in imperative languages. Similar ideas—if not the same techniques—are used in Prolog, where the method is known as *partial execution*. Pereira and Shieber (1987) say that the partial execution of a Prolog program 'involves the replacing of certain computations that would normally be performed at execution time by changes to the program itself' (p. 98, see also Section 6.4, "Partial Execution and Compilers", pp. 172–178; Shapiro (1987), pp. 300–301, also mentions the idea). But it would not be appropriate for me to explore the use of partial evaluation in imperative or logic programming in greater detail here. What I propose to do in the rest of this Section is to mention how the ideas of partial evaluation can be used to provide meaningful error message in a combinator-based functional language compiler.

11.4.7 Diagnostic Run-time Error Message

One of the problems with combinator-based compilers for functional languages is that it is difficult to give meaningful run-time error messages. There are two main reasons for this. The first is that the functional program is translated into an incomprehensible CL-term and the second is that this CL-term is then repeatedly transformed by head reduction, so that if an error occurs, the program graph is far removed from what it was originally.

In order to remedy this situation Turner (1981a), p. 140, suggests—following an idea of Hamilton Richards Jr—introducing a combinator *AB-STR*, which I will write as **A**. This has the reduction properties

$$\mathbf{A}xPQ \quad \rightarrow \quad PQ, \tag{11.41}$$

$$\mathbf{A}xPQ \quad \rightarrow \quad Px \ \mathbf{whererec} \ x = Q. \tag{11.42}$$

Rule (11.41) is used when everything is going smoothly, but rule (11.42) is followed when an error occurs (for example, when we try to take the head of a number or add two lists together). In (11.41) and (11.42) x is a variable and the purpose of the **A** combinator is to keep a record of the names that the programmer actually used in his program, although the **whererec**-clauses introduced by (11.42) will rarely be the same as he used.

The **A** combinator is introduced into the CL-term through the abstraction algorithm. For example, algorithm (C) would have to be modified as follows in order to use this idea:

$$[x]E \quad \rightarrow \quad \mathbf{A}x(\mathbf{K}E),$$
$$[x]x \quad \rightarrow \quad \mathbf{A}x\mathbf{I},$$
$$[x]Ex \quad \rightarrow \quad \mathbf{A}xE,$$
$$[x]EFX \quad \rightarrow \quad \mathbf{A}x(\mathbf{B}'EF([x]X)),$$
$$[x]EXF \quad \rightarrow \quad \mathbf{A}x(\mathbf{C}'E([x]X)F),$$

$$[x]EXY \rightarrow \mathbf{A}x(\mathbf{S}'E([x]X)([x]Y)),$$
$$[x]EX \rightarrow \mathbf{A}x(\mathbf{B}E([x]X)),$$
$$[x]XE \rightarrow \mathbf{A}x(\mathbf{C}([x]X)E),$$
$$[x]XY \rightarrow \mathbf{A}x(\mathbf{S}([x]X)([x]Y)).$$

Here, E and F are CL-terms which definitely do not contain x and X and Y are CL-terms which definitely do contain x.

In order to see how this idea works I shall consider the translation and evaluation of a faulty program, namely

$$f1 \ \mathbf{whererec} \ f = \lambda(i).cons((head \ i),(f(i+1))).$$

This is translated into

$$([f]f1)(\mathbf{Y}([f][i]CONS(HEAD \ i)(f(ADD \ i \ 1)))).$$

Let α and β be the following CL-terms:

$$\alpha \equiv \mathbf{A}f(\mathbf{C}(\mathbf{A}f\mathbf{I})1),$$
$$\beta \equiv \mathbf{A}f(\mathbf{B}'\mathbf{A}i(\mathbf{A}f(\mathbf{B}'(\mathbf{S}'CONS)(\mathbf{A}i \ HEAD)$$
$$(\mathbf{A}f(\mathbf{B}'\mathbf{A}i(\mathbf{A}f(\mathbf{C}'\mathbf{B}(\mathbf{A}f\mathbf{I})(\mathbf{A}i(\mathbf{C}'ADD(\mathbf{A}i\mathbf{I}) \ 1)))))))))).$$

Then the above program becomes $\alpha(\mathbf{Y}\beta)$. Reduction of this proceeds smoothly until we get to the stage

$$CONS \ (HEAD \ 1) \ (\mathbf{A}f(\underbrace{\mathbf{B}'\mathbf{A}i(\mathbf{A}f(\mathbf{C}'\mathbf{B}(\mathbf{A}f\mathbf{I})(\mathbf{A}i(\mathbf{C}'ADD(\mathbf{A}i\mathbf{I})1)))))}_{\gamma}) \ (\mathbf{Y}\beta)1).$$

We now have to use rule (11.42), which results in

$$CONS \ (HEAD \ 1)(\gamma f \ \mathbf{whererec} \ f = \mathbf{Y}\beta) \ 1,$$

and eventually we arrive at

$$CONS \ (HEAD \ 1)) \ (f(ADD \ i \ 1) \ \mathbf{whererec} \ f = \mathbf{Y}\beta,$$

from which the programmer should be able to work out his error. It should be noticed that when an error occurs not only do we use the reduction (11.42) but also source reduction—which Turner calls formal reduction—is used wherever possible. More sophisticated versions of this technique are presented by Toyn and Runciman (1986) and Henson (1987), pp. 305–306, who adds that the method—which he calls *symbolic decompilation*—could also be used to provide a pretty-printing facility for functional languages.

Chapter 12

Strictness Analysis

12.1 Introduction

Strictness analysis is a method of finding some of the strict argument-places of a function. A one-place function f is *strict* iff $f\bot = \bot$ and an n-place function g is strict in its i-th argument-place iff

$$gx_1 \ldots x_{i-1}\bot x_{i+1} \ldots x_n = \bot.$$

A *non-strict* function is one that can return a value even if some of its arguments are undefined.

One of the uses to which strictness analysis can be put is in the way that a functional program, written in a lazy language, can be evaluated on a parallel machine. There is no problem about incorporating parallelism into a compiler for a language that makes use of applicative order reduction (AOR). For example, let f be a 5-place function. Then in order to evaluate $fa_1a_2a_3a_4a_5$, a reducer using AOR would first evaluate all five arguments, namely a_1, a_2, a_3, a_4 and a_5, then it would evaluate f, and after that it would apply the result of evaluating f to the results of evaluating its arguments. If the language in which the compiler is written incorporates parallel constructs, then all we have to do is to evaluate the five arguments in parallel and then evaluate f and apply the result to them. Using AOR corresponds to treating f as being strict in each of its five argument-places.

In the case of a reducer using normal order reduction (NOR) the situation is not so simple. There will be occasions when we do not require some of the arguments to a function, and hence we do not want the reducer to try to evaluate them. The reason for this concerns the termination properties of certain programs. Some programs terminate when evaluated on a reducer employing NOR, but not when evaluated on one using AOR. For example, consider the following function definition in KRC:

$$bot \ a \ = \ tom \ (a + 1),$$
$$tom \ a \ = \ bot \ (a - 1),$$
$$\mathbf{K} \ x \ y \ = \ x.$$

An attempt to evaluate:

$$\mathbf{K} \ (3 + 5) \ (bot \ 7),$$

on a reducer employing AOR will result in eternal silence, for the attempt to evaluate this function application will never terminate; but if the reducer employs NOR then the evaluation will terminate with the result 8. In this case, the reducer will not even try to evaluate the second argument to the **K** function, namely *bot* 7.

Languages employing NOR have a non-strict semantics. As already mentioned, strictness analysis is a way of locating some of the strict argument-places of a function defined in an applicative language.[1] When that function is then applied to some arguments it is then safe to evaluate those in strict argument-places simultaneously.

Strictness analysis also has other uses. In an SECD machine-based implementation of a functional language it is more expensive to pass arguments to a function using call-by-name—or even call-by-need—than it is to pass them by the call-by-value mechanism. This is because each passed argument needs to carry around a closure with it, according to Mycroft (1981), p. 64. It is, therefore, advantageous to be able to convert call-by-name and call-by-need into call-by-value wherever possible, and strictness analysis finds many of the occasions when this is possible. This was, indeed, Mycroft's motivation for applying the technique of strictness analysis to functional programs.

The most efficient implementations of lazy functional languages at present are based on the G-machine and—as Peyton Jones (1987), p. 5, points out—strictness analysis 'is crucial to many of the optimizations of the G-machine'.

---

[1] The reason I say *some* strict argument-places and not *all* is that the problem of finding all of a function's strict argument-places is—in general—undecidable.

Strictness analysis is a form of abstract interpretation and that is a compile-time technique which works on the text of the program being analyzed and derives properties of the program by executing it on a restricted domain of values.

The structure of this Chapter is as follows. First, I say what abstract interpretation is by considering the example of the rule of signs for multiplication. Then, I explain the basic ideas of domain theory, paying special attention to the finding of least fixed-points. After that I present the abstraction rules that are used in the simplest kinds of strictness analysis and illustrate their use by means by a few easy examples.

12.2   What is Abstract Interpretation?

A simple example of abstract interpretation concerns the familiar rule of signs when multiplying together two integers. Let us assume that we want to know the sign of the result of a multiplication. One way of getting this answer is to first multiply the two integers together and then to take the sign of the result. An example of this is

$$abs\ (387 \times -1154) = abs\ (-446598) = \textbf{neg},$$

where abs is the function from integers to their signs. The sign of an integer can be either **neg** (negative), **pos** (positive) or **zero**, since I assume that 0 is neither negative nor positive. But given the signs of the two numbers involved it is possible to work out the sign of the result without actually having to perform the multiplication. In this case we proceed as follows:

$$abs\ (387 \times -1154) = abs\ (387) \otimes abs\ (-1154) = \textbf{pos} \otimes \textbf{neg} = \textbf{neg},$$

where, $\otimes$ is the operator corresponding to the rule of signs for multiplication. Its definition is as follows:

$$
\begin{aligned}
\textbf{pos} \otimes \textbf{pos} &= \textbf{pos,} \\
\textbf{pos} \otimes \textbf{neg} &= \textbf{neg,} \\
\textbf{pos} \otimes \textbf{zero} &= \textbf{zero,} \\
\textbf{neg} \otimes \textbf{pos} &= \textbf{neg,} \\
\textbf{neg} \otimes \textbf{neg} &= \textbf{pos,} \\
\textbf{neg} \otimes \textbf{zero} &= \textbf{zero,} \\
\textbf{zero} \otimes \textbf{pos} &= \textbf{zero,}
\end{aligned}
$$

$$\textbf{zero} \otimes \textbf{neg} \;\; = \;\; \textbf{zero},$$

$$\textbf{zero} \otimes \textbf{zero} \;\; = \;\; \textbf{zero}.$$

What is going on in the rule of signs for multiplication is that we have a function *abs* from the integers to the set **sign** = {**pos**, **neg**, **zero**}, that is to say,

$$abs : \mathbb{Z} \rightarrow \textbf{sign},$$

where *abs* is defined by these equations:

$$abs \; n = \begin{cases} \textbf{pos}, & \text{if } n > 0, \\ \textbf{zero}, & \text{if } n = 0, \\ \textbf{neg}, & \text{if } n < 0. \end{cases}$$

The result of applying *abs* to the result of a multiplication is the same as combining the results of applying *abs* to the two arguments of the multiplication function and combining them with $\otimes$. In symbols, this is represented by the identity

$$abs \; (x \times y) = (abs \; x) \otimes (abs \; y).$$

Summarizing, then, if we are interested in the sign of a multiplication then it is more efficient to first work out the sign of the numbers we are interested in multiplying together and only then to work out the sign of the result of the multiplication.

12.3 The Basic Ideas of Domain Theory

Model theory is that branch of mathematical logic in which the formulas or terms of some formal system are associated with objects in an algebraic structure. In the case of the λ-calculus—and functional languages in general—the algebraic structures involved make use of domains or complete partial orders (cpos). The purpose of this Section is to introduce the basic ideas of domain theory.

12.3.1 Partial Orders and Posets

A relation $\sqsubseteq$ is a *partial order* on a set D if the following three conditions are satisfied:[2]

---

[2]In the literature a *partial order* $\sqsubseteq$ on a set D is sometimes defined to be a transitive relation such that it is not the case that $x \sqsubseteq x$ for any $x \in D$. If this terminology is used, then the relation $\sqsubseteq$ defined in the text is known as a *reflexive partial order*. Mendelson (1964), p. 9, for example, uses this alternative terminology.

1. $\sqsubseteq$ is reflexive, that is to say, for all $d \in D$, $d \sqsubseteq d$.

2. $\sqsubseteq$ is antisymmetric, that is to say, for all $d, e \in D$, $d \sqsubseteq e$ and $e \sqsubseteq d$ implies that $d = e$.

3. $\sqsubseteq$ is transitive, that is to say, for all $d, e, f \in D$, $d \sqsubseteq e$ and $e \sqsubseteq f$ implies that $d \sqsubseteq f$.

Some examples may make this idea clearer. The relation *is a factor of* on the set of natural numbers is a partial order. The three conditions given above are easily verified. Every number is a factor of itself. If p is a factor of q and q is a factor of p, then p is the same number as q. If p is a factor of q and q is a factor of r, then p is a factor of r.

As another example let X be any set. Then the subset relation $\subseteq$ is a partial order on the powerset of X, namely $P(X)$.

Both these examples also illustrate the important point that a partial order does not have to hold between every pair of elements of the set on which it is a partial order. Let $X = \{1, 2, 3, 4\}$. Then $\subseteq$ is a partial order on $P(\{1, 2, 3, 4\})$, but neither is $\{1, 2\}$ a subset of $\{3, 4\}$ nor is $\{3, 4\}$ a subset of $\{1, 2\}$. Such elements are said to be *incomparable* or *unconnected*. (A relation $\sqsubseteq$ is *connected* if, for all $d, e \in D$, either $d \sqsubseteq e$ or $e \sqsubseteq d$. If a relation $\sqsubseteq$ is connected—in addition to being reflexive, antisymmetric and transitive—then it is called a *linear order*.)

A *partially ordered set* or *poset* is an ordered pair $(D, \sqsubseteq)$, where $\sqsubseteq$ is a partial order on the set D. One example of a poset is $(P(X), \subseteq)$, where X is any set, $P(X)$ is the powerset of X and $\subseteq$ is set inclusion. Another example of a poset is **bool** $= (\{\bot, t, f\}, \sqsubseteq)$, where $\bot \sqsubseteq t$ and $\bot \sqsubseteq f$ and $\sqsubseteq$ does not hold between any other elements of **bool**.

12.3.2 Bounds, Directed Subsets and Cpos

Let $(D, \sqsubseteq)$ be a poset and let S be a subset of D, $S \subseteq D$. Then we say that u is an *upper bound* of S if, for all $s \in S, s \sqsubseteq u$ and l is a *lower bound* of S if, for all $s \in S, l \sqsubseteq s$. There is no guarantee that an arbitrary subset S of D will have either an upper or a lower bound.

Let $(D, \sqsubseteq)$ be a poset and let S be a subset of D, $S \subseteq D$. Then we say that l is the *least upper bound* or *lub* of S if l is an upper bound of S and, furthermore, for all upper bounds u of S, $l \sqsubseteq u$. The least upper bound of a set S is also known as the *supremum* of S and is represented as $\sqcup S$. If the set S just contains two members, say a and b, then $\sqcup \{a, b\}$ can be written as $a \sqcup b$, the *join* of a and b.

175

Let $(D, \sqsubseteq)$ be a poset and let $S \subseteq D$. Then g is the *greatest lower bound* or *glb* of S if g is a lower bound of S and for all lower bounds l of S, $l \sqsubseteq g$. The greatest lower bound of a set S is also known as the *infimum* of S and is represented as $\sqcap S$. If the set S just contains two members, say a and b, then $\sqcap\{a, b\}$ can be written as $a \sqcap b$, the *meet* of a and b.

Let $(D, \sqsubseteq)$ be a poset. Then a subset $X \subseteq D$ is *directed* if $X \neq \{\}$ and

$$(\forall x, y \in X)(\exists z \in X)(x \sqsubseteq z \land y \sqsubseteq z).$$

A *complete partial order* or *cpo* is a poset $(D, \sqsubseteq)$ with the following additional properties:

1. There exists a least element in D. This is called *bottom* and is conventionally represented as $\bot$. Because $\bot$ is the least element of D we have that $(\forall x \in D)\, \bot \sqsubseteq x$.

2. Every directed subset $X \subseteq D$ has a supremum in D. This is represented as $\bigsqcup X$.

The relation $x \sqsubseteq y$ is variously read as 'x is less defined than y' (O'Donnell (1977), p. 14), 'x is weaker than y' (Stoy (1977), p. 82) and 'x approximates y' (Bird (1976), p. 148). The posets $(P(X), \subseteq)$ and **bool** are also examples of cpos. Complete partial orders are also known as *domains*.

12.3.3 Sums and Products of Cpos

There are two main ways of defining the sum of two cpos. The *coalesced disjoint sum* $(D, \sqsubseteq)$ of two cpos $(D_1, \sqsubseteq_1)$ and $(D_2, \sqsubseteq_2)$ is such that:

$$D = D_1 + D_2 = \{< a, 1 >|\ a \in D_1\} \cup \{< b, 2 >|\ b \in D_2\},$$

where the following conditions hold:

$$< \bot_1, 1 >=< \bot_2, 2 >= \bot,$$

$$< a, 1 >\sqsubseteq< a', 1 > \text{ iff } a \sqsubseteq_1 a',$$

$$< b, 2 >\sqsubseteq< b', 2 > \text{ iff } b \sqsubseteq_2 b',$$

but $< a, 1 >$ and $< b, 2 >$ are otherwise incomparable.

The *separated disjoint sum* $(D, \sqsubseteq)$ of two cpos $(D_1, \sqsubseteq_1)$ and $(D_2, \sqsubseteq_2)$ is such that:

$$D = D_1 + D_2 = \{< a, 1 >|\ a \in D_1\} \cup \{< b, 2 >|\ b \in D_2\} \cup \{\bot\},$$

where $\perp \sqsubseteq < \perp_1, 1 >$ and $\perp \sqsubseteq < \perp_2, 2 >$, otherwise $\sqsubseteq$ is as before. When the sum of two domains is used in this book—as in Chapter 6—it is to be understood as being the separated disjoint sum.

There are two main ways of defining the product of two cpos. The first is the *non-strict product*. Let $(D_1, \sqsubseteq_1)$ and $(D_2, \sqsubseteq_2)$ be two cpos. Then their non-strict product is $(D, \sqsubseteq)$, where:

$$D = D_1 \times D_2 = \{< d_1, d_2 > \mid d_1 \in D_1 \wedge d_2 \in D_2\},$$

and $< d_1, d_2 > \sqsubseteq < d_1', d_2' >$ iff $d_1 \sqsubseteq d_1'$ and $d_2 \sqsubseteq d_2'$.

The *strict* product is similar, except that it has to satisfy the additional property that for all $d_1 \in D_1$ and $d_2 \in D_2$:

$$< d_1, \perp_2 > = \perp = < \perp_1, d_2 >,$$

where $\perp_1$ is the least element of D_1, $\perp_2$ of D_2 and $\perp$ of $D_1 \times D_2$.

It is easy to verify that $D_1 \times D_2$ is a cpo in both cases. In what follows it is to be assumed that products are strict.

12.3.4   Monotonicity, Continuity and Function Spaces

Let $(D, \sqsubseteq_D)$ and $(E, \sqsubseteq_E)$ be cpos. Then a function $f : D \to E$ is *monotonic* if

$$(\forall x \in D, y \in E)(x \sqsubseteq_D y \Rightarrow fx \sqsubseteq_E fy).$$

Let $(D, \sqsubseteq)$ be a poset. A sequence of elements of D , say $x_0, x_1, x_2, x_3, \ldots$, is an *ascending chain of approximations* (or an *ascending chain* or simply a *chain*) if $x_i \sqsubseteq x_{i+1}$ for all $i \geq 0$.[3] This can be written as:

$$x_0 \sqsubseteq x_1 \sqsubseteq x_2 \sqsubseteq x_3 \sqsubseteq \ldots$$

Such a chain of elements of D has a *unique limit x in D* if $x \in D$ and

1. $x_i \sqsubseteq x$, for all $i \geq 0$.

2. If $x_i \sqsubseteq y$, for all $i \geq 0$, then $x \sqsubseteq y$.

If the chain $x_0 \sqsubseteq x_1 \sqsubseteq x_2 \sqsubseteq x_3 \sqsubseteq \ldots$ has a unique limit x in D, then x is denoted by $\bigsqcup_{n=0}^{\infty} x_i$. Such a limit is also the least upper bound of the set $\{x_0, x_1, x_2, x_3, \ldots\}$ under the relation $\sqsubseteq$.

---

[3] Another characterization of a chain is possible. A subset X of D is a *chain* iff it is totally ordered by $\sqsubseteq$.

Let $(D, \sqsubseteq_D)$ and $(E, \sqsubseteq_E)$ be cpos, then a function $f : D \rightarrow E$ is *continuous* if it is monotonic and for every chain $x_0 \sqsubseteq x_1 \sqsubseteq x_2 \sqsubseteq x_3 \ldots$ of elements of D we have:

$$f(\bigsqcup_{n=0}^{\infty} x_n) = \bigsqcup_{n=0}^{\infty} f(x_n).$$

The notation $D \rightarrow E$ usually means the set of *all* functions from D to E, but this set is too large to be of use in domain theory—one of the reasons for this is that we require $D \rightarrow D$ to be isomorphic to D—so we must restrict the size of $D \rightarrow E$ in some way. When D and E are domains, then we define $D \rightarrow E$ to be the set of all *continuous* functions from D to E. We can define a partial order $\sqsubseteq$ on $D \rightarrow E$. Let $f, g \in D \rightarrow E$, then if, for all $x \in D$, $fx \sqsubseteq_E gx$, then $f \sqsubseteq_{D \rightarrow E} g$. The least element of $D \rightarrow E$ is $\lambda x.\perp_E$ and it is possible to prove that $D \rightarrow E$, as defined here, is a complete partial order. Barendregt (1984), p. 12, contains a proof.

Let $(D, \sqsubseteq_D)$ be a cpo and let g be a continuous function of type $D \rightarrow D$, then a *fixed-point* of the function g is an object z, such that $z = gz$. Define g^n as follows:

$$\begin{aligned} g^0 &= \lambda x.x, \\ g^n &= g \circ g^{n-1}, \text{ for } n > 0. \end{aligned}$$

Let *Fix* be the following function:

$$\text{Fix } g = \bigsqcup_{n=0}^{\infty} g^n(\perp).$$

It can be proved that every continuous function g has a least fixed-point, namely *Fix* g. (See, for example, Paulson (1987), p. 66.)

12.3.5 Deriving Least Fixed-points

The most complicated part of strictness analysis is that of finding the strict argument-places of recursively defined functions. The method employed to do this involves working out the least fixed-point of a functional—that is to say, a higher-order function obtained by a systematic method from the function we are analysing—and what I propose to do now is to explain how least fixed-points can be derived for numerical functions. It will then be easier to understand the method when it is applied in the context of abstract interpretation. But in order to use domain theory on numerical functions we first have to make certain changes to the familiar arithmetical operators.

The set $\mathbb{N}$ of non-negative natural numbers is not a cpo, but the lifted set $\mathbb{N}_\perp$ is. The lifting operation can be applied to any set X. It involves adding a bottom element $\perp$ and a partial order $\sqsubseteq$. The lifted version of X is represented as $X_\perp = (X \cup \{\perp\}, \sqsubseteq)$, where for all $x, y \in X \cup \{\perp\}$, $x \sqsubseteq y$ iff $x = \perp$ or $x = y$. It is easy to verify that $X_\perp$ is a cpo. A cpo such as $X_\perp$ is known as a *flat domain*.

Addition—and the other arithmetical operators—are functions of type $\mathbb{N} \times \mathbb{N} \to \mathbb{N}$, but we need to extend them to be of type $\mathbb{N}_\perp \times \mathbb{N}_\perp \to \mathbb{N}_\perp$, where $\times$ is now the strict product of two cpos and $\to$ is restricted to continuous functions. Assuming that this has been done, I will continue to use the signs $+, -$, etc., but now they will refer to these extended functions. I will use $\mathbb{N}$ for $\mathbb{N}_\perp$, if no confusion can arise.

The derivation of least fixed-points depends upon Kleene's fixed-point theorem, which states that if D is a cpo with least element $\perp$ and $f : D \to D$ is a continuous function, then f has a fixed-point x which is such that

$$x = \bigsqcup_{n=0}^{\infty} f^n(\perp),$$

where $f^0 x = x$ and $f^{n+1} x = f(f^n x)$. In fact, x is the least fixed-point of f. This is proved, for example, by Bird (1976), pp. 158–159. Now I will consider some examples of how all this theory can be put into practice.

Consider the following function, which is taken from Stoy (1977), p. 79:

$$g = \lambda x. \text{if } x = 0 \text{ then } 1 \text{ else if } x = 1 \text{ then } g(3) \text{ else } g(x - 2).$$

What we are interested in are the fixed-points of the functional G defined by:

$$G \equiv \lambda g x. \text{if } x = 0 \text{ then } 1 \text{ else if } x = 1 \text{ then } g(3) \text{ else } g(x - 2).$$

This has several solutions, for example, one fixed-point of G is:

$$g'(x) = \begin{cases} 1, & \text{if } x = 0 \text{ or } x \text{ is even,} \\ \perp, & \text{if } x \text{ is odd.} \end{cases}$$

Another is given by:

$$g_1(x) = 1, \text{for all } x.$$

For every value of a the following is also a fixed-point of G:

$$g_a(x) = \begin{cases} 1, & \text{if } x = 0 \text{ or } x \text{ is even,} \\ a, & \text{if } x \text{ is odd.} \end{cases}$$

Of these solutions, g' is the minimal one. It is the least fixed-point of the functional G and it is the one that a computer would produce if g was represented in some programming language.

The functions Fix_D, of type $(D \to D) \to D$, calculate the least fixed-points of continuous functions of type $D \to D$:

$$Fix_D(f) = \bigsqcup_{i=0}^{\infty} f^i(\bot),$$

where $\bot$ is the least element of D and $f^0 = \lambda x.x$ and $f^{n+1} = f \circ f^n$.

Now let us work out the successive approximations of the functional G. These approximations will be called g_i, for $i \geq 0$. We know that $g_0 = G(\lambda y.\bot) = \lambda x.\bot$:

$$
\begin{aligned}
g_1 &= G(g_0), \\
&= \lambda x.\textbf{if } x = 0 \textbf{ then } 1 \textbf{ else} \\
&\qquad \textbf{if } x = 1 \textbf{ then } (\lambda y.\bot)(3) \textbf{ else } (\lambda y.\bot)(x-2), \\
&= \lambda x.\textbf{if } x = 0 \textbf{ then } 1 \textbf{ else } \bot.
\end{aligned}
$$

The next approximation is given by:

$$
\begin{aligned}
g_2 &= G(g_1), \\
&= \lambda x.\textbf{if } x = 0 \textbf{ then } 1 \textbf{ else if } x = 1 \textbf{ then } g_1(3) \textbf{ else } g_1(x-2), \\
&= \lambda x.\textbf{if } x = 0 \textbf{ then } 1 \textbf{ else} \\
&\qquad \textbf{if } x = 1 \textbf{ then } \bot \textbf{ else if } x - 2 = 0 \textbf{ then } 1 \textbf{ else } \bot, \\
&= \lambda x.\textbf{if } x = 0 \textbf{ then } 1 \textbf{ else if } x = 2 \textbf{ then } 1 \textbf{ else } \bot.
\end{aligned}
$$

The next approximation is given by:

$$
\begin{aligned}
g_2 &= G(g_1), \\
&= \lambda x.\textbf{if } x = 0 \textbf{ then } 1 \textbf{ else} \\
&\qquad \textbf{if } x = 2 \textbf{ then } 1 \textbf{ else if } x = 4 \textbf{ then } 1 \textbf{ else } \bot.
\end{aligned}
$$

By Kleene's theorem we know that the limit of the sequence

$$g_0 \sqsubseteq g_1 \sqsubseteq g_2 \sqsubseteq g_3 \sqsubseteq \cdots,$$

180

is the least fixed-point of G, and in this case it is g', where

$$g'(x) = \begin{cases} 1, & \text{if } x = 0 \text{ or } x \text{ is even,} \\ \bot, & \text{if } x \text{ is odd.} \end{cases}$$

As another example I shall consider the following function g, which is taken from Bird (1976), p. 162:

$$\lambda x.\text{if } x = 0 \text{ then } 0 \text{ else } (2x - 1) + g(x - 1).$$

The normal functional here is G:

$$G \equiv \lambda gx.\text{if } x = 0 \text{ then } 0 \text{ else } (2x - 1) + g(x - 1).$$

As in the previous example, if we want to discover the least fixed-point of G, then we need to construct the series of approximations:

$$g_0 \sqsubseteq g_1 \sqsubseteq g_2 \sqsubseteq g_3 \sqsubseteq \cdots,$$

where $g_0 = \lambda x.\bot$ and $g_{n+1} = G(g_n)$, for all $n \geq 0$.

The second approximation is g_1:

$$\begin{aligned} g_1 &= \lambda x.\text{if } x = 0 \text{ then } 0 \text{ else } (2x - 1) + g_0(x - 1), \\ &= \lambda x.\text{if } x = 0 \text{ then } 0 \text{ else } \bot. \end{aligned}$$

since $(2x - 1) + \bot = \bot$ when we extend addition to the domain of natural numbers. The third approximation is:

$$\begin{aligned} g_2 &= \lambda x.\text{if } x = 0 \text{ then } 0 \text{ else } (2x - 1) + g_1(x - 1), \\ &= \lambda x.\text{if } x = 0 \text{ then } 0 \text{ else } (2x - 1) + (\text{if } x - 1 = 0 \text{ then } 0 \text{ else } \bot), \\ &= \lambda x.\text{if } x = 0 \text{ then } 0 \text{ else if } x = 1 \text{ then } 1 \text{ else } \bot. \end{aligned}$$

Continuing in this way we see that:

$$\bigsqcup_{i=0}^{\infty} g_i(\bot) = x^2.$$

Hence, the least fixed-point of the functional G is $\lambda x.x^2$.

So far I have only considered the method of finding the least fixed-point of a functional G corresponding to a function g which is just defined recursively in terms of itself, but mutually recursive functions are also common in functional programming. The following example of mutual recursion comes from Brady (1977), p. 144, and the theory is well-explained in Bird (1976), pp. 166–167:

$$f = \lambda x.\textbf{if } x = 0 \textbf{ then } 1 \textbf{ else } f(x-1) \times g(x),$$
$$g = \lambda x.\textbf{if } x \leq 1 \textbf{ then } 2 \textbf{ else } f(x-2) \times g(x-1).$$

It is possible to define f and g in terms of functionals F and G as follows: $f = Ffg$ and $g = Gfg$, where

$$F \equiv \lambda fgx.\textbf{if } x = 0 \textbf{ then } 1 \textbf{ else } f(x-1) \times g(x),$$
$$G \equiv \lambda fgx.\textbf{if } x \leq 1 \textbf{ then } 2 \textbf{ else } f(x-2) \times g(x-1).$$

The "trick" in finding the least fixed-points of F and G is to combine them into a single recursive definition, thus:

$$H(f,g) = (Ffg, Gfg),$$

where—putting $D = \mathbb{N} \to \mathbb{N}$—$H : D \times D \to D \times D$. Let us define

$$h_0 = (\lambda x.\bot, \lambda x.\bot),$$
$$h_{n+1} = Hh_n.$$

Now, let $h_n = (f_n, g_n)$, where f_n is the $(n+1)$-th approximation of f and g_n is the $(n+1)$-th approximation of g. Then $h_{n+1} = (Ff_ng_n, Gf_ng_n)$. Thus $f_{n+1} = Ff_ng_n$ and $g_{n+1} = Gf_ng_n$. The first approximations of f and g are $f_0 = \lambda x.\bot$ and $g_0 = \lambda x.\bot$.

The second approximation to f is calculated thus:

$$
\begin{aligned}
f_1 = Ff_0g_0 &= \lambda x.\textbf{if } x = 0 \textbf{ then } 1 \textbf{ else } f_0(x-1) \times g_0(x),\\
&= \lambda x.\textbf{if } x = 0 \textbf{ then } 1 \textbf{ else } \bot \times \bot,\\
&= \lambda x.\textbf{if } x = 0 \textbf{ then } 1 \textbf{ else } \bot.
\end{aligned}
$$

The second approximation to g is derived as follows:

$$
\begin{aligned}
g_1 = Gf_0g_0 &= \lambda x.\textbf{if } x \leq 1 \textbf{ then } 2 \textbf{ else } f_0(x-2) \times g_0(x-1),\\
&= \lambda x.\textbf{if } x \leq 1 \textbf{ then } 2 \textbf{ else } \bot \times \bot,\\
&= \lambda x.\textbf{if } x \leq 1 \textbf{ then } 2 \textbf{ else } \bot.
\end{aligned}
$$

The calculation of the third approximations proceeds similarly:

$$
\begin{aligned}
f_2 = Ff_1g_1 &= \lambda x.\textbf{if } x = 0 \textbf{ then } 1 \textbf{ else } f_1(x-1) \times g_1(x),\\
&= \lambda x.\textbf{if } x = 0 \textbf{ then } 1 \textbf{ else if } x = 1 \textbf{ then } 2 \textbf{ else } \bot.
\end{aligned}
$$

$$g_2 = Gf_1g_1 \quad = \quad \lambda x.\text{if } x \leq 1 \text{ then } 2 \text{ else } f_1(x-2) \times g_1(x-1),$$
$$= \quad \lambda x.\text{if } x \leq 1 \text{ then } 2 \text{ else if } x = 2 \text{ then } 2 \text{ else } \bot,$$

as does that of the fourth approximations:

$$f_3 = Ff_2g_2 \quad = \quad \lambda x.\text{if } x = 0 \text{ then } 1 \text{ else } f_2(x-1) \times g_2(x),$$
$$= \quad \lambda x.\text{if } x = 0 \text{ then } 1 \text{ else}$$
$$\text{if } x = 1 \text{ then } 2 \text{ else if } x = 2 \text{ then } 4 \text{ else } \bot.$$

$$g_3 = Gf_2g_2 \quad = \quad \lambda x.\text{if } x \leq 1 \text{ then } 2 \text{ else } f_2(x-2) \times g_2(x-1),$$
$$= \quad \lambda x.\text{if } x \leq 1 \text{ then } 2 \text{ else}$$
$$\text{if } x = 2 \text{ then } 2 \text{ else if } x = 3 \text{ then } 4 \text{ else } \bot,$$

and we could carry on in this fashion indefinitely.

12.4 Abstract Interpretation in Practice

Now I am going to discuss how the method strictness analysis works. In Mycroft's work functions are mapped to abstract functions defined over a two-element domain $\{\bot, \top\}$, which is ordered by the relation $\bot \sqsubseteq \top$. When x is a value of the original domain, then the idea is that:

$$\text{abs } x = \begin{cases} \bot, & \text{if } x \text{ necessarily fails to terminate,} \\ \top, & \text{if } x \text{ may terminate.} \end{cases}$$

Often, this two-element domain is taken to be $\{0, 1\}$, with $0 \equiv \bot$ and $1 \equiv \top$. $\top$ can be thought of as *truth* and $\bot$ as *falsity*.

The abstraction function for non-recursive definitions is given by the following equations:[4]

1. If k is a constant, then abs $k = \top$, because constants always terminate.

2. If x is a variable, then abs $x = x$.

3. If $\square$ is a binary built-in operator which is strict in both its arguments, like addition or multiplication, then

$$\text{abs } (x \square y) = (\text{abs } x) \wedge (\text{abs } y).$$

---

[4]A very clear account of the following rules can be found in Wray (1986), pp. 35–36.

4. If f is a function, then abs $f = f^\sharp$.

5. abs $(\lambda x.e) = \lambda x.\text{abs } e$.

6. abs $(fa) = (\text{abs } f)(\text{abs } a)$.

7. abs $(\textbf{if } b \textbf{ then } p \textbf{ else } q) = (\text{abs } b) \wedge ((\text{abs } p) \vee (\text{abs } q))$.

There is nothing special about the symbol $f^\sharp$: just think of it as an abbreviation for abs f. The operators $\wedge$ and $\vee$ used in some of the above equations are the usual logical ones:

$$x \wedge y = \begin{cases} \top, & \text{if } x = y = \top, \\ \bot, & \text{otherwise.} \end{cases}$$

$$x \vee y = \begin{cases} \bot, & \text{if } x = y = \bot, \\ \top, & \text{otherwise.} \end{cases}$$

The way in which these abstraction rules are used can be seen by considering a simple example, and for this purpose I use one taken from Peyton Jones (1987), p. 388:

$$f \; x \; y \; z = \textbf{if } y = 0 \textbf{ then } f \; 0 \; 1 \; x \textbf{ else } x.$$

This is clearly equivalent to

$$f = \lambda xyz.\textbf{if } y = 0 \textbf{ then } f \; 0 \; 1 \; x \textbf{ else } x.$$

To find out if any of the argument-places of the function f are strict, we first apply the abstraction transformation to it, obtaining

$$f^\sharp = \lambda xyz.y \wedge (f^\sharp \; \top\top x \vee x).$$

This is the same as $f^\sharp = Ff^\sharp$, where

$$F = \lambda fxyz.y \wedge (f\top\top x \vee x).$$

Thus $f^\sharp$ is a fixed-point of F. In order to work out the fixed-point of F we construct successive approximations $f_i^\sharp = Ff_{i-1}^\sharp$, for $i \geq 1$, where $f_0^\sharp = \lambda xyz.\bot$. Thus,

$$\begin{aligned} f_1^\sharp &= Ff_0^\sharp, \\ &= \lambda xyz.y \wedge (\bot \vee x), \\ &= \lambda xyz.y \wedge x. \end{aligned}$$

Now, we test $f_0^\sharp$ and $f_1^\sharp$ for equality, that is to say, whether

$$f_0^\sharp xyz = f_1^\sharp xyz, \text{ for all } x, y, z \in \{\top, \bot\}.$$

They are different, so we proceed to construct the third approximation:

$$
\begin{aligned}
f_2^\sharp &= F f_1^\sharp, \\
&= \lambda xyz.y \wedge (f_1^\sharp \top \top x \vee x), \\
&= \lambda xyz.y \wedge ((\top \wedge \top) \vee x), \\
&= \lambda xyz.y.
\end{aligned}
$$

Again we test $f_1^\sharp$ and $f_2^\sharp$ for equality. They are different, so we proceed to construct the fourth approximation $f_3^\sharp$:

$$
\begin{aligned}
f_3^\sharp &= F f_2^\sharp, \\
&= \lambda xyz.y \wedge (f_2^\sharp \top \top x \vee x), \\
&= \lambda xyz.y \wedge (\top \vee x), \\
&= \lambda xyz.y.
\end{aligned}
$$

Testing $f_2^\sharp$ and $f_3^\sharp$ for equality, we find that they are the same. Thus $f_3^\sharp$ is the least fixed-point of F, therefore $f^\sharp = \lambda xyz.y$. Evaluating $f^\sharp \bot \top \top$, $f^\sharp \top \bot \top$ and $f^\sharp \top \top \bot$ we see that $f^\sharp$ is strict only in its second argument-place, therefore the second argument-place of f is strict. The others may or may not be.

In some cases, applying the abstraction transformation to a recursive function results in a non-recursive definition. Consider the definition of the exponential function exp:

$$exp = \lambda xy.\textbf{if } y = 0 \textbf{ then } 1 \textbf{ else } x \times exp\ x\ (y-1).$$

This is transformed into:

$$exp^\sharp = \lambda xy.(y \wedge \top) \wedge (\top \vee (x \wedge exp^\sharp x(y \wedge \top))).$$

Using familiar truth-functional equalities, this becomes

$$exp^\sharp = \lambda xy.y.$$

The function $exp^\sharp$ is not recursive. Some of the equalities used are:

$$
\begin{aligned}
y \wedge \top &= y, \\
\bot \vee x &= \bot.
\end{aligned}
$$

The pattern of definition exemplified by exp is quite common.

12.5 Conclusion

The method of strictness analysis presented in this Chapter has certain limitations. It only works for functions defined by first-order recursion equations defined over flat domains. Since the pioneering work of Mycroft (1981) the technique has been extended to cope with functions defined by higher-order recursion equations over arbitrary domains. See, especially, Burn, Hankin and Abramsky (1985) and the papers in Abramsky and Hankin (1987).

Chapter 13

Type Systems

13.1 Introduction

I begin this Chapter by motivating the inclusion of a polymorphic type discipline in a functional programming language. I do this by pointing out the limitations of both a typeless language like Lispkit and a monomorphically typed language like Pascal. Then I discuss some of the choices that have to be made by designers of polymorphic type systems and that is followed by an example of type inference.

13.2 Motivation

Polymorphic type systems are—at present—very popular amongst designers of functional programming languages. There are two main considerations that contribute to this popularity. On the one hand, there is the realization that many programming errors are typing errors and that these can be very difficult to track down without assistance. On the other, there is also the realization that a language in which every identifier is just assigned a single type is far too restrictive and constraining and leads to much duplication in some programs. I will now elaborate these points in greater detail.

Having no type-checking in a programming language is not good, because many programming errors are typing errors and also because in a language without type-checking it is possible to define functions that are difficult to understand and hard to reason about. For example, in an interactive Lispkit system we could define the following function:

187

```
(def funny (lambda (x)
            (if (not (leq (quote 0) x))
                (cons x (quote NIL))
                (if (eq x (quote 0))
                    (quote 0)
                    (lambda (y) (add y x))))))
```

This is a function which takes a number as its argument, but its value is a list if its argument is less than 0, a number if its argument is equal to 0 and a function if its argument is greater than 0. Thus, it could be used in each of the following three ways:

```
(cons (funny (quote -1)) (quote NIL))

(mul (funny (quote 0)) (quote 3))

((funny (quote 5)) (quote 7))
```

I shall illustrate the restrictiveness of a monomorphic type discipline by considering Pascal's type system. In this context it is not important that Pascal is an imperative language because there is no essential connection between a particular kind of type system and any one class of programming language.

Let us consider the definition of a list of integers in Pascal as a dynamic data structure. I shall use the built-in Pascal constant **nil** to represent the empty list. A list of integers is either the empty list or it is constructed by putting an integer at the front of a list. The following type declarations are suitable for representing such lists:

CellPtr = ↑ Cell;
Cell = **record**
        value: Integer;
        next: CellPtr
      end;

and the following function declarations define some of the operations that can be performed on this data structure:[1]

---

[1] Although I use the function names *Cons*, *Car* and *Cdr* that are used in Lisp, these

```
function Cons (h: Integer; t: CellPtr): CellPtr;
    var p: CellPtr;
begin
   New (p);
   with p↑ do
     begin
        value := h;
        next := t
     end;
   Cons := p
end;

function Car (p: CellPtr): Integer;
begin Car := p↑.value end;

function Cdr (p: CellPtr): CellPtr;
begin Cdr := p↑.next end;
```

Let us now consider the definition of a function that returns the length of an arbitrary list of integers:

```
function CLength (p: CellPtr): Integer;
begin
   if p = nil then
     CLength := 0
   else
     CLength := 1 + CLength (Cdr (p))
end;
```

But what happens when we find that we also want to manipulate lists of characters in the same program? What we would have to do is to define an entirely new data structure and new list-manipulating operations on it. Thus, a list of characters is either the empty list or it is constructed by putting a character at the front of a list. The following type declarations are suitable for representing lists of characters:

```
KellPtr = ↑ Kell;
Kell = record
```

Pascal functions are much less general. In particular, the elements of a list here have to integers; they cannot themselves be lists.

```
      value: Char;
    next: KellPtr
  end;
```

The following function declarations define the familiar list constructor and destructor operations on this data structure:

```
function Kons (h: Char; t: KellPtr): KellPtr;
  var p: KellPtr;
begin
  New (p);
  with p↑ do
    begin
      value := h;
      next := t
    end;
  Kons := p
end;

function Kar (p: KellPtr): Char;
begin Kar := p↑.value end;

function Kdr (p: KellPtr): KellPtr;
begin Kdr := p↑.next end;
```

If we again need to know the length of an arbitrary list of characters, then we have to define another function to perform this task, such as the following:

```
function KLength (p: KellPtr): Integer;
begin
  if p = nil then
    KLength := 0
  else
    KLength := 1 + KLength (Kdr (p))
end;
```

Whenever we want to deal with a list consisting of elements of a new type, then we will have to define all the list-manipulating functions all over again. We also have to define new versions of functions like those that return the length of a list of integers or of characters. This is clearly neither an economical nor an efficient way to proceed. The various list-manipulating and length functions involved are only slightly different from one another. This shows that a type system as incorporated into Pascal is far too restrictive.

By contrast, in a language like ML or Miranda—which has a polymorphic type system—all the basic list-manipulating functions work on lists whose members are elements of any type and it is only necessary to define a single *length* function. Such a function will then work on lists of any type of element. The only constraint is that each element in the list must be of the same type. The function *length*, for example, could be defined thus:

$$length\ [\ ] \quad = \quad 0,$$
$$length\ (a : x) \quad = \quad 1 + length\ x,$$

and its type is *list* $\alpha \rightarrow int$.[2] When the *length* function is applied to a list of numbers, as when we ask for

$$length\ [1, 3, 6, 23, 1, 34],$$

to be evaluated, then the type of the *length* function is instantiated to *list int* $\rightarrow$ *int*, and when it is applied to a list of characters, as when we ask for

$$length\ "character",$$

to be evaluated, then the type of the *length* function is instantiated to *list char* $\rightarrow$ *int*.

This discussion has shown that, although there are good reasons for having a type system in a programming language, a monomorphic type system is far too restrictive. Therefore, designers of functional languages have recently favoured the inclusion of some kind of polymorphic type system and some of the possibilities in this area are discussed in the next Section.

13.3   Choices to be Made about Type Systems

The considerations of the previous Section show the desirability of having a type discipline in a programming language and they also indicate that a monomorphic type discipline is far too restrictive. The conclusion that should be drawn from this is that we need to incorporate a polymorphic

---

[2]This is not the syntax that is used in Miranda for types; it is, rather, similar to the notation used by Milner, which is—in any case—fairly standard.

type system into our functional language, but such type systems are not made in heaven. There are many possible polymorphic type systems and what I want to do next is to single out the choices that we have to make in order to design a type discipline that we find acceptable.

In the remainder of this Chapter I shall use the following notational conventions. α, β and γ will stand for type variables and *int*, *char* and *bool* will be type constants, representing—respectively—the types of integers, characters and booleans. Only two type constructors are allowed, namely the two-place infix operator $\rightarrow$, which is right associative and denotes a function type, and the one-place prefix operator *list*, which makes—not surprisingly—list types out of arbitrary types. Finally, arbitrary types, that is to say, any types that can be constructed from the type variables and constants by means of the type constructors, will be represented by σ and τ.

It should be noted that—in the interests of simplicity and clarity—I do not allow product types. This has necessitated the making of a few minor alterations to the syntax of Lispkit used in this Chapter.

13.3.1 Abstractions

Consider the λ-abstraction $\lambda x.e$, and assume that x occurs several times in e. Does each occurrence of x have to have exactly the same type or can the types associated with different occurrences of x be instances of a more general type? For example, let the most general type of x be $\alpha \rightarrow \alpha$, does it have to be of the same type each time it occurs? Or can it be of type $\beta \rightarrow \beta$, say, on one occasion and $(\beta \rightarrow \beta) \rightarrow (\beta \rightarrow \beta)$, say, on another? Do we allow

$$\lambda x_{\alpha \rightarrow \alpha}.x_{(\beta \rightarrow \beta) \rightarrow (\beta \rightarrow \beta)} x_{\beta \rightarrow \beta},$$

to be well-typed? A type system in which $\lambda x.e$ is well-typed even though x is used polymorphically in e—as in $\lambda x.xx$—is studied in Coppo, Dezani-Ciancoglini and Venneri (1980). The resulting type system is, however, not decidable. The usual decision made by designers of type systems for functional languages is to insist that $\lambda x.e$ is well-typed only if each occurrence of x in e has the same type.[3]

---

[3]An alternative approach is to say that $(\lambda x.e)f$ is well-typed iff $[f/x]e$ is well-typed. This, again, results in a system which is not decidable. See Yelles (1979) for details.

13.3.2 Let-clauses

Consider the let-clause

$$\textbf{let } x = e \textbf{ in } f, \tag{13.1}$$

and assume that x occurs several times in f. Does it have to have the same type each time or can the types of the several occurrences of x in f just be instances of a more general type? For example, should we allow

$$\textbf{let } i_{\alpha\to\alpha} = (\lambda y_\alpha.y_\alpha)_{\alpha\to\alpha} \textbf{ in } i_{(\beta\to\beta)\to(\beta\to\beta)}i_{\beta\to\beta},$$

to be well-typed?

If we say no, then the clause (13.1) is identical to $(\lambda x.f)e$ and the inclusion of let-clauses in our language is purely cosmetic. Milner's answer was to allow x to occur polymorphically in f in expressions of the form (13.1) and others have generally followed his lead. This has the consequence that (13.1) can be well-typed even if $(\lambda x.f)e$ cannot. As we wish reduction and conversion to preserve the property of being well-typed we cannot allow (13.1) and $(\lambda x.f)e$ to be interconvertible. Damas (1985), pp. 17 and 32, uses the following reduction rule for let-clauses:

$$\textbf{let } x = e \textbf{ in } f \to [f/x]e,$$

and this does preserve the property of being well-typed.

No new considerations arise in the case of having multiple declarations in the let-clause,

$$\textbf{let } x_1 = e_1 \textbf{ and } x_2 = e_2 \textbf{ and } \ldots \textbf{ and } x_n = e_n \textbf{ in } e.$$

13.3.3 Letrec-clauses

The general form of letrec-clauses is

$$\textbf{letrec } x_1 = e_1 \textbf{ and } x_2 = e_2 \textbf{ and } \ldots x_n = e_n \textbf{ in } e. \tag{13.2}$$

Consider the following example:

$$\textbf{letrec } map = \lambda fx.\textbf{if } null \ x \textbf{ then } NIL$$
$$\textbf{else } cons \ (f(head \ x))(map \ f(tail \ x))$$
$$\textbf{in } map \ chr \ (map \ (\lambda x.2 \times x) \ \phi),$$

where ϕ is an arbitrary list of integers. Clearly, we want this to be allowed, although *map* occurs once with type:

$$(int \rightarrow char) \rightarrow list\ int \rightarrow list\ char,$$

and once with type:

$$(int \rightarrow int) \rightarrow list\ int \rightarrow list\ int.$$

Clearly we want to allow:

$$\textbf{letrec}\ length\ =\ \lambda x.\textbf{if}\ null\ x\ \textbf{then}\ 0$$
$$\textbf{else}\ 1 + length\ (tail\ x)\ \textbf{in}\ length\ \phi + length\ \psi,$$

where ϕ and ψ are lists of different kinds of things. Say, ϕ is a list of integers and ψ is a list of characters. So, in (13.2) we allow x_i to have different types in e, but what about in e_i and in e_j when $i \neq j$? The usual decision is to insist that x_i has the same type both in e_i and also in e_j when $i \neq j$. Mycroft (1984) has investigated the consequences of letting x_i occur polymorphically in e_j when $i \neq j$, but the resulting type system is not decidable.

13.3.4 Quantified Types

Following Milner (1978), I have only considered types that can be constructed from type variables and type constants by means of the constructors *list* and $\rightarrow$, but it is also possible to include quantified types, like $\forall \alpha.\sigma$, in a type system. Damas (1985), Chapter II, pp. 65–87, considers the case in which quantifiers are only allowed at the outermost level, that is to say, types of the form

$$(\forall \alpha)(\alpha \rightarrow (\forall \beta)(\beta \rightarrow \alpha \rightarrow \beta)),$$

are *not* allowed. Henson (1987), p. 325, gives a set of rules for constructing types which allow such embedded quantifiers, but he makes no interesting use of them. Neither ML nor Miranda allow embedded quantifiers in types.

13.3.5 Discussion

One of the arguments used in favour of making one choice rather than another in the alternatives mentioned is that the resulting type system should be decidable. This is supposed to be a good thing because then the programmer does not have to specify the type to which his functions belong.

An algorithm can be devised for *assigning* types to functions and not just for checking them. But people who use this argument also urge programmers to specify the types of the functions they define for pragmatic reasons. This seems to invalidate the original argument. If you are urged to specify types—as good programming practice—in any case, then surely a semi-decidable system is acceptable? My advice to designers of functional programming languages would be to experiment with various type systems, even the semi-decidable ones, because—although it is very good—I do not think Milner's type system is necessarily the best.

13.4   Type Inference

The rules for type inference are all straightforward. In what follows I shall use Δ, Γ and Σ to represent sets of type assignments of the form $x : \sigma$ and Δ^x means the set Δ from which all propositions involving x have been removed. The notation $\Delta \vdash x : \sigma$ means that the type assignment $x : \sigma$ follows from the set of assignments Δ by the following rules:

1. The first rule simply states that if $x : \sigma \in \Delta$, then $\Delta \vdash x : \sigma$.

2. The rule for function application states that if $\Delta \vdash f : \sigma \rightarrow \tau$ and $\Gamma \vdash x : \sigma$, then it follows that $\Delta \cup \Gamma \vdash fx : \tau$.

3. The rule for the conditional is that if $\Delta \vdash b : bool$, $\Gamma \vdash p : \sigma$ and $\Sigma \vdash q : \sigma$, then it follows that

$$\Delta \cup \Gamma \cup \Sigma \vdash \textbf{if } b \textbf{ then } p \textbf{ else } q : \sigma.$$

4. The rule for λ-abstraction states that if $\Delta^x \cup \{x : \sigma\} \vdash e : \tau$, then $\Delta \vdash \lambda x.e : \sigma \rightarrow \tau$.

5. The rule for **let**-clauses is that if all the following hold, where—without loss of generality—we can assume that x does not occur in any proposition in Δ_i, for $1 \leq i \leq n$,

$$\Delta_1 \vdash e : \tau_1,$$
$$\Delta_2 \vdash e : \tau_2,$$
$$\vdots$$
$$\Delta_n \vdash e : \tau_n,$$
$$\Gamma^x \cup \{x : \tau_1, x : \tau_2, \ldots, x : \tau_n\} \vdash f : \sigma,$$

then we can infer that

$$\Delta_1 \cup \Delta_2 \cup \ldots \cup \Delta_n \cup \Gamma \vdash \mathbf{let}\ x = e\ \mathbf{in}\ f : \sigma.$$

Here, the τ_i are assumed to be polymorphic instances of some more general type τ.

6. The rule for **letrec**-clauses is that if $\Delta^x \cup \{x : \sigma\} \vdash e : \sigma$ and $\Gamma^x \cup \{x : \sigma_1, x : \sigma_2, \ldots, x : \sigma_n\} \vdash f : \tau$, then $\Delta \cup \Gamma^x \vdash \mathbf{letrec}\ x = e\ \mathbf{in}\ f : \tau$. Here, the σ_i are assumed to be polymorphic instances of σ.

As an example of a type inference I shall consider the following program:

$$\mathbf{letrec}\ map\ =\ \lambda f y.\mathbf{if}\ null\ y\ \mathbf{then}\ NIL$$
$$\mathbf{else}\ cons\ (f(head\ y))(map\ f(tail\ y))\ \mathbf{in}\ map\ decode\ (map\ code\ \phi).$$

Here, *decode* is a function which maps a number to the character which has that number as its ASCII value, *code* takes a character as its argument and returns its numerical ASCII value and ϕ is a list of characters. A combination of the form

$$map\ decode\ (map\ code\ \phi),$$

is more efficiently represented as

$$map\ (decode\ o\ code)\ \phi,$$

where o is functional composition, but one of the purposes of this example is to illustrate polymorphism in action.

I begin by considering each of the parts of the conditional subexpression first. The type of *null* is given by

$$null : list\ \alpha \rightarrow bool. \tag{13.3}$$

We instantiate this by replacing α with a new type variable, say β, to give

$$null : list\ \beta \rightarrow bool. \tag{13.4}$$

We also have that

$$y : list\ \beta. \tag{13.5}$$

From (13.4) and (13.5) by means of the rule for function application we can infer that

$$null\ y : bool. \tag{13.6}$$

The empty list *NIL* belongs to every type of the form *list α*, but in the conditional it has to be instantiated to *list γ*, giving

$$NIL : list\ \gamma. \tag{13.7}$$

Now, I turn my attention to the final clause of the conditional. The type of *head* is *list α → α*, but here we require an instantiated version of this:

$$head\ :\ list\ \beta \rightarrow \beta. \tag{13.8}$$

From (13.8) and (13.5) by the rule for function application we can infer that

$$head\ y : \beta. \tag{13.9}$$

Using this same rule five more times we conclude that

$$cons\ (f(head\ y))(map\ f(tail\ y)) : list\ \gamma. \tag{13.10}$$

This assumes that we have made use of the following premises:

$$\begin{array}{lll} tail & : & list\ \beta \rightarrow list\ \beta, & (13.11) \\ map & : & (\beta \rightarrow \gamma) \rightarrow list\ \beta \rightarrow list\ \gamma, & (13.12) \\ f & : & \beta \rightarrow \gamma, & (13.13) \\ cons & : & \gamma \rightarrow list\ \gamma \rightarrow list\ \gamma. & (13.14) \end{array}$$

From (13.6), (13.7) and (13.10) we can infer the type of the conditional expression. For brevity, I will use the abbreviation

$$B \equiv \textbf{if}\ null\ y\ \textbf{then}\ NIL\ \textbf{else}\ cons\ (f(head\ y))(map\ f(tail\ y)).$$

We, thus, have that

$$B : list\ \gamma. \tag{13.15}$$

From (13.5) and (13.15) by the rule for λ-abstraction we infer

$$\lambda y.B : list\ \beta \rightarrow list\ \gamma. \tag{13.16}$$

From (13.13) and (13.16) by the rule for λ-abstraction we have that

$$\lambda fy.B : (\beta \rightarrow \gamma) \rightarrow list\ \beta \rightarrow list\ \gamma. \tag{13.17}$$

In a similar fashion, but just using the rule for function application, it is possible to conclude

$$map\ decode\ (map\ code\ \phi) : list\ char, \tag{13.18}$$

197

on the assumption that

$$decode \quad : \quad char \rightarrow int,$$
$$code \quad : \quad int \rightarrow char,$$
$$\phi \quad : \quad list\ char.$$

We now know the types of all the constituents of the **letrec**-clause, so from (13.12), (13.17) and (13.18) we can conclude that the type of the entire program is *list char*.

13.5 Conclusion

In this Chapter I have given a brief account of the desirability of incorporating a type system into a functional language and I have spelled out some of the choices that have to be made in choosing a suitable type discipline. Many topics have not been covered. In particular, Milner's type-assignment algorithm has not been included. This is readily available elsewhere, for example, in Milner (1978), Damas (1985), Mycroft (1984) and Chapters 8 and 9 of Peyton Jones (1987), written by Peter Hancock. I would just like to mention one interesting development in type systems here and that is the introduction by Turner (1985b) of algebraic data types with associated laws into Miranda. These are studied by Thompson (1985), but it is too early to pass any final judgment on their utility.

Appendix A

Simple Lispkit System

A.1   Introduction

In this Appendix I include the Pascal[1] source code of a compiler and reducer
for a non-interactive version of Lispkit based on the material covered in
Chapters 2 to 5 of this book. This program is not particularly efficient and
some people may criticize its inclusion here. I therefore begin this Appendix
by giving my reasons for including it.

In general, I believe that it is a good idea for books on the implementation of programming languages to contain the source code of a compiler,
because having a concrete program to look at puts flesh on the rather skele-
tal expositions that such books necessarily contain. This is, I believe, even
more important in a book about implementing functional languages, since
the methods employed in this area tend to be fairly mathematical. Accept-
ing this point, one is faced with the problem of how *sophisticated* a program
to include. In deciding to include a very simple program I was greatly influenced by Terry (1987), in which a number of simple compilers are included.
In a sophisticated program it is rarely obvious what is going on, and the
writers of such programs invariably begin by writing naïve ones first. One
learns a lot by doing this, and in writing a series of programs one finds
that each program's successor is better than its predecessor. By including a
rudimentary compiler for Lispkit here I hope to save the reader some of the
trouble of going through the first few iterations of that learning process. I
am sure that my decision will be criticized by some, as Terry's was.

---

[1]I use standard Pascal except for one occasion and that is when I perform a *Reset*
operation on the file *lispCode*.

Now I want to be a bit more specific about the value and utility of this program to the reader. The program included here is—I believe—a good Pascal program, but—as already mentioned—it is not particularly efficient. By studying it—in connection with Chapters 2 to 5—I hope that the reader will grasp the main ideas involved in the compilation and evaluation of a program written in an applicative language. A highly efficient compiler would not serve this purpose, because efficient programs are difficult to understand. This is usually because they contain non-intuitive auxiliary data structures for the sole purpose of improving their performance. Having understood the implementation technique involved, then the reader will be better prepared to refine and develop it. Therefore, the main reason for including this program here is to help the reader understand the main ideas involved in implementing a functional language by means of combinators.

Furthermore, I believe it to be generally true that the ability to intelligently criticize any idea shows that you thoroughly understand it. Therefore, I hope that readers will study critically the program included here, all the time looking out for ways in which the techniques that it contains can be improved and enhanced.

The structure of the remainder of this Appendix follows the organization of the program that it describes. In successive Sections I describe the parser, the translator and the reducer of an implementation that compiles and evaluates programs written in Lispkit.

A.2 The Parser

The function *Parse* takes as its single argument a file of characters and—if that file contains a valid S-expression—it returns as its value the abstract syntax tree of that S-expression.

The function *Parse*, therefore, carries out the analytic stage of the translation process. This consists of character handling, lexical analysis and syntax analysis. (Sometimes the semantic analyser is included in the analytic part of the translation process.) The synthetic stage of code generation will be carried out by the translator. It should be noted that here the analytic stage of the translation process results in an explicit parse tree. In most compilers the parse tree is never actually constructed, being only implicit in the recursive calls of the syntactic and semantic analysers.

The character handler is the subprocedure *GetChar*, which reads the next character from the file f and puts its ASCII value into the integer variable *ch*. If the end of the file *f* is encountered, then the value −1 is returned. This way of dealing with character handling was strongly influenced by Chapter 1 and the Appendix of Kernighan and Plauger (1981). I use the convention that the variable *ch* always contains an unprocessed character value.

The subprocedure *GetToken* is the lexical analyser or scanner and it constructs tokens from the file *f* that is being read. Six tokens are recognized and these are *Numeric*, *Literal*, *LeftParen*, *FullStop*, *RightParen* and *EndOfFile*. The meaning of the first five tokens should be self-evident. The idea of considering the end of a file as a token comes from Henderson (1980), p. 292, although how I treat the end of a file is different from his.

The subprocedure *GetToken* leaves a token in the variable *curTok* after it is called. If the token is *Numeric*, then its attribute-value is put into the integer variable *numVal* and if it is *AlphaNumeric*, then its attribute-value is put into the character array *symb*. Note that *ch* is an integer, but *symb* is a packed array of characters. This was decided because Pascal treats packed arrays of characters—as opposed to arrays of integers, say—in a special way. They can, for example, be written directly to a file, unlike other kinds of arrays. If the token is either a *LeftParen*, *RightParen* or *EndOfFile*, then there is no corresponding attribute-value.

The subprocedure *GetToken* is straightforwardly coded from the transition diagram shown in Fig. A.1, which corresponds to the conventions given in Aho, Ullman and Sethi (1986), pp. 99–104.

The syntax analyser is made up out of the four functions *SAAtom*, *SASexp*, *SASexpListPlus* and *SATemp*. In order to explain their significance recall that the syntactic description of an S-expressions is as shown in Fig. A.2, which is from Henderson (1980), p. 289. In order to write a recursive descent syntax analyser we have to transform the above grammar into the equivalent form shown in Fig. A.3. The syntax analyser can straightforwardly be coded from this with one Pascal function corresponding to each expression enclosed in pointed brackets <>.

As already mentioned, the value of the function *Parse* is an abstract syntax tree. This is stored as a dynamic Pascal data structure. The vertices of the tree are records of type *Node*. I decided not to make use of the variant record in Pascal, because it complicates the processing of individual vertices and for small programs there is not much space saving.

There are three kinds of vertex. Two of these are for atoms and one for *cons* vertices. In the case of a numeric atom the vertex is an *Nint* one and only the fields *kind* and *val* are significant. A literal atom is kept in

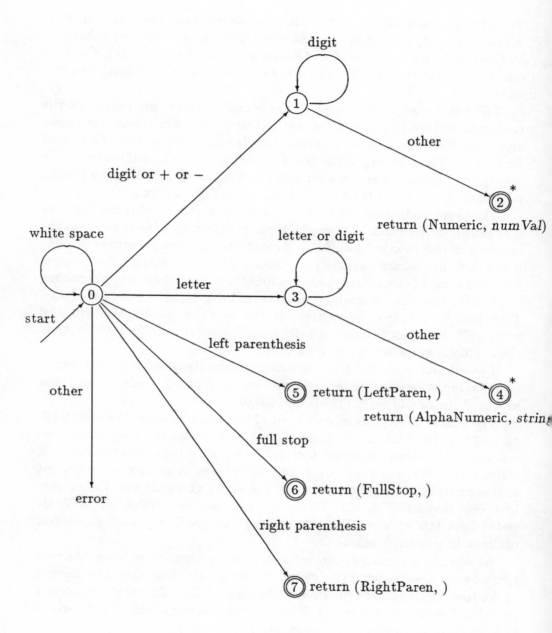

Figure A.1: Transition diagram for Lispkit tokens.

202

```
<S-expression> ::= <atom>

    |  ( <S-expression list> )

<S-expression list> ::= <S-expression>

    |  <S-expression> . <S-expression>

    |  <S-expression> <S-expression list>
```

Figure A.2: The syntax of S-expressions.

```
<S-expression> ::= <atom>

    |  ( <S-expression-list-plus> )

<S-expression-list-plus> ::= <S-expression> <temp>

<temp> ::= )

    |  . <S-expression>

    |  <S-expression-list-plus>
```

Figure A.3: The transformed syntax of S-expressions.

an *Nsymb* record in which only the fields *kind* and *symb* are significant. In the case of a *cons* vertex—of kind *Ncons*—only the *kar* and *kdr* fields are significant. When records of these kinds are created non-significant fields are set to particular values: the integer field is set to 0, the string field to blanks and pointer fields to **nil**.

In order to manipulate the parse tree we need constructors to build it, predicates to distinguish between nodes, selectors to extract information from nodes, and various other kinds of functions and procedures. The function *NextNode* makes a fresh record of type *Node* available. This is made use of in the constructor functions *MkSymbNode* and *MkNumbNode*. The constructor function *Cons* makes a cons *Node* with its first argument as the car and its second argument as the cdr. The function *pair* makes a 2-list, that is to say, a list of length 2 whose elements are made up out of its two arguments and *unit* make a 1-list. The predicate *IsAtom* returns the value true if its argument is an atomic *Node* and false otherwise. Various boolean-valued functions or predicates are available for testing for particular sorts of *Node* and these are *IsNilNode*, *IsSymbol*, *IsNumber* and *IsCons*. The selectors *Head* and *Tail* take cons *Nodes* apart. *Snd* returns the second element of a list, which does not have to be a 2-list. The selector function *PullOutInt* extracts the integer value from a *Node* and *PullOutString* is a procedure for extracting the *String* from a *Node*. The function *SameNode* returns true if its two arguments are the same and false otherwise.

A.3   The Translator

The function *Parse* builds an explicit abstract syntax tree of the S-expression contained in the file *f*, but before this can be evaluated it has to translated into a term of combinatory logic. This translation is performed by the function *Tr*, which takes a tree made up out of *Nodes* and returns a tree made up out of applicative nodes or *AppNodes*. One of the most important components of the translator is the bracket abstraction algorithm. This is contained in the function *Ba*, which encodes algorithm (C) of Chapter 7.

If the function *Tr* is applied to a list, then it calls one of the functions *TrLetRec*, *TrLet*, *TrLambda*, *TrQuote* or *TrApp* depending on the first item of the list. If the first item is the literal 'letrec', then *TrLetRec* is called. If it is 'let', then *TrLet* is called. If 'lambda', then *TrLambda* and if 'quote', then *TrQuote*. Every other case is handled by the procedure *TrApp*. The nature of the translations that each of these must perform has been explained in

Chapter 4. Here, I just want to say more about the translation of **let**-clauses.
The syntax of **let**-clauses in Lispkit is

$$\textbf{let } x_1 = e_1 \textbf{ and } x_2 = e_2 \textbf{ and } \ldots \textbf{ and } x_n = e_n \textbf{ in } e. \qquad (A.1)$$

According to the translation scheme proposed in Chapter 4, the translation
of (A.1) in the cases when $n = 1, 2$ and 3 are, respectively,

$$[e_1/x_1]e,$$
$$[e_1/x_1, e_2/x_2]e,$$
$$[e_1/x_1, e_2/x_2, e_3/x_3]e,$$

and these are—again respectively—equivalent to

$$([x_1]e)e_1,$$
$$([x_1][x_2]e)e_1 e_2,$$
$$([x_1][x_2][x_3]e)e_1 e_2 e_3.$$

The pattern in this sequence of expressions is best captured by means of the
higher-order functions *AppReduce* and *AppAccumulate*.[2] *AppAccumulate*
is a Pascal version of the KRC function *foldright* and *AppReduce* is closely
related to *foldleft*. Whereas *foldleft* is defined in this way:

$$\begin{aligned}
\textit{foldleft } f \, b \, [\,] &= b, \\
\textit{foldleft } f \, b \, (a : x) &= \textit{foldleft } f \, (f \, a \, b) \, x,
\end{aligned}$$

the KRC version of *AppReduce* would have the following definition:

$$\begin{aligned}
\textit{reduce } f \, b \, [\,] &= b, \\
\textit{reduce } f \, b \, (a : x) &= \textit{reduce } f \, (f \, b \, a) \, x.
\end{aligned}$$

Thus, *reduce* $f \, a \, y = $ *foldleft* $(\textbf{C} \, f) \, a \, y$.

The vertices of the program graph are records of type *AppNode* (applicative node) and there are five kinds of these, namely those of *Combinator*,
IntConst, *StrConst*, *Variable* and *Application*. It was decided to represent
each kind of vertex by a fixed size record and not a variant record in order
to make the manipulation of the graph more straightforward. In order not
to unduly complicate the program strings are kept in the records themselves

---

[2]See the function *TrLet* on lines 780–787 in the program contained in Section 6.

and not in a symbol table. This is, after all, an experimental program and not a production compiler.

In the case of a *Combinator* node only the *symb* field is initially significant. This contains the characters making up the combinator. By convention, combinators are represented by capital letters, whereas the corresponding Lispkit functions are kept in lower case. In the case of an *IntConst*—integer constant—vertex only the *kind* and *val* fields are significant. The field *val* contains the value of the integer in question. For *StrConst* vertices *kind* contains the sort of vertex it is and *symb* the actual string in question. In a *Variabler* node the field *symb* contains the character making up the variable and in an *Application* node the *rator* and *rand* fields contain pointers to the function and argument of the application.

The function *NextAppNode* makes the next application node available. It is used by the constructor functions that create the various kinds of node, namely *MkComb*, which makes a combinator node, *MkIntConst*, which makes a node containing an integer, *MkStrConst*, which creates a node containing a string, *MkVar*, which makes a node for a variable, and *MkApp*, which makes an application node from its two arguments. In order to represent a list using application nodes we have to use the combinator *CONS* and the empty list *NIL*. The function *AppCons* makes a dotted pair out of its two arguments.

The predicate *IsAppNode* tests to see whether a node is atomic and the function *SameAppNode* whether two application nodes are the same. The predicate *IsAppNil* tests to see if its argument is the empty list. Applied to lists stored in application nodes the selector functions *Car* and *Cdr* select the head and tail of the list, respectively.

The functions *AppReduce* and *AppAccumulate* are higher-order functions, as already mentioned.

A.4   The Reducer

The method of graph-reduction has been explained in Chapter 5. The function *EvalFun* takes a graph as its argument and returns the evaluated form of it. It repeatedly calls the procedure *OneRed* which performs a single reduction. Particular reductions are performed by procedures with names like *RedHead* and *RedB*. *RedHead* performs the reduction associated with the combinator *HEAD* and *RedB* that associated with **B** and similarly for all the other combinators that there are.

A.5 Discussion

I hope the reader profits from reading and studying the program included in the next Section. It has been deliberately simplified in order to be easy to understand. Thus, it should be noted that no garbage collector is provided in this program and indirection nodes are also not included. The reader is urged either to modify the program to include these features or to write his own program into which they are incorporated. I would also urge him to write a compiler for the interactive version of Lispkit described at the ends of Chapters 2 and 5.

A.6 The Program

```
1   PROGRAM Lispkit (lispCode, input, output);

3       LABEL 5;

5       CONST
6           Tab = 9;
7           NewLine = 13;
8           Space = 32;
9           LParen = 40;      { ( }
10          RParen = 41;      { ) }
11          Plus = 43;        { + }
12          Minus = 45;       { - }
13          Period = 46;      { . }
14          Zero = 48;        { 0 }
15          Nine = 57;        { 9 }
16          CapA = 65;        { A }
17          CapZ = 90;        { Z }
18          LitA = 97;        { a }
19          LitZ = 122;       { z }
20          StringMax = 10;
21          LineMax = 79;
22          CmdMax = 7;
23          CTabMax = 20;
24          EndInfo = '%';
25          EndFile = -1;
```

```
26        AStackMax = 1000;

28    TYPE
29        StringRange = 1..StringMax;
30        String = PACKED ARRAY [StringRange] OF Char;

32        Token = (Numeric, Literal, LeftParen,
33                  FullStop, RightParen, EndOfFile);

35        NodeType = (NInt, NSymb, NCons);
36        NodePtr = ^Node;
37        Node = RECORD
38                  kind: NodeType;
39                  symb: String;
40                  val: Integer;
41                  kar: NodePtr;
42                  kdr: NodePtr
43              END;

45        LineRange = 1..LineMax;
46        Line = PACKED ARRAY [LineRange] OF Char;

48        CmdRange = 1..CmdMax;
49        Cmd = PACKED ARRAY [CmdRange] OF Char;

51        CTabRange = 1..CTabMax;
52        CTab = ARRAY [CTabRange] OF Cmd;

54        AppNodeType = (Combinator, IntConst,
55                        StrConst, Variable, Application);

57        AppNodePtr = ^AppNode;
58        AppNode = RECORD
59                    kind: AppNodeType;
60                    rator, rand: AppNodePtr;
61                    val: Integer;
62                    symb: String
63                END;
```

```
65      AStackRange = 1..AStackMax;
66      AStack = ARRAY [AStackRange] OF AppNodePtr;
67        { The type of the left ancestors' stack. }

69    VAR
70      lispCode: Text;
71      last: LineRange;
72      uLine, lineSpaces: Line;
73      cmdSpaces, globCmd: Cmd;
74      uCT: CTab;
75      stringSpaces: String;
76      root: NodePtr;
77      symbOnLine: Integer;
78      ready: Boolean;
79      appRoot: AppNodePtr;

81    PROCEDURE Skip; BEGIN END;

83    PROCEDURE Error (i: Integer);
84    BEGIN
85      WriteLn;
86      WriteLn ('Error code: ', i);
87      WriteLn;
88      GOTO 5;
89    END;   { Error }

91    PROCEDURE IncL (VAR i: LineRange);
92    BEGIN IF i <> LineMax THEN i := i + 1 ELSE Error (1) END;

94    FUNCTION IsNumeral (c: Integer): Boolean;
95    BEGIN IsNumeral := c IN [Zero..Nine] END;

97    FUNCTION IsLetter (c: Integer): Boolean;
98    BEGIN IsLetter := c IN [LitA..LitZ, CapA..CapZ] END;

100   FUNCTION IsWhiteSpace (x: Integer): Boolean;
101   BEGIN IsWhiteSpace :=
102     (x = Space) OR (x = Tab) OR (x = NewLine) END;
```

```
104    FUNCTION NextNode: NodePtr;
105      VAR y: NodePtr;
106    BEGIN
107      New (y);
108      NextNode := y;
109    END;   { NextNode }

111    FUNCTION MkSymbNode (s: String): NodePtr;
112      VAR y: NodePtr;
113    BEGIN
114      y := NextNode;
115      WITH y^ DO
116        BEGIN
117          kind := NSymb;
118          symb := s;
119          val := 0;
120          kar := Nil;
121          kdr := Nil;
122        END;
123      MkSymbNode := y;
124    END;   { MkSymbNode }

126    FUNCTION MkNumNode (i: Integer): NodePtr;
127      VAR y: NodePtr;
128    BEGIN
129      y := NextNode;
130      WITH y^ DO
131        BEGIN
132          kind := NInt;
133          symb := stringSpaces;
134          val := i;
135          kar := Nil;
136          kdr := Nil;
137        END;
138      MkNumNode := y;
139    END; { MkNumNode }

141    FUNCTION Cons (x, y: NodePtr): NodePtr;
142      VAR z: NodePtr;
```

```
143     BEGIN
144       z := NextNode;
145       WITH z^ DO
146         BEGIN
147           kind := NCons;
148           symb := stringSpaces;
149           val := 0;
150           kar := x;
151           kdr := y;
152         END;
153       Cons := z;
154     END;   { Cons }

156     FUNCTION IsSymbol (p: NodePtr): Boolean;
157     BEGIN
158       IF p^.kind = NSymb THEN
159         IsSymbol := True
160       ELSE
161         IsSymbol := False
162     END;

164     FUNCTION IsNumber (p: NodePtr): Boolean;
165     BEGIN
166       IF p^.kind = NInt THEN
167         IsNumber := True
168       ELSE
169         IsNumber := False
170     END;

172     FUNCTION IsCons (p: NodePtr): Boolean;
173     BEGIN
174       IF p^.kind = NCons THEN
175         IsCons := True
176       ELSE
177         IsCons := False
178     END;

180     FUNCTION IsNilNode (p: NodePtr): Boolean;
181     BEGIN IsNilNode :=
```

```
182          (p^.kind = NSymb) AND (p^.symb = 'NIL         ') END;

184    FUNCTION IntLength (l: NodePtr): Integer;
185    BEGIN
186      IF IsNilNode (l) THEN
187        IntLength := 0
188      ELSE
189        IntLength := 1 + IntLength (l^.kdr);
190    END;  { IntLength }

192    PROCEDURE ToString (x: Integer; VAR y: String);
193      VAR z: StringRange;

195      FUNCTION Itoc (n: Integer;
196                     VAR s: String;
197                     i: StringRange): StringRange;
198    { This function is based on that given by
199      Kernighan and Plauger (1981) on p. 58. }
200    BEGIN
201      IF n >= 10 THEN i := Itoc (n DIV 10, s, i);
202      s [i] := Chr (n MOD 10 + Ord ('0'));
203      Itoc := i + 1;
204    END; { Itoc }

206    BEGIN { ToString }
207      y := stringSpaces;
208      IF x = 0 THEN
209        y [1] := '0'
210      ELSE IF x < 0 THEN
211        BEGIN
212          y [1] := '-';
213          z := Itoc (-x, y, 2);
214        END
215      ELSE
216        z := Itoc (x, y, 1);
217    END;  { ToString }

219    FUNCTION PullOutInt (x: NodePtr): Integer;
220    BEGIN PullOutInt := x^.val END;
```

212

```
222     PROCEDURE PullOutString (x: NodePtr; VAR s: String);
223     BEGIN s := x^.symb END;




225     { The Parser. }

227     FUNCTION Parse (VAR f: Text): NodePtr;
228       VAR
229         ch,
230         numVal: Integer; { Last numeric atom read. }
231         curTok: Token;   { Last token read. }
232         symb: String;    { Last literal atom read. }

234       PROCEDURE GetChar;
235       { Character handler. }
236         VAR k: Char;
237       BEGIN
238         IF Eof (f) THEN
239           ch := EndFile
240         ELSE
241           BEGIN
242             Read (f, k);
243             ch := Ord (k);
244           END;
245       END;   { GetChar }

247       PROCEDURE GetToken;
248       { This is the lexical analyser for Lispkit. }
249         PROCEDURE GetLiteral;
250           VAR i: Integer;
251         BEGIN
252           curTok := Literal;
253           symb := stringSpaces;
254           symb [1] := Chr (ch);
255           i := 2;
256           GetChar;
257           WHILE (IsLetter (ch) OR IsNumeral (ch))
```

```
258              AND (i <= StringMax) DO
259              BEGIN
260                symb [i] := Chr (ch);
261                i := i + 1;
262                GetChar;
263              END;
264            WHILE IsLetter (ch) OR IsNumeral (ch) DO GetChar;
265          END;   { GetLiteral }

267          PROCEDURE GetNumeric;
268            VAR i: Integer;
269          BEGIN
270            curTok := Numeric;
271            i := 1;
272            IF ch = Plus THEN
273              GetChar
274            ELSE IF ch = Minus THEN
275              BEGIN
276                i := -1;
277                GetChar;
278              END
279            ELSE
280              Skip;
281            IF NOT IsNumeral (ch) THEN Error (2);
282            numVal := ch - Zero;
283            GetChar;
284            WHILE IsNumeral (ch) DO
285              BEGIN
286                numVal := 10 * numVal + (ch - Zero);
287                GetChar;
288              END;
289            numVal := numVal * i;
290          END;   { GetNumeric }

292          PROCEDURE GetLeftParen;
293          BEGIN curTok := LeftParen; GetChar END;

295          PROCEDURE GetFullStop;
296          BEGIN curTok := FullStop; GetChar END;
```

```
298        PROCEDURE GetRightParen;
299        BEGIN curTok := RightParen; GetChar END;


301     BEGIN  { GetToken }
302       WHILE IsWhiteSpace (ch) DO GetChar;
303       IF IsLetter (ch) THEN
304         GetLiteral
305       ELSE IF (ch IN [Plus, Minus]) OR IsNumeral (ch) THEN
306         GetNumeric
307       ELSE IF ch = LParen THEN
308         GetLeftParen
309       ELSE IF ch = Period THEN
310         GetFullStop
311       ELSE IF ch = RParen THEN
312         GetRightParen
313       ELSE IF ch = EndFile THEN
314         curTok := EndOfFile
315       ELSE
316         Error (3);
317     END;    { GetToken }


319     { Lispkit syntax analyser. }


321     FUNCTION SAAtom: NodePtr;
322     BEGIN
323       IF curTok = Literal THEN
324         SAAtom := MkSymbNode (symb)
325       ELSE IF curTok = Numeric THEN
326         SAAtom := MkNumNode (numVal)
327       ELSE
328         Error (4);
329       GetToken;
330     END;  { SAAtom }


332     FUNCTION SASexpListPlus: NodePtr; FORWARD;


334     FUNCTION SASexp: NodePtr;
335     BEGIN
```

215

```
336        IF (curTok = Literal) OR (curTok = Numeric) THEN
337          SASexp := SAAtom
338        ELSE IF curTok = LeftParen THEN
339          BEGIN
340            GetToken;
341            SASexp := SASexpListPlus;
342          END
343        ELSE
344          Error (5);
345      END;  { SASexp }

347      FUNCTION SATemp (p: NodePtr): NodePtr; FORWARD;

349      FUNCTION SASexpListPlus;
350        VAR p: NodePtr;
351      BEGIN
352        p := SASexp;
353        SASexpListPlus := SATemp (p);
354      END;  { SASexpListPlus }

356      FUNCTION SATemp;
357      BEGIN
358        IF curTok = RightParen THEN
359          BEGIN
360            SATemp := Cons (p, MkSymbNode ('NIL        '));
361            GetToken;
362          END
363        ELSE IF curTok = FullStop THEN
364          BEGIN
365            GetToken;
366            SATemp := Cons (p, SASexp);
367            IF curTok <> RightParen THEN Error (6);
368            GetToken;
369          END
370        ELSE IF (curTok = Literal) OR
371                (curTok = Numeric) OR
372                (curTok = LeftParen) THEN
373          SATemp := Cons (p, SASexpListPlus)
374        ELSE
```

216

```
375          Error (7);
376        END;  { SATemp }

378    BEGIN { Parse }
379      GetChar;
380      GetToken;
381      Parse := SASexp;
382    END;  { Parse }

384    { Procedures for applicative structures. }

386    FUNCTION NextAppNode: AppNodePtr;
387      VAR p: AppNodePtr;
388    BEGIN
389      New (p);
390      NextAppNode := p;
391    END; { NextAppNode }

393    FUNCTION MkComb (x: String): AppNodePtr;
394      VAR p: AppNodePtr;
395    BEGIN
396      p := NextAppNode;
397      WITH p^ DO
398        BEGIN
399          kind := Combinator;
400          rator := Nil;
401          rand := Nil;
402          val := 0;
403          symb := x;
404        END;
405      MkComb := p;
406    END;  { MkComb }

408    FUNCTION MkIntConst (x: Integer): AppNodePtr;
409      VAR p: AppNodePtr;
410    BEGIN
411      p := NextAppNode;
412      WITH p^ DO
413        BEGIN
```

```
414        kind := IntConst;
415        rator := Nil;
416        rand := Nil;
417        val := x;
418        symb := stringSpaces;
419      END;
420    MkIntConst := p;
421  END;  { MkIntConst }

423  FUNCTION MkStrConst (x: String): AppNodePtr;
424    VAR p: AppNodePtr;
425  BEGIN
426    p := NextAppNode;
427    WITH p^ DO
428      BEGIN
429        kind := StrConst;
430        rator := Nil;
431        rand := Nil;
432        val := 0;
433        symb := x;
434      END;
435    MkStrConst := p;
436  END;  { MkStrConst }

438  FUNCTION MkVar (x: String): AppNodePtr;
439    VAR p: AppNodePtr;
440  BEGIN
441    p := NextAppNode;
442    WITH p^ DO
443      BEGIN
444        kind := Variable;
445        rator := Nil;
446        rand := Nil;
447        val := 0;
448        symb := x;
449      END;
450    MkVar := p;
451  END;  { MkVar }
```

```
453    FUNCTION MkApp (x, y: AppNodePtr): AppNodePtr;
454      VAR p: AppNodePtr;
455    BEGIN
456      p := NextAppNode;
457      WITH p^ DO
458        BEGIN
459          kind := Application;
460          rator := x;
461          rand := y;
462          val := 0;
463          symb := '        ';
464        END;
465      MkApp := p;
466    END;  { MkApp }

468    FUNCTION AppCons (alpha, beta: AppNodePtr): AppNodePtr;
469    BEGIN AppCons :=
470      MkApp (MkApp (MkComb ('CONS    ')), alpha), beta) END;

472    FUNCTION IsAppAtom (p: AppNodePtr): Boolean;
473    BEGIN IsAppAtom := p^.kind IN [Combinator,
474                                   IntConst,
475                                   StrConst,
476                                   Variable] END;

478    FUNCTION SameAppNode (p,q: AppNodePtr): Boolean;
479    BEGIN
480      IF p = Nil THEN
481        SameAppNode := q = Nil
482      ELSE IF q = Nil THEN
483        SameAppNode := p = Nil
484      ELSE
485        SameAppNode := (p^.kind = q^.kind) AND
486                       SameAppNode (p^.rator, q^.rator) AND
487                       SameAppNode (p^.rand, q^.rand) AND
488                       (p^.val = q^.val) AND
489                       (p^.symb = q^.symb);
490    END;  { SameAppNode }
```

```
492     { The Translator. }

494     FUNCTION Tr (x: NodePtr): AppNodePtr; FORWARD;

496     FUNCTION Fsa (x: NodePtr): AppNodePtr;
497     { From S-expression list to applicative list. }
498     BEGIN
499       IF IsNilNode (x) THEN
500         Fsa := MkStrConst ('NIL        ')
501       ELSE
502         Fsa := AppCons (Tr (x^.kar), Fsa (x^.kdr));
503     END;  { Fsa }

505     FUNCTION Car (p: AppNodePtr): AppNodePtr;
506     BEGIN Car := p^.rator^.rand END;

508     FUNCTION Cdr (p: AppNodePtr): AppNodePtr;
509     BEGIN Cdr := p^.rand END;

511     FUNCTION IsAppNil (p: AppNodePtr): Boolean;
512     BEGIN IsAppNil :=
513       (p^.kind = StrConst) AND (p^.symb = 'NIL        ') END;

515     FUNCTION AppReduce
516       (FUNCTION f (x, y: AppNodePtr): AppNodePtr;
517        a, xs: AppNodePtr): AppNodePtr;
518     BEGIN
519       IF IsAppNil (xs) THEN
520         AppReduce := a
521       ELSE
522         AppReduce := AppReduce (f, f (a, Car (xs)), Cdr (xs));
523     END;  { AppReduce }

525     FUNCTION AppAccumulate
526       (FUNCTION f (x, y: AppNodePtr): AppNodePtr;
527        b, xs: AppNodePtr): AppNodePtr;
528     BEGIN
529       IF IsAppNil (xs) THEN
```

```
530        AppAccumulate := b
531    ELSE
532        AppAccumulate :=
533          f (Car (xs), AppAccumulate (f, b, Cdr (xs)));
534    END;  { AppAccumulate }

536    FUNCTION TrApp (x: NodePtr): AppNodePtr;
537      VAR p: AppNodePtr;
538    BEGIN
539      p := Fsa (x);
540      TrApp := AppReduce (MkApp, p^.rator^.rand, p^.rand);
541    END;  { TrApp }

543    PROCEDURE Clas (o: AppNodePtr;
544                       VAR p: AStack;
545                       VAR top: AStackRange);
546    { Create Left Ancestors' Stack.
547      'o' is the root of the graph.
548      On termination 'p' contains the spine. }
549      VAR i: AStackRange;
550    BEGIN
551      FOR i := 1 TO AStackMax DO p [i] := Nil;
552      i := 1;
553      p [i] := o;
554      WHILE p [i]^.kind = Application DO
555        BEGIN
556          p [i + 1] := p [i]^.rator;
557          i := i + 1;
558        END;
559      top := i;
560    END;  { Clas }

562    PROCEDURE Tulas (VAR p: AStack; VAR top: AStackRange);
563    { Top Up Left Ancestors' Stack.
564      On termination 'p' contains the spine. }
565      VAR i: AStackRange;
566    BEGIN
567      i := top;
568      WHILE p [i]^.kind = Application DO
```

```
569        BEGIN
570          p [i + 1] := p [i]^.rator;
571          i := i + 1;
572        END;
573      top := i;
574    END;  { Tulas }

576    PROCEDURE SplitIntoLines;
577    BEGIN
578      IF symbOnLine = 20 THEN
579        BEGIN
580          symbOnLine := 0;
581          WriteLn (output);
582        END
583      ELSE
584        symbOnLine := symbOnLine + 1;
585    END;  { SplitIntoLines }

587    PROCEDURE PrStr (w: String);
588      VAR i: Integer;
589    BEGIN
590      SplitIntoLines;
591      i := 1;
592      WHILE (w [i] <> ' ') AND (i <> 10) DO
593        BEGIN
594          Write (output, w [i]);
595          i := i + 1;
596        END;
597      IF (w [i] <> ' ') AND (i = 10) THEN
598        Write (output, w [i]);
599      Write (output, ' ');
600    END;  { PrStr }

602    PROCEDURE PrApp (p: AppNodePtr);
603      VAR q: String;
604    BEGIN
605      IF (p^.kind = Combinator) OR
606         (p^.kind = StrConst) OR
607         (p^.kind = Variable) THEN
```

222

```
608        PrStr (p^.symb)
609      ELSE IF (p^.kind = IntConst) THEN
610        BEGIN
611          ToString (p^.val, q);
612          PrStr (q);
613        END
614      ELSE
615        BEGIN
616          PrStr ('(          ');
617          PrApp (p^.rator);
618          PrApp (p^.rand);
619          PrStr (')          ');
620        END;
621    END;   { PrApp }


623    FUNCTION IsAppList (o: AppNodePtr): Boolean;
624    BEGIN
625      IF IsAppAtom (o) THEN
626        IsAppList := False
627      ELSE IF IsAppAtom (o^.rator) THEN
628        IsAppList := False
629      ELSE
630        IsAppList := o^.rator^.rator^.symb = 'CONS       ';
631    END;   { IsAppList }


633    FUNCTION EvalFun (VAR g: AppNodePtr): AppNodePtr; FORWARD;


635    PROCEDURE PrAppAll (q: AppNodePtr); FORWARD;


637    PROCEDURE PrAppList (o: AppNodePtr);
638      VAR p: AStack; top, len: AStackRange;
639    BEGIN
640      Clas (o, p, top);
641      PrStr ('(          ');
642      PrAppAll (EvalFun (p [top - 1]^.rand));
643      len := top;
644      WHILE len <> 3 DO
645        BEGIN
646          PrAppAll (EvalFun (p [len - 2]^.rand));
```

```
647            len := len - 1;
648        END;
649      IF IsAppNil (p [len - 2]^.rand) THEN
650        PrStr (')            ')
651      ELSE
652        BEGIN
653          PrStr ('.            ');
654          PrAppAll (EvalFun (p [len - 2]^.rand));
655          PrStr (')            ')
656        END;
657    END;  { PrAppList }


659    PROCEDURE PrAppAll;
660    BEGIN
661      IF IsAppList (q) THEN
662        PrAppList (q)
663      ELSE
664          PrApp (q);
665    END;  { PrAppAll }


667    FUNCTION MakeAppList (p, q: AppNodePtr): AppNodePtr;
668    { Makes an app-list out of 'p' and 'q'. }
669    BEGIN MakeAppList :=
670      MkApp (MkApp (MkComb ('CONS        '), p),
671            MkApp (MkApp (MkComb ('CONS        '), q),
672                  MkStrConst ('NIL        ')));
673    END;  { MakeAppList }


675    FUNCTION GetExpList (p: NodePtr): AppNodePtr;
676    { Given an S-expression list of declarations 'p'
677      this returns an app-list of expressions. }
678    BEGIN
679      IF IsNilNode (p) THEN
680        GetExpList := MkStrConst ('NIL        ')
681      ELSE
682        GetExpList := AppCons (Tr (p^.kar^.kdr),
683                              GetExpList (p^.kdr));
684    END;  { GetExpList }
```

```
686    FUNCTION GetNameList (p: NodePtr): AppNodePtr;
687    { Given an S-expression list of declarations 'p' this
688       returns an app-list of names. }
689    BEGIN
690      IF IsNilNode (p) THEN
691        GetNameList := MkStrConst ('NIL        ')
692      ELSE
693        GetNameList := AppCons (Tr (p^.kar^.kar),
694                                    GetNameList (p^.kdr));
695    END;  { GetNameList }

697    FUNCTION Occurs (x, y: AppNodePtr): Boolean;
698    { 'True' if 'x' occurs in 'y'. }
699    BEGIN
700      IF IsAppAtom (y) THEN
701        Occurs := SameAppNode (x, y)
702      ELSE
703        Occurs := Occurs (x, y^.rator) OR Occurs (x, y^.rand);
704    END;  { Occurs }

706    FUNCTION Ba (x, e: AppNodePtr): AppNodePtr;
707      FUNCTION IsThree (p: AppNodePtr): Boolean;
708      BEGIN
709        IF IsAppAtom (p) THEN
710          IsThree := False
711        ELSE IF IsAppAtom (p^.rator) THEN
712          IsThree := False
713        ELSE IF occurs (x, p^.rator^.rator) THEN
714          IsThree := False
715        ELSE
716          IsThree := True;
717      END;  { IsThree }
718      FUNCTION IsTwo (p: AppNodePtr): Boolean;
719      BEGIN
720        IF IsAppAtom (p) THEN
721          IsTwo := False
722        ELSE
723          IsTwo := True;
724      END;  { IsTwo }
```

```
725        FUNCTION Third (p: AppNodePtr): AppNodePtr;
726        BEGIN Third := p^.rand END;
727        FUNCTION Second (p: AppNodePtr): AppNodePtr;
728        BEGIN Second := p^.rator^.rand END;
729        FUNCTION First (p: AppNodePtr): AppNodePtr;
730        BEGIN First := p^.rator^.rator END;
731        FUNCTION Oneth (p: AppNodePtr): AppNodePtr;
732        BEGIN Oneth := p^.rator END;
733        FUNCTION Twoth (p: AppNodePtr): AppNodePtr;
734        BEGIN Twoth := p^.rand END;
735     BEGIN
736        IF NOT Occurs (x, e) THEN
737          Ba := MkApp (MkComb ('K          '), e)
738        ELSE IF IsThree (e) THEN
739          BEGIN
740            IF NOT Occurs (x, Second (e)) THEN
741              Ba := MkApp (MkApp (MkApp (MkComb ('B1        '),
742                                          First (e)),
743                                Second (e)),
744                      Ba (x, Third (e)))
745            ELSE IF NOT Occurs (x, Third (e)) THEN
746              Ba := MkApp (MkApp (MkApp (MkComb ('C1        '),
747                                          First (e)),
748                                Ba (x, Second (e))),
749                      Third (e))
750            ELSE
751              Ba := MkApp (MkApp (MkApp (MkComb ('S1        '),
752                                          First (e)),
753                                Ba (x, Second (e))),
754                      Ba (x, Third (e)));
755          END
756        ELSE IF IsTwo (e) THEN
757          BEGIN
758            IF NOT Occurs (x, Twoth (e)) THEN
759              Ba := MkApp (MkApp (MkComb ('C         '),
760                                Ba (x, Oneth (e))),
761                      Twoth (e))
762            ELSE IF NOT Occurs (x, Oneth (e)) THEN
763              BEGIN
```

226

```
764            IF IsAppAtom (Twoth (e)) THEN
765                Ba := Oneth (e)
766            ELSE
767                Ba := MkApp (MkApp (MkComb ('B        ')),
768                                    Oneth (e)),
769                            Ba (x, Twoth (e)));
770          END
771        ELSE
772          Ba := MkApp (MkApp (MkComb ('S        ')),
773                              Ba (x, Oneth (e))),
774                          Ba (x, Twoth (e)));
775        END
776      ELSE
777        Ba := MkComb ('I        ');
778    END; { Ba }

780    FUNCTION TrLet (p: NodePtr): AppNodePtr;
781      VAR e, decs: NodePtr; phi: AppNodePtr;
782    BEGIN
783      e := p^.kdr^.kar;
784      decs := p^.kdr^.kdr;
785      phi := AppAccumulate (Ba, Tr (e), GetNameList (decs));
786      TrLet := AppReduce (MkApp, phi, GetExpList (decs));
787    END; { TrLet }

789    FUNCTION TrLambda (p: NodePtr): AppNodePtr;
790      VAR s, argList: NodePtr;
791    BEGIN
792      s := p^.kdr^.kdr^.kar;
793      argList := p^.kdr^.kar;
794      TrLambda := AppAccumulate (Ba, Tr (s), Fsa (argList));
795    END; { TrLambda }

797    FUNCTION TrQuote (x: NodePtr): AppNodePtr;
798      VAR ed: NodePtr;

800      FUNCTION MiniTr (y: NodePtr): AppNodePtr;
801      BEGIN
802        IF IsCons (y) THEN
```

```
803         MiniTr := AppCons (MiniTr (y^.kar), MiniTr (y^.kdr))
804       ELSE IF IsNilNode (y) THEN
805         MiniTr := MkStrConst ('NIL        ')
806       ELSE IF IsNumber (y) THEN
807         MiniTr := MkIntConst (y^.val)
808       ELSE IF IsSymbol (y) THEN
809         MiniTr := MkStrConst (y^.symb)
810       ELSE
811         Error (8);
812     END; { MiniTr }

814   BEGIN { TrQuote }
815     ed := x^.kdr^.kar;
816     TrQuote := MiniTr (ed);
817   END; { TrQuote }

819   FUNCTION TrLetRec (p: NodePtr): AppNodePtr;
820     VAR
821       e, decs: NodePtr;
822       nameList, expList, one, two: AppNodePtr;

824     FUNCTION LetRecG (x, y: AppNodePtr): AppNodePtr;
825     BEGIN LetRecG :=
826       MkApp (MkComb ('U          '), Ba (x, y)) END;

828   BEGIN  { TrLetRec }
829     e := p^.kdr^.kar;
830     decs := p^.kdr^.kdr;
831     IF IntLength (decs) = 0 THEN
832       TrLetRec := Tr (e)
833     ELSE
834       BEGIN
835         namelist := GetNameList (decs);
836         expList := GetExpList (decs);
837         IF IntLength (decs) = 1 THEN
838           TrLetRec := MkApp (Ba (Car (namelist), Tr (e)),
839                              MkApp (MkComb ('Y          '),
840                                        Ba (Car (namelist),
841                                            Car (expList))))
```

```
842      ELSE
843        BEGIN
844          one := AppAccumulate
845                    (LetRecG,
846                     MkApp (MkComb ('K        '), Tr (e)),
847                     namelist);
848          two := AppAccumulate
849                    (LetRecG,
850                     MkApp (MkComb ('K        '), expList),
851                     namelist);
852          TrLetRec := MkApp
853              (one, MkApp (MkComb ('Y        '), two));
854        END;
855      END;
856   END;  { TrLetRec }


858   FUNCTION Tr;
859     VAR tt: NodePtr; uu: NodeType; vv: String;
860   BEGIN
861     uu := x^.kind;
862     vv := x^.symb;
863     IF uu = NSymb THEN
864       BEGIN
865         IF vv = 'add       ' THEN
866           Tr := MkComb ('ADD       ')
867         ELSE IF vv = 'sub      ' THEN
868           Tr := MkComb ('SUB      ')
869         ELSE IF vv = 'mul      ' THEN
870           Tr := MkComb ('MUL      ')
871         ELSE IF vv = 'div      ' THEN
872           Tr := MkComb ('DIV      ')
873         ELSE IF vv = 'rem      ' THEN
874           Tr := MkComb ('REM      ')
875         ELSE IF vv = 'sq       ' THEN
876           Tr := MkComb ('SQ       ')
877         ELSE IF vv = 'odd      ' THEN
878           Tr := MkComb ('ODD      ')
879         ELSE IF vv = 'even     ' THEN
880           Tr := MkComb ('EVEN     ')
```

```
881          ELSE IF vv = 'leq        ' THEN
882            Tr := MkComb ('LEQ          ')
883          ELSE IF vv = 'eq         ' THEN
884            Tr := MkComb ('EQ           ')
885          ELSE IF vv = 'head       ' THEN
886            Tr := MkComb ('HEAD         ')
887          ELSE IF vv = 'tail       ' THEN
888            Tr := MkComb ('TAIL         ')
889          ELSE IF vv = 'atom       ' THEN
890            Tr := MkComb ('ATOM         ')
891          ELSE IF vv = 'null       ' THEN
892            Tr := MkComb ('NULL         ')
893          ELSE IF vv = 'if         ' THEN
894            Tr := MkComb ('IF           ')
895          ELSE IF vv = 'not        ' THEN
896            Tr := MkComb ('NOT          ')
897          ELSE IF vv = 'and        ' THEN
898            Tr := MkComb ('AND          ')
899          ELSE IF vv = 'or         ' THEN
900            Tr := MkComb ('OR           ')
901          ELSE IF vv = 'chr        ' THEN
902            Tr := MkComb ('CHR          ')
903          ELSE IF vv = 'cons       ' THEN
904            Tr := MkComb ('CONS         ')
905          ELSE IF vv = 'NIL        ' THEN
906            Tr := MkStrConst ('NIL          ')
907          ELSE IF vv = 'TRUE       ' THEN
908            Tr := MkStrConst ('TRUE          ')
909          ELSE IF vv = 'FALSE      ' THEN
910            Tr := MkStrConst ('FALSE        ')
911          ELSE
912            Tr := MkVar (vv)
913        END
914      ELSE IF uu = NCons THEN
915        BEGIN
916          tt := x^.kar;
917          IF tt^.symb = 'letrec     ' THEN
918            Tr := TrLetRec (x)
919          ELSE IF tt^.symb = 'let        ' THEN
```

230

```
920            Tr := TrLet (x)
921         ELSE IF tt^.symb = 'lambda    ' THEN
922            Tr := TrLambda (x)
923         ELSE IF tt^.symb = 'quote     ' THEN
924            Tr := TrQuote (x)
925         ELSE
926            Tr := TrApp (x);
927       END;
928    END; { Tr }


930    PROCEDURE ReadCmd (row: Line;
931                         VAR i: LineRange;
932                         VAR x: Cmd);
933      VAR j: CmdRange; carryOn: Boolean;
934    BEGIN
935      carryOn := True;
936      x := cmdSpaces;
937      j := 1;
938      WHILE row [i] = ' ' DO IncL (i);
939      WHILE (row [i] <> ' ') AND
940            (row [i] <> EndInfo) AND
941            carryOn DO
942        BEGIN
943          x [j] := row [i];
944          IncL (i);
945          IF j <> CmdMax THEN
946            j := j + 1
947          ELSE
948            carryOn := False;
949        END;
950      WHILE row [i] <> ' ' DO IncL (i);
951    END;   { ReadCmd }



953    { The Reduction Machine. }

955    PROCEDURE RedS (VAR p: AStack; VAR top: AStackRange);
956    BEGIN
```

231

```
957      p [top - 3]^.rator :=
958         MkApp (p [top - 1]^.rand, p [top - 3]^.rand);
959      p [top - 3]^.rand :=
960         MkApp (p [top - 2]^.rand, p [top - 3]^.rand);
961      top := top - 3;
962   END;   { RedS }


964   PROCEDURE RedK (VAR p: AStack; VAR top: AStackRange);
965   BEGIN
966      p [top - 2]^ := p [top - 1]^.rand^;
967      top := top - 2;
968   END;   { RedK }


970   PROCEDURE RedI (VAR p: AStack; VAR top: AStackRange);
971   BEGIN
972      p [top - 1]^ := p [top - 1]^.rand^;
973      top := top - 1;
974   END;   { RedI }


976   PROCEDURE RedB (VAR p: AStack; VAR top: AStackRange);
977   BEGIN
978      p [top - 3]^.rator := p [top - 1]^.rand;
979      p [top - 3]^.rand :=
980         MkApp (p [top - 2]^.rand, p [top - 3]^.rand);
981      top := top - 3;
982   END;   { RedB }


984   PROCEDURE RedC (VAR p: AStack; VAR top: AStackRange);
985   BEGIN
986      p [top - 3]^.rator :=
987         MkApp (p [top - 1]^.rand, p [top - 3]^.rand);
988      p [top - 3]^.rand := p [top - 2]^.rand;
989      top := top - 3;
990   END;   { RedC }


992   PROCEDURE RedS1 (VAR p: AStack; VAR top: AStackRange);
993   BEGIN
994      p [top - 4]^.rator :=
995         MkApp (p [top - 1]^.rand,
```

232

```
996                      MkApp (p [top - 2]^.rand, p [top - 4]^.rand));
997          p [top - 4]^.rand :=
998            MkApp (p [top - 3]^.rand, p [top - 4]^.rand);
999          top := top - 4;
1000       END;    { RedS1 }

1002     PROCEDURE RedB1 (VAR p: AStack; VAR top: AStackRange);
1003     BEGIN
1004       p [top - 4]^.rator :=
1005         MkApp (p [top - 1]^.rand, p [top - 2]^.rand);
1006       p [top - 4]^.rand :=
1007         MkApp (p [top - 3]^.rand, p [top - 4]^.rand);
1008       top := top - 4;
1009     END;    { RedB1 }

1011     PROCEDURE RedC1 (VAR p: AStack; VAR top: AStackRange);
1012     BEGIN
1013       p [top - 4]^.rator :=
1014         MkApp (p [top - 1]^.rand,
1015                   MkApp (p [top - 2]^.rand, p [top - 4]^.rand));
1016       p [top - 4]^.rand := p [top - 3]^.rand;
1017       top := top - 4;
1018     END;    { RedC1 }

1020     PROCEDURE RedY (VAR p: AStack; VAR top: AStackRange);
1021     BEGIN
1022       p [top - 1]^.rator := p [top - 1]^.rand;
1023       p [top - 1]^.rand := p [top - 1];
1024       top := top - 1;
1025     END;    { RedY }

1027     PROCEDURE RedAdd (VAR p: AStack; VAR top: AStackRange);
1028        VAR arg1, arg2, other: AppNodePtr;
1029     BEGIN
1030       arg1 := EvalFun (p [top - 1]^.rand);
1031       arg2 := EvalFun (p [top - 2]^.rand);
1032       other := MkIntConst (arg1^.val + arg2^.val);
1033       p [top - 2]^ := other^;
1034       top := top - 2;
```

233

```
1035    END;    { RedAdd }

1037    PROCEDURE RedSub (VAR p: AStack; VAR top: AStackRange);
1038      VAR arg1, arg2, other: AppNodePtr;
1039    BEGIN
1040      arg1 := EvalFun (p [top - 1]^.rand);
1041      arg2 := EvalFun (p [top - 2]^.rand);
1042      other := MkIntConst (arg1^.val - arg2^.val);
1043      p [top - 2]^ := other^;
1044      top := top - 2;
1045    END;  { RedSub }

1047    PROCEDURE RedMul (VAR p: AStack; VAR top: AStackRange);
1048      VAR arg1, arg2, other: AppNodePtr;
1049    BEGIN
1050      arg1 := EvalFun (p [top - 1]^.rand);
1051      arg2 := EvalFun (p [top - 2]^.rand);
1052      other := MkIntConst (arg1^.val * arg2^.val);
1053      p [top - 2]^ := other^;
1054      top := top - 2;
1055    END;  { RedMul }

1057    PROCEDURE RedDiv (VAR p: AStack; VAR top: AStackRange);
1058      VAR arg1, arg2, other: AppNodePtr;
1059    BEGIN
1060      arg1 := EvalFun (p [top - 1]^.rand);
1061      arg2 := EvalFun (p [top - 2]^.rand);
1062      other := MkIntConst (arg1^.val DIV arg2^.val);
1063      p [top - 2]^ := other^;
1064      top := top - 2;
1065    END;  { RedDiv }

1067    PROCEDURE RedRem (VAR p: AStack; VAR top: AStackRange);
1068      VAR arg1, arg2, other: AppNodePtr;
1069    BEGIN
1070      arg1 := EvalFun (p [top - 1]^.rand);
1071      arg2 := EvalFun (p [top - 2]^.rand);
1072      other := MkIntConst (arg1^.val MOD arg2^.val);
1073      p [top - 2]^ := other^;
```

```
1074        top := top - 2;
1075      END;  { RedRem }

1077      PROCEDURE RedSq (VAR p: AStack; VAR top: AStackRange);
1078        VAR other: AppNodePtr;
1079      BEGIN
1080        other := EvalFun (p [top - 1]^.rand);
1081        IF other^.kind = IntConst THEN
1082          other := MkIntConst (other^.val * other^.val)
1083        ELSE
1084          Error (9);
1085        p [top - 1]^ := other^;
1086        top := top - 1;
1087      END;   { RedSq }

1089      PROCEDURE RedOdd (VAR p: AStack; VAR top: AStackRange);
1090        VAR other: AppNodePtr;
1091      BEGIN
1092        other := EvalFun (p [top - 1]^.rand);
1093        IF other^.kind <> IntConst THEN
1094          Error (10)
1095        ELSE IF odd (other^.val) THEN
1096          other := MkStrConst ('TRUE       ')
1097        ELSE
1098          other := MkStrConst ('FALSE      ');
1099        p [top - 1]^ := other^;
1100        top := top - 2;
1101      END;   { RedOdd }

1103      PROCEDURE RedEven (VAR p: AStack; VAR top: AStackRange);
1104        VAR other: AppNodePtr;
1105      BEGIN
1106        other := EvalFun (p [top - 1]^.rand);
1107        IF other^.kind <> IntConst THEN
1108          Error (11)
1109        ELSE IF odd (other^.val) THEN
1110          other := MkStrConst ('FALSE      ')
1111        ELSE
1112          other := MkStrConst ('TRUE       ');
```

```
1113        p [top - 1]^ := other^;
1114        top := top - 2;
1115     END;   { RedEven }

1117     PROCEDURE RedLeq (VAR p: AStack; VAR top: AStackRange);
1118        VAR other1, other2: AppNodePtr;
1119     BEGIN
1120        other1 := EvalFun (p [top - 1]^.rand);
1121        other2 := EvalFun (p [top - 2]^.rand);
1122        IF other1^.val <= other2^.val THEN
1123          other1 := MkStrConst ('TRUE      ')
1124        ELSE
1125          other1 := MkStrConst ('FALSE     ');
1126        p [top - 2]^ := other1^;
1127        top := top - 2;
1128     END;   { leq }

1130     PROCEDURE RedEq (VAR p: AStack; VAR top: AStackRange);
1131        VAR other: AppNodePtr;
1132     BEGIN
1133        IF SameAppNode (EvalFun (p [top - 1]^.rand),
1134                        EvalFun (p [top - 2]^.rand)) THEN
1135          other := MkStrConst ('TRUE      ')
1136        ELSE
1137          other := MkStrConst ('FALSE     ');
1138        p [top - 2]^ := other^;
1139        top := top - 2;
1140     END;   { RedEq }

1142     PROCEDURE RedHead (VAR p: AStack; VAR top: AStackRange);
1143        VAR other: AppNodePtr;
1144     BEGIN
1145        other := EvalFun (p [top - 1]^.rand);
1146        p [top - 1]^ := other^.rator^.rand^;
1147        top := top - 1;
1148     END;   { RedHead }

1150     PROCEDURE RedTail (VAR p: AStack; VAR top: AStackRange);
1151        VAR other: AppNodePtr;
```

```
1152    BEGIN
1153      other := EvalFun (p [top - 1]^.rand);
1154      p [top - 1]^ := other^.rand^;
1155      top := top - 1;
1156    END;   { RedTail }

1158    PROCEDURE RedAtom (VAR p: AStack; VAR top: AStackRange);
1159      VAR other: AppNodePtr;
1160    BEGIN
1161      other := EvalFun (p [top - 1]^.rand);
1162      IF other^.kind = Application THEN
1163        other := MkStrConst ('FALSE      ')
1164      ELSE
1165        other := MkStrConst ('TRUE       ');
1166      p [top - 1]^ := other^;
1167      top := top - 1;
1168    END;   { RedAtom }

1170    PROCEDURE RedNull (VAR p: AStack; VAR top: AStackRange);
1171      VAR other: AppNodePtr;
1172    BEGIN
1173      other := EvalFun (p [top - 1]^.rand);
1174      IF other^.symb = 'NIL        ' THEN
1175        other := MkStrConst ('TRUE       ')
1176      ELSE
1177        other := MkStrConst ('FALSE      ');
1178      p [top - 1]^ := other^;
1179      top := top - 1;
1180    END;   { RedNull }

1182    PROCEDURE RedU (VAR p: AStack; VAR top: AStackRange);
1183    BEGIN
1184      p [top - 2]^.rator :=
1185        MkApp (p [top - 1]^.rand,
1186                MkApp (MkComb ('HEAD      '),
1187                        p [top - 2]^.rand));
1188      p [top - 2]^.rand :=
1189        MkApp (MkComb ('TAIL      '), p [top - 2]^.rand);
1190      top := top - 2;
```

```
1191    END;    { RedU }

1193    PROCEDURE RedIf (VAR p: AStack; VAR top: AStackRange);
1194      VAR other: AppNodePtr;
1195    BEGIN
1196      other := EvalFun (p [top - 1]^.rand);
1197      IF other^.symb = 'TRUE     ' THEN
1198        other := p [top - 2]^.rand
1199      ELSE IF other^.symb = 'FALSE     ' THEN
1200        other := p [top - 3]^.rand
1201      ELSE
1202        Error (12);
1203      p [top - 3]^ := other^;
1204      top := top - 3;
1205    END;    { RedIf }

1207    PROCEDURE RedNot (VAR p: AStack; VAR top: AStackRange);
1208      VAR other: AppNodePtr;
1209    BEGIN
1210      other := EvalFun (p [top - 1]^.rand);
1211      IF other^.symb = 'TRUE     ' THEN
1212        other := MkStrConst ('FALSE     ')
1213      ELSE IF other^.symb = 'FALSE     ' THEN
1214        other := MkStrConst ('TRUE     ')
1215      ELSE
1216        Error (13);
1217      p [top - 1]^ := other^;
1218      top := top - 1;
1219    END;    { RedNot }

1221    PROCEDURE RedAnd (VAR p: AStack; VAR top: AStackRange);
1222      VAR arg1, arg2, other: AppNodePtr;
1223    BEGIN
1224      arg1 := EvalFun (p [top - 1]^.rand);
1225      arg2 := EvalFun (p [top - 2]^.rand);
1226      IF arg1^.symb = 'TRUE     ' THEN
1227        BEGIN
1228          IF other^.symb = 'TRUE     ' THEN
1229            other := MkStrConst ('TRUE     ')
```

238

```
1230        ELSE
1231            other := MkStrConst ('FALSE      ');
1232          END
1233      ELSE
1234        other := MkStrConst ('FALSE      ');
1235      p [top - 2]^ := other^;
1236      top := top - 2;
1237    END;    { RedAnd }

1239    PROCEDURE RedOr (VAR p: AStack; VAR top: AStackRange);
1240      VAR arg1, arg2, other: AppNodePtr;
1241    BEGIN
1242      arg1 := EvalFun (p [top - 1]^.rand);
1243      arg2 := EvalFun (p [top - 2]^.rand);
1244      IF arg1^.symb = 'FALSE     ' THEN
1245        BEGIN
1246          IF arg2^.symb = 'FALSE     ' THEN
1247            other := MkStrConst ('FALSE     ')
1248          ELSE
1249            other := MkStrConst ('TRUE     ');
1250        END
1251      ELSE
1252        other := MkStrConst ('TRUE     ');
1253      p [top - 2]^ := other^;
1254      top := top - 2;
1255    END;    { RedOr }

1257    PROCEDURE RedChr (VAR p: AStack; VAR top: AStackRange);
1258      VAR s: String; other: AppNodePtr;
1259    BEGIN
1260      s := stringSpaces;
1261      other := EvalFun (p [top - 1]^.rand);
1262      s [1] := Chr (other^.val);
1263      other := MkStrConst (s);
1264      p [top - 1]^ := other^;
1265      top := top - 1;
1266    END;    { RedChr }

1268    PROCEDURE OneRed (VAR spine: AStack; VAR tspi: AStackRange);
```

```
1269        VAR curPtr: AppNodePtr; s: String;
1270      BEGIN
1271        curPtr := spine [tspi];
1272        s := CurPtr^.symb;
1273        IF s = 'S       ' THEN RedS (spine, tspi)
1274        ELSE IF s = 'K       ' THEN RedK (spine, tspi)
1275        ELSE IF s = 'I       ' THEN RedI (spine, tspi)
1276        ELSE IF s = 'B       ' THEN RedB (spine, tspi)
1277        ELSE IF s = 'C       ' THEN RedC (spine, tspi)
1278        ELSE IF s = 'S1      ' THEN RedS1 (spine, tspi)
1279        ELSE IF s = 'B1      ' THEN RedB1 (spine, tspi)
1280        ELSE IF s = 'C1      ' THEN RedC1 (spine, tspi)
1281        ELSE IF s = 'Y       ' THEN RedY (spine, tspi)
1282        ELSE IF s = 'ADD     ' THEN RedAdd (spine, tspi)
1283        ELSE IF s = 'SUB     ' THEN RedSub (spine, tspi)
1284        ELSE IF s = 'MUL     ' THEN RedMul (spine, tspi)
1285        ELSE IF s = 'DIV     ' THEN RedDiv (spine, tspi)
1286        ELSE IF s = 'REM     ' THEN RedRem (spine, tspi)
1287        ELSE IF s = 'SQ      ' THEN RedSq (spine, tspi)
1288        ELSE IF s = 'ODD     ' THEN RedOdd (spine, tspi)
1289        ELSE IF s = 'EVEN    ' THEN RedEven (spine, tspi)
1290        ELSE IF s = 'LEQ     ' THEN RedLeq (spine, tspi)
1291        ELSE IF s = 'EQ      ' THEN RedEq (spine, tspi)
1292        ELSE IF s = 'HEAD    ' THEN RedHead (spine, tspi)
1293        ELSE IF s = 'TAIL    ' THEN RedTail (spine, tspi)
1294        ELSE IF s = 'ATOM    ' THEN RedAtom (spine, tspi)
1295        ELSE IF s = 'NULL    ' THEN RedNull (spine, tspi)
1296        ELSE IF s = 'U       ' THEN RedU (spine, tspi)
1297        ELSE IF s = 'IF      ' THEN RedIf (spine, tspi)
1298        ELSE IF s = 'NOT     ' THEN RedNot (spine, tspi)
1299        ELSE IF s = 'AND     ' THEN RedAnd (spine, tspi)
1300        ELSE IF s = 'OR      ' THEN RedOr (spine, tspi)
1301        ELSE IF s = 'CHR     ' THEN RedChr (spine, tspi)
1302        ELSE skip;
1303        Tulas (spine, tspi);
1304      END;    { OneRed }

1306      FUNCTION EvalFun;
1307        VAR a: AStack; b: AStackRange; c: AppNodePtr;
```

```
1308    BEGIN
1309      Clas (g, a, b);
1310      c := a [b];
1311      WHILE (c^.kind = Combinator)
1312        AND (c^.symb <> 'CONS      ') DO
1313        BEGIN
1314          OneRed (a, b);
1315          c := a [b];
1316        END;
1317      EvalFun := g;
1318    END;  { EvalFun }


1320    PROCEDURE Eval;
1321      VAR root: NodePtr; fileName: Cmd;
1322    BEGIN
1323      symbOnLine := 0;
1324      ReadCmd (uLine, last, fileName);
1325      Reset (lispCode, fileName); { Non-standard Pascal. }
1326      root := Parse (lispCode);
1327      appRoot := Tr (root);
1328      appRoot := EvalFun (appRoot);
1329      PrAppAll (appRoot);
1330      WriteLn;
1331    END;  { Eval }


1333    PROCEDURE ReadLine (VAR x: Text; VAR y: Line);
1334      VAR z: Char; a: LineRange;
1335    BEGIN
1336      y := lineSpaces;
1337      a := 1;
1338      WHILE (NOT Eof (x)) AND (NOT Eoln (x)) DO
1339        BEGIN
1340          Read (x, z);
1341          y [a] := z;
1342          IncL (a);
1343        END;
1344      IF Eof (x) THEN Error (14);
1345      IF a >= LineMax - 2 THEN Error (15);
1346      y [LineMax - 1] := EndInfo;
```

```
1347        ReadLn (x);
1348     END;   { ReadLine }


1350     PROCEDURE Initialise;
1351        VAR i: Integer; j: LineRange; k: CmdRange;
1352     BEGIN
1353        FOR j := 1 TO LineMax DO lineSpaces [j] := ' ';
1354        FOR k := 1 TO CmdMax DO cmdSpaces [k] := ' ';
1355        FOR i := 1 TO StringMax DO stringSpaces [i] := ' ';
1356        symbOnLine := 0;
1357        ready := True;
1358     END;  { Initialise }


1360  BEGIN { LispKit }
1361     Initialise;
1362     WriteLn;
1363     WriteLn ('Hello from the LispKit system.');
1364     WriteLn;
1365     WHILE ready DO
1366        BEGIN
1367           WriteLn ('What next?');
1368           ReadLine (input, uLine);
1369           last := 1;
1370           ReadCmd (uLine, last, globCmd);
1371           IF globCmd = 'eval   ' THEN Eval
1372           ELSE IF globCmd = 'quit   ' THEN ready := False
1373           ELSE WriteLn (output, 'Unknown command');
1374        5: Skip;
1375           END;
1376     WriteLn;
1377     WriteLn ('Goodbye from the LispKit system.');
1378     WriteLn;
1379  END. { LispKit }
```

Glossary

Applicative order reduction This is a reduction strategy in which the arguments of a function are evaluated before the function body is evaluated and applied to the results of evaluating its arguments. Its main advantage is that each actual parameter of a function call is only evaluated once, but its main disadvantage is that actual parameters may be evaluated even when they are not used in the function body and some of these may be non-terminating. Another disadvantage is that languages which make use of AOR—such as Scheme—have to have *special forms*, *q.v.*, which are not evaluated in this way. An example of such a special form is the conditional **if**. Clearly we not want both p and q to be evaluated every time a conditional **if** b **then** p **else** q is called. No such problem with the conditional exists in languages employing normal order reduction. Applicative order reduction is also known as *call-by-value*, *q.v.* Usually the actual parameters are evaluated from left to right; in this case it can also be referred to as a *leftmost-innermost* evaluation strategy. Clearly, a *rightmost-innermost* strategy is also possible in which the actual parameters are evaluated from right to left.

Bag A *bag* is a collection of objects which is like a set in that the ordering of elements is not important, but it is like a list in that duplicate members are allowed. Bags are also known as *multi-sets* or *families*.

Bracket abstraction A method used in combinatory logic to remove variables from a CL-term. It is conventionally represented as $[x]M$, thus the name. It *roughly* corresponds to abstraction, $\lambda x.M$, in the λ-calculus.

Call-by-name A parameter-passing mechanism for procedures in Algol 60. It is described in the Algol report—Naur (1963)—as follows:

4.7.3.2 Name replacement (call by name). Any formal parameter not quoted in the value list is replaced, throughout the procedure body, by the corresponding actual parameter, after enclosing this latter in parentheses wherever syntactically possible. Possible conflicts between identifiers inserted through this process and other identifiers already present within the procedure body will be avoided by suitable systematic changes of the formal or local identifiers involved.

This replacement technique is known as the *copy rule* and it has the effect that an actual parameter is not evaluated unless a reference to it is met whilst the procedure body is being executed, but if several references to it are met, then it is re-evaluated. The term *call-by-name* has been taken over by the functional programming community to refer to *normal order reduction, q.v.*

Call-by-need A parameter-passing mechanism introduced by Wadsworth (1971), pp. 183–184, which combines the advantages of call-by-name—actual parameters are only evaluated if used in the evaluation of the procedure body—and call-by-value—actual parameters are only evaluated once. In a functional language implemented by means of graph-reduction call-by-need corresponds to normal order graph-reduction, an idea also introduced by Wadsworth (1971), pp. 171ff.

Call-by-value A parameter-passing mechanism for procedures in Algol 60. It is described in the Algol report—Naur (1963)—in these terms:

4.7.3.1 Value assignment (call by value). All formal parameters quoted in the value part of the procedure declaration heading are assigned the value of the corresponding actual parameters, these assignments being considered as being performed explicitly before entering the procedure body. The effect is as though an additional block embracing the procedure body were created in which these assignments were made to variables local to this fictitious block with types as given in the corresponding specifications. As a consequence, variables called by value are to be considered as nonlocal to the body of the procedure, but local to the fictitious block.

In other words, each actual parameter is evaluated before the procedure body is executed and that value is used throughout the procedure. The term *call-by-value* has been taken over by the functional programming community to describe *applicative order reduction, q.v.*

Church–Rosser property Let $\rightarrow$ be a binary relation over Δ, $\rightarrow^*$ its reflexive, transitive closure and $=$ the reflexive, symmetric and transitive closure of $\rightarrow$. Then $\rightarrow$ has the *Church–Rosser property* or is said to be *Church–Rosser* iff for all $P, Q \in \Delta$, whenever $P = Q$ holds, then there exists an element of Δ, say N, such that $P \rightarrow^* N$ and $Q \rightarrow^* N$.

Combinator (1) A very general one-place function that can be defined in terms of the combinators **S** and **K** (combinatory logic). (2) A λ-term with no free variables and whose body contains no constants (lambda calculus). See also *supercombinator*. (3) The term is also used loosely to describe a primitive operator in some domain or other, with the connotation that the operator in question has been particularly well chosen to capture a specific feature of that domain.

Confluent Let $\rightarrow$ be a binary relation over Δ and $\rightarrow^*$ its reflexive, transitive closure. In these circumstances, we say that $\rightarrow$ is *confluent* iff for all $M, P, Q \in \Delta$, whenever both $M \rightarrow^* P$ and $M \rightarrow^* Q$ hold, then there exists an element of Δ, say N, such that $P \rightarrow^* N$ and $Q \rightarrow^* N$. If a relation $\rightarrow$ is confluent, then $\rightarrow^*$ has the *diamond property, q.v.*

Currying This is the process of replacing a function of several variables by a (higher-order) one-place function. For example, let $f(x, y)$ be a two-place function. First, we define $f_x \triangleq \lambda y.f(x, y)$ and then $g \triangleq \lambda x.f_x$. The function g is the *curried* version of f and the following holds:

$$(gx)y = f_x(y) = f(x, y).$$

The general case of an n-place function is treated similarly. See also the entry under *section*.

Definition A method of program transformation which allows us to add an equation $E = E'$ to our program if E is not an instance of the left-hand side of any existing equation in the program.

Diamond property Let $\rightarrow$ be a binary relation over Δ. Then $\rightarrow$ has the *diamond property* iff for all M, P and Q in Δ, whenever $M \rightarrow P$ and $M \rightarrow Q$ both hold, then there exists an element of Δ, say N, such that $P \rightarrow N$ and $Q \rightarrow N$. This terminology is used, for example, by Barendregt (1984), pp. 53–54.

Dynamic binding Under dynamic binding a free variable is bound to its value when it is used and not when it is declared, that is to say, its value is only fixed in the calling environment and not in the environment where it was declared. It is contrasted with static binding. Dynamic binding is also known as *fluid binding* (for example, in Henderson (1980), p. 123).

Eager evaluation Same as *call-by-value, q.v.*, or *applicative order reduction, q.v.*

Expansion Let $\rightarrow$ be a reduction relation. Then the replacement of a redex M by its corresponding contractum N is known as a reduction and is symbolized $M \rightarrow N$. By contrast, *expansion* involves the replacement of a contractum N by any one of the terms that can reduce to it by means of a single contraction. For example, in the λ-calculus the λ-term $xy(xz)$ expands to $(\lambda u.u(xz))(xy)$ and also to $(\lambda v.xyv)(xz)$, because

$$
\begin{aligned}
(\lambda u.u(xz))(xy) &\rightarrow xy(xz), \\
(\lambda v.xyv)(xz) &\rightarrow xy(xz).
\end{aligned}
$$

The term *expansion* comes from Curry and Feys (1958), p. 91. Peyton Jones (1987), p. 18, calls it β-abstraction—in the λ-calculus case—and O'Donnell (1985) refers to it as backwards reduction, p. 85, or reverse reduction, p. 226.

Family See under *bag*.

Fluid binding The same as *dynamic binding, q.v.*

Folding Let $E = E'$ be the definition that we want to fold, where the expression E is defined as E', and let $G = G'$ be the equation that is to be transformed. For this to be possible an instance of E', say E'_1, must occur in G'. Let E_1 be the corresponding instance of E. To fold the definition $E = E'$ in the equation $G = G'$ we replace the occurrence of E' in G', namely E'_1, with E_1. Call the result of this substitution G'', then we can add the equation $G = G''$ to our program.

Full section See *section*.

Fully lazy evaluation Hughes (1984a) introduced the concept of *fully lazy evaluation*. In lazy evaluation *every argument of a function* is evaluated at most once, whereas in fully lazy evaluation every expression is evaluated at most once after the variables in it have been bound. In order to illustrate this, let consider an example. Define the power function y^x as follows:

$$
\begin{aligned}
power\ x\ y &= 1,\ x = 0, \\
&= square\ (power\ (x/2)\ y),\ even\ x, \\
&= y * power\ (x - 1)\ y.
\end{aligned}
$$

Say that you now map *power* over a list:

$$map\ (power\ 5)\ [1, 3, 7, 11, 23, 5].$$

In this case a fully lazy evaluator would not calculate *power* 5 six times. All combinator-based implementations for functional languages are fully lazy, as is the supercombinator version described in this book, though some supercombinator implementations are not fully lazy.

Function There are two main ways of looking at functions in mathematics. We can think of a function as a rule or as a graph, that is to say, a set of ordered pairs in which no two distinct pairs have the same first element or argument. The concept of a function as a graph is dominant in most of mathematics, but the λ-calculus is based on the notion of a function as a rule according to which the value of the function can be derived from its argument.

General recursive function The class of *general recursive functions* is obtained from the same initial functions as define the class of *primitive recursive function*, *q.v.*, except that now three ways of making functions out of functions are allowed. In addition to substitution and recursion, new functions can be created by means of the μ-*operation*.

Assume that $f(x_1, \ldots, x_n, y)$ is a number-theoretic function such that for all $x_1, \ldots, x_n$, there exists at least one y such that $f(x_1, \ldots, x_n, y) = 0$. Then $\mu y(f(x_1, \ldots, x_n, y) = 0)$ is the least number y such that $f(x_1, \ldots, x_n, y) = 0$. Let $g(x_1, \ldots, x_n) = \mu y(f(x_1, \ldots, x_n, y) = 0)$. Then g is said to be obtained from f by means of the μ-operator. See Mendelson (1964), pp. 121ff., and Kleene (1952), Chapter XI, for more information.

Head It is easy to see—and straightforward to prove by induction on its length—that every CL-term X can be expressed in the form $X \equiv aX_1 \ldots X_n$, where a is an atom—possibly a combinator—and $n \geq 0$. This occurrence of a is called the *head* or *leading element* of X and X_i is its i-th argument.

Higher-order function A *higher-order function* is one whose arguments and/or values can themselves be functions. Frege (1893)—see, for example, §§21–23—was the first to clearly see the difference between first- and higher-order functions.

Homomorphism This term—taken from algebra—describes a particular kind of higher-order function which is best explained by means of an example. Consider the following definition in KRC:

$$\text{hom } f\, g\, b\, [\,] \;=\; b,$$
$$\text{hom } f\, g\, b\, (a:x) \;=\; f\,(g\,a)\,(\text{hom } f\, g\, b\, x).$$

The function *hom* is an example of a homomorphism. Given an arbitrary list y, what *hom* does is to replace each occurrence of *cons* in y by f, each occurrence of an element u of the list by gu and the empty list in y by b. The type of *hom* is

$$(\alpha \to \beta \to \beta) \to (\gamma \to \alpha) \to \beta \to \text{list } \gamma \to \beta.$$

The function *foldright*, which is widely used in functional programming —see, for example, the SASL prelude in Turner (1976)—can be defined in terms of *hom* thus:

$$\text{foldright } f = \text{hom } f\, \mathbf{I}.$$

Clearly, a homomorphism can be defined for any abstract data type. For example, in Miranda the type of binary trees can be defined, following Turner (1985b), p. 7, as

$$\text{tree } * ::= \text{Niltree} \,|\, \text{Node } * (\text{tree } *)\,(\text{tree } *).$$

In this case the homomorphism for binary trees is

$$\text{treehom } f\, g\, j\, \text{Niltree} \;=\; j,$$
$$\text{treehom } f\, g\, j\, (\text{Node } a\, l\, r) \;=\; f\,(ga)\,(\text{treehom } f\, g\, j\, l)$$
$$(\text{treehom } f\, g\, j\, r).$$

In a call involving *treehom*, say *treehom f g j b*, every occurrence of *Niltree* in *b* is replaced by *j*, every item *a* that occurs at a node is replaced by *ga*, and every node is replaced by *f*. The type of *treehom* is

$$(\alpha \to \beta \to \beta \to \beta) \to (\gamma \to \alpha) \to \beta \to \text{tree } \gamma \to \beta.$$

See Henson (1987), pp. 126–133, for more details.

Bird (1986), p. 9, defines what a homomorphism is differently. Let $\Box$ be an associative binary operator with identity element e:

$$x \Box (y \Box z) \;=\; (x \Box y) \Box z,$$
$$x \Box e \;=\; x,$$
$$e \Box x \;=\; x.$$

Then h is a *homomorphism* iff

$$h\,[\,] \;=\; e,$$
$$h\,(x + + y) \;=\; hx \Box hy,$$

where x and y are arbitrary finite lists and $++$ is list addition.

Hope A functional programming language described in Burstall, MacQueen and Sannella (1981). According to Sadler and Eisenbach (1987), p. 16, it is named after Hope Park Square, where Edinburgh University's Department of Computer Science is situated.

Illative combinatory logic The word 'illative' means *pertaining to infer-ence*. Combinatory logic can be sub-divided into two branches, namely *pure* and *illative* combinatory logic. The pure part deals with the properties of those combinators that can be defined in terms of **S** and **K**, whereas the illative part seeks to formalize those notions that we normally think of as logical; for example, *implication, generality* and *existence*. To begin with, Curry restricted illative combinatory logic to the study of such notions in the framework of pure combinatory logic—which can, in fact, be thought of as a *pre-logical* system—but later he extended it to encompass also arithmetical notions and those connected with the theory of functionality, that is to say, type theory.

Instantiation A method of program transformation. Let $E = E'$ be an equation in our program. Then the program transformation *instantia-tion* allows us to add a substitution instance of $E = E'$ to the program.

Kent Recursive Calculator See *KRC*.

KRC Abbreviation for *Kent Recursive Calculator*. A functional programming language designed by Turner. It is similar to the earlier SASL, but its concrete syntax is a great improvement. It also improves on SASL in that it contains ZF-expressions, but one of its defects is that it is not possible to make local definitions. For more details see Turner (1982b).

Lattice A poset $(D, \sqsubseteq)$ is a *lattice* iff for all $d, e \in D$, there exist $f, g \in D$, such that $f = d \sqcup e$ and $g = d \sqcap e$, where $d \sqcup e$ is the join or least upper bound of d and e and $d \sqcap e$ is the meet or greatest lower bound of d and e.

Laws A method of program transformation. Let $E = E'$ be an equation in our program. Then the program transformation *laws* allows us to add $E = E''$ to our system of equations, where E'' has been obtained from E' by making use of any of the properties of the primitive operators of our language. For example, we might use the fact that addition is commutative and associative to transform E' into E''.

Lazy evaluation A reduction strategy which proceeds by performing head reductions on the functional program being evaluated. Internal reductions are only performed when a strict function is encountered or when the head redex is shared. Intuitively, this means that each expression is only evaluated when the result is needed (and every argument of a function is evaluated at most once).

LCF Abbreviation for *Logic of Computable Functions*. LCF is a family of interactive theorem-provers based on Scott's logic PPλ, that is to say, polymorphic predicate λ-calculus. See Paulson (1987) for details. It is important for many reasons, one of which is that it led to the development of the functional programming language ML. Initially, this was just used to guide proofs, but—as Wikström (1987) testifies— it has grown into a general purpose programming language in its own right.

Leftmost-innermost See under *applicative order reduction*.

Leftmost-outermost See under *normal order reduction*.

Lexical scoping Exactly the same as *static binding, q.v.*

Lexicographic binding Synonymous with *static binding, q.v.*

Linear order Same as *total order, q.v.*

Lispkit Lisp A purely functional version of Lisp devised by Henderson (1980). Some of its distinctive features are that it is lexically scoped, the implemented version is subject to lazy evaluation, it is untyped, it supports higher-order functions as first-class citizens and it contains both global and local **let**- and **letrec**-clauses.

Local confluence Let $\rightarrow$ be a binary relation over Δ and $\rightarrow^*$ its reflexive, transitive closure. Then $\rightarrow$ is said to be *locally confluent* iff, for all $M, P, Q \in \Delta$, whenever both $M \rightarrow P$ and $M \rightarrow Q$ hold, then there exists an element of Δ, say N, such that both $P \rightarrow^* N$ and $Q \rightarrow^* N$ hold. Some writers use an alternative terminology and say that a relation satisfies the *weak diamond property* if it is locally confluent. For example, Barendregt (1984), p. 58, uses this alternative terminology.

Miranda A functional programming language designed by Turner (1985b, 1986) and succeeding KRC, to which it is very similar, except that local definitions are now allowed. The major addition, however, is the type system, which is based on Milner (1978), but allows both algebraic and abstract types. These contain some novel features, which are discussed in Thompson (1985).

ML Abbreviation for *meta-language*. A functional programming language that was a spin-off of the LCF project. The first applicative language to use the type system described in Milner (1978). See Wikström (1987) for a thorough account and both Gordon, Milner and Wadsworth (1979) and Paulson (1987) describe its use in the LCF framework.

Multi-set See under *bag*.

Normal order reduction This is a reduction strategy in which the redexes in a term—be it a λ-term or a CL-term or whatever—are evaluated from left to right. Evaluation proceeds until all the redexes have been contracted. The main advantages of NOR are that unnecessary arguments are not evaluated and that if either a λ-term or a CL-term has a normal form then NOR will find it. Its main disadvantage is that often the same redex will be evaluated several times. This means that

251

the length of a NOR path is usually longer than the corresponding applicative order reduction path. In a language with imperative features, such as Franz Lisp, there are circumstances in which a program would terminate under AOR, but employing NOR would result in eternal silence. See Allen (1978), p. 227, for more information. NOR is also known as *call-by-name, q.v.,* or *leftmost-outermost* reduction.

Offside rule This was introduced by Landin (1966), p. 160, to account for the scope of such constructs as **whererec**-clauses in the extension of KRC proposed in Chapter 1. Landin's own explanation is clear and succinct:

> The southeast quadrant that just contains the phrase's first symbol must contain the entire phrase, except possibly for bracketed subsegments.

Operator section See *section.*

Overloading An *overloaded* operator is one 'whose meaning depends on the type of its operands', according to Ghezzi and Jazayeri (1982), p. 65. Arithmetic operators, like + and *, are usually overloaded, being defined and (usually) implemented differently for real numbers and for integers.

Peano's axioms A group of five postulates attributed to Peano which define the properties of the natural numbers up to isomorphism.

Let Nat be a set, 0 a designated member of Nat, $0 \in Nat$, and $succ$ a (partial) function from Nat to itself, $succ : Nat \rightarrow Nat$. Then the set Nat is isomorphic to the natural numbers if the following hold:

(1) $0 \in Nat$;

(2) $x \in Nat \Rightarrow succ\ (x) \in Nat$;

(3) $x \in Nat \wedge y \in Nat \wedge x \neq y \Rightarrow succ\ (x) \neq succ\ (y)$;

(4) $x \in Nat \Rightarrow 0 \neq succ\ (x)$;

(5) $\phi(0) \wedge (\forall x \in Nat)(\phi(x) \Rightarrow \phi(succ\ (x)) \Rightarrow (\forall x \in Nat)\phi(x)$.

Clauses (5) here is the induction axiom and the quantification involved has to be understood as over all the elements of Nat and ϕ is a property of the elements of Nat.

Postsection See *section*

Presection See *section*

Primitive recursive function The *primitive recursive functions* are those that can be obtained by *substitution* and *primitive recursion* from a set of *initial functions*. The following are the permissible initial functions:

(I) The successor function: $S(x) = x + 1$, for all x.

(II) The constant functions C_q^n, which are such that $C_q^n(x_1, \ldots, x_n) = q$.

(III) The projection or identity functions U_i^n, which are such that $U_i^n(x_1, \ldots, x_n) = x_i$, for all $x_1, \ldots, x_n$.

And the following are the ways in which new functions can be generated from these initial functions:

(IV) In order to explain definition by substitution consider the equation:

$$f(x_1, \ldots, x_n) = g(h_1(x_1, \ldots, x_n), \ldots, h_m(x_1, \ldots, x_n)).$$

Here, $f(x_1, \ldots, x_n)$ has been obtained from $g(y_1, \ldots, y_m)$ and the m functions $h_1(x_1, \ldots, x_n), \ldots, h_m(x_1, \ldots, x_n)$ by substitution.

(Va) In order to explain the generation of new functions from old ones by primitive recursion without parameters consider the functions:

$$
\begin{aligned}
f(0) &= q, \\
f(y + 1) &= g(y, f(y)).
\end{aligned}
$$

Here, f has been obtained from the function $g(x, y)$ and the constant q by primitive recursion (without parameters).

(Vb) In order to explain primitive recursion with parameters, consider the functions:

$$
\begin{aligned}
f(x_1, \ldots, x_n, 0) &= g(x_1, \ldots, x_n), \\
f(x_1, \ldots, x_n, y + 1) &= h(x_1, \ldots, x_n, y, f(x_1, \ldots, x_n, y)).
\end{aligned}
$$

Here, the function $f(x_1, \ldots, x_{n+1})$ has been obtained from the two functions $g(x_1, \ldots, x_n)$ and $h(z_1, \ldots, z_{n+2})$ by primitive recursion. The parameters of the recursion are $x_1, \ldots, x_n$. See Kleene (1952), Chapter IX, for more discussion and examples.

Proper binding Synonymous with *static binding, q.v.* Used by Henderson (1980), p. 47.

Recursion equation Let $\Sigma = \{l_i = r_i | 1 \leq i \leq n\}$, then Σ is a set of *recursion equations* if each l_i is of the form of a function application $f_i x_{i_1} x_{i_2} \ldots x_{i_m}$, where the x_{i_j} are variables, and each r_k is an expression built up out of variables, primitive built-in operators—such as the conditional and arithmetical operators—and function names f_i occurring on the left hand sides of equations. In KRC the x_{i_j} can be arbitrary patterns built up out of variables, constants and the list constructor, whereas in Miranda user-defined type constructors are also allowed to appear in patterns. A set of recursion equations is higher-order if the x_{i_j} are allowed to range over functions and not just objects or individuals.

Rightmost-innermost See under *applicative order reduction.*

Referential transparency A notation is *referentially transparent* if it satisfies the following two conditions:

1. Different occurrences of the same expression in a single scope have the same meaning.

2. Two different expressions which have the same meaning anywhere in a single scope have the same meaning throughout that scope and, hence, can be substituted for each other anywhere in that scope.

St Andrews Static Language See *SASL.*

SASL Abbreviation for *St Andrews Static Language.* A purely functional language designed by Turner (1976), though largely influenced by PAL, for details of which see Evans (1968). From PAL it takes over the use of higher-order recursion equations to define functions and pattern-matching.

Section Let $\square$ be an infix binary operator. There may be occasions on which we want to use a partially parameterized version of $\square$. This can be done by defining two infix operators:

$$\begin{aligned}
\textit{one } x \ y &\triangleq x \square y, \\
\textit{two } x \ y &\triangleq y \square x,
\end{aligned}$$

254

then *one z* and *two z* are the two possible partial parameterizations of
$\Box$. For example, if $\Box$ is division $\div$, then *one* 7 is a one-place function
which returns seven times the reciprocal of its argument and *two* 7
returns a seventh of its argument. An alternative method—due to
Bird—is to use sections. The function *one z* is now represented as
$(z\Box)$ and *two z* as $(\Box z)$. The partial parameterizations $(z\Box)$ and $(\Box z)$
are called *sections*. $(z\Box)$ is a *presection* and $(\Box z)$ is a *postsection*. For
example, in the case of division we would write $(7\div)$ for the function
which returns seven times the reciprocal of its argument and $(\div 7)$ for
the function which returns a seventh of its argument.

The *full section* of the infix operator $\Box$ is written $(\Box)$ and is defined
so that $(\Box)xy = x\Box y$, thus $(\Box)$ is just the prefix curried version of
the infix operator $\Box$. See Bird and Hughes (1987) and Bird (1986) for
examples of the utility of sections.

Semi-standard reduction A *semi-standard reduction* is one in which every
head contraction is performed before any internal contractions.

Side effect A function or procedure in an imperative language has a *side
effect* when it alters a non-local variable.

Source reduction This is an implementation technique for functional languages which involves no compilation. (Alternatively, this is a method
of compilation in which the translation function from source code to
object code is the identity function.) Let Σ be a set of recursion equations. A source reduction implementation would simply regard each
function definition $l_i = r_i$ as a rewrite rule $l_i \rightarrow r_i$ to be applied as
necessary when a request to evaluate an expression e is made. According to Hughes (1984), pp. 119–121, KRC was implemented by Turner
using source reduction. O'Donnell (1977, 1985) are also useful.

Special form Most versions of Lisp are implemented using applicative order
reduction. This gives rise to the following evaluation strategy. First,
evaluate all of a function's arguments and then apply the function to
them. Unfortunately, there are Lisp primitives for which this evaluation method would give the wrong result or simply not work. These
are called *special forms*, and the way they are treated by the Lisp
system differs from the usual applicative order reduction method.

Standard reduction A *standard reduction* is similar to normal order reduction in that redexes are contracted from left to right. The only

difference is that not all redexes have to be contracted in a standard reduction, thus a terminating standard reduction path does not necessarily terminate in a normal form.

Static binding Under static binding a free variable is bound to its value when it is declared and not when it is used. By way of contrast, under dynamic binding the value of a variable depends on the calling environment. The difference can be brought out in the following Lispkit program:

$$\textbf{let } x = 7 \textbf{ in (let } g = \lambda(z).(x \times z) \textbf{ in (let } x = 3 \textbf{ in } g(5))).$$

Under static binding the result is 35, but under dynamic binding the result would be 15. Static binding is also known as *proper binding*, for example, by Henderson (1980), p. 47; *lexical binding*, for example, by Allen (1978), p. 150; and *lexicographic binding*, for example, by Turner (1981a), p. 3.

Strictness A one-place function f is *strict* iff $f\bot = \bot$ and an n-place function g is strict in its i-th argument-place iff

$$gx_1 \ldots x_{i-1} \bot x_{i+1} \ldots x_n = \bot.$$

A non-strict function is one that can return a value even if some of its arguments are undefined.

Strong reduction The reduction relation studied in Chapter 3 is *weak* reduction. *Strong* reduction is weak reduction to which is added the property known as (ξ): if $M \to N$, then $[x]M \to [x]N$. It is often represented by the sign $\succ$. If M strongly reduces to N, it does not follow that M weakly reduces to N. A counterexample is provided by the fact that **SK** strongly reduces to **KI**, but not weakly. We have—and this is taken from Hindley, Lercher and Seldin (1972), p. 53—the following:

$$\textbf{SK} \equiv [x][y]\textbf{SK}xy \succ [x][y]\textbf{K}y(yx) \succ [x][y]y \equiv \textbf{KI}.$$

For more information about strong reduction, see Chapter 7 of Hindley, Lercher and Seldin (1972).

Supercombinator In the λ-calculus a *supercombinator* α of *arity n*, where $n \geq 0$, is a closed λ-term $\lambda x_1 x_2 \ldots x_n.E$, where E is not a λ-abstraction and—furthermore—if E contains any subexpressions which are themselves λ-abstractions, then they must be supercombinators as well. The difference between a combinator in the λ-calculus and a supercombinator is that the body E of a supercombinator may contain constants, whereas the body E of a combinator can only contain free variables.

Surjective pairing A group of list-manipulating operations $CONS$, $HEAD$ and $TAIL$ have the surjective pairing property if the following reduction holds:

$$CONS\ (HEAD\ x)(TAIL\ x) \rightarrow x,$$

for all x and not just for those values constructed out of $CONS$. If a relation $\rightarrow$ has the surjective pairing property, then it lacks the Church–Rosser property. See Barendregt (1984), p. 133, for more information about this.

Topological sort *Topological sort* is the name given to the process of turning a partially ordered set into a totally—or linearly—ordered one.

Total order A *total order* is a relation $\sqsubseteq$ which, in addition to being a partial order, is also such that every pair of elements in the field of $\sqsubseteq$ are related by $\sqsubseteq$, that is to say,

$$(\forall d, e \in D)(d \sqsubseteq e \vee e \sqsubseteq d).$$

A *totally ordered set* is a pair $(D, \sqsubseteq)$ such that $\sqsubseteq$ is a total order over D.

Unfolding Let $E = E'$ be the definition that we wish to unfold, where the expression E is defined as E', and let $F = F'$ be the equation that is to be transformed. For this to be possible an instance of E, say E_1, must occur in F'. Let E_1' be the corresponding instance of E'. To unfold the definition $E = E'$ in the equation $F = F'$ we replace the occurrence of E in F', namely E_1, with E_1'. Call the result of this substitution F''. Then we can add the equation $F = F''$ to our program.

Weak Church–Rosser property A binary relation $\rightarrow$ is said to be *weakly Church–Rosser* iff it satisfies the weak diamond property.

Weak diamond property See *local confluence*.

Annotated Bibliography

Annotations

Chapter 1: Introduction

The concept of referential transparency was introduced into computing in Landin (1964). Stoy (1977) contains a good discussion. After a little uncertainty about its significance, a consensus is now emerging about what transparency amounts to. A programming language is referentially transparent if it admits of equational reasoning, that is to say, if you can substitute equals for equals in the same scope with impunity. Josephs (1986) investigates the consequences of adding side-effects to a purely functional language.

The language KRC is described in Turner (1982b), Miranda in Turner (1985b, 1986) and Orwell in Wadler (1985a, 1985b). Orwell is presently in a state of flux, but should stabilize soon as it metamorphoses into the Oxford Language (OL).

Chapter 2: Lispkit Lisp

The Lispkit language and its SECD machine implementation are fully described in Henderson (1980) and the two volumes of *The LispKit Manual*, which are Henderson, Jones and Jones (1983a, 1983b). Although it is a very simple language, Lispkit is not a toy one; it is actually being used currently to do serious work in computing, especially in the area of the specification of what programs should do. The language **me-too** was developed to be used in the design of software components and it 'is supported by a range of tools written in Lispkit including a translator which translates **me-too** into Lispkit and the shell of an interactive prototyping tool, ProtoKit, which allows **me-too** specifications to be executed' (Henderson (1984), p. 2). The reports by Henderson and Minkowitz (1985), Minkowitz (1984) and Clark (1985) give more details. The last report should be more widely known, if only for its title, which is *Ada as a Complement to Lispkit for the Prototyping of Software Design*! The **me-too** language is similar to the specification language VDM, which is described in Jones (1986); and Naftalin (1986) briefly describes the semantics of both Lispkit and **me-too**.

There are few books which deal with the issues involved in writing programs in a lazy functional language, but luckily there is an excellent book, namely Bird and Wadler (1988). Glaser, Hankin and Till (1984) and Henson (1987) both contain chapters on applicative programming in a lazy language. Hughes's monograph (1984b) is also useful, but very short. Several books deal with programming in a strict functional language. Wikström (1987) is a thorough recent book which is an introduction to programming using Standard ML. Abelson and Sussman (1985) is an excellent book which uses Scheme and much of Allen (1978) is very useful.

Chapter 3: Combinatory Logic

Combinatory logic was first studied by Schönfinkel (1924), but most of the early work was done by Curry. Curry and Feys (1958) and Curry, Hindley and Seldin (1972) form a comprehensive treatment, although the former is a little dated now. A very good recent introduction to the subject is Hindley and Seldin (1986), which is an updated and improved version of Hindley, Lercher and Seldin (1972). Other useful introductions are Stenlund (1972) and Fitch (1974). Seldin and Hindley (1980) is a collection of papers on various aspects of combinatory logic.

Chapter 4: Translating Lispkit into Combinators

According to Turner (1984), p. 5.28, it was Petznick (1970) who first had the idea of using combinatory logic as the machine code of an abstract machine, but it was Turner (1979a, 1979b, 1981a) who made it into a practicable implementation method by devising an efficient abstraction algorithm. Turner (1979b) contains all the information you need in order to translate a language like Lispkit or SASL into combinators.

Chapter 5: Graph-reduction

The method of graph-reduction was first put forward by Wadsworth (1971) for the λ-calculus and it was used by Turner (1981a) in order to evaluate CL-terms.

Fasel and Keller (1987) is a recent collection of papers devoted to the subject. Barendregt, *et al.* (1987) provides a rigorous foundation for the technique when cyclic graphs are allowed.

A related topic is that of subtree replacement systems and generalizations of these. Useful publications in this area include Brainerd (1969), Rosen (1973), O'Donnell (1977, 1985), Staples (1980a, 1980b, 1980c), Raoult (1984) and Kennaway (1987). I only came across such systems a few months ago. If I had known of them when I started writing this book, then I would have used them as a unifying framework for the discussion of such subjects as the reduction of CL-terms, λ-terms and source reduction.

Chapter 6: The Lambda Calculus

Hindley and Seldin (1986) is an excellent introduction to the λ-calculus, whereas Barendregt (1984) is an encyclopaedic coverage of the whole field.

Chapter 7: Bracket Abstraction Algorithms

Bracket abstraction algorithms are briefly discussed in Curry and Feys (1958) and Curry, Seldin and Hindley (1972), although they made their first appearance much earlier. The search for efficient algorithms only started when their utility in computing was appreciated. Abdali (1976) presents a linear algorithm, as do Castan, Durand and Lemaître (1987) and Piperno (1987). All of these algorithms make use of finitely generated infinite sets of combinators, though the sets are different in each case.

Turner (1979a) devised an algorithm which made use of only a finite set of combinators, yet which was usable in a compiler for a functional language. It is also linear. Joy, Rayward-Smith and Burton (1985) survey about fifteen algorithms that only use a finite set of combinators and establish their complexity.

An interesting idea due to Kennaway and Sleep (1987a, 1987b) is the use of director strings. This leads to a more efficient algorithm than Turner's.

Chapter 8: Supercombinators

Supercombinators—by that name—were introduced by Hughes (1982, 1984a) and they have generated a lot of interest. See, for example, Peyton Jones (1986, 1987). The latter contains a great deal of information about the G-machine—introduced by Augustsson (1984) and Johnsson (1984)—which is the most efficient lazy implementation technique at present for purely applicative languages. A related idea is the technique of lambda lifting, which is described in Johnsson (1986).

Chapter 9: Pattern-matching

The treatment of pattern-matching presented in Chapter 9 is based on that found in Turner (1981a). A slightly different approach is presented by Wadler in Peyton Jones (1987). He also extends the method to deal with data types other than lists. Boutel (1987) is—amongst other things—an elementary introduction to pattern-matching and Abramson (1986) generalizes the technique—in a different way from Wadler—to what he calls one-way unification by introducing a unification-based conditional binding expression into SASL.

Chapter 10: Categorical Combinators

Categorical combinatory logic was first introduced in Curien (1985a, 1985b) and it is fully explained in Curien (1986). It is based on category theory—explained, for example, in MacLane (1971)—and especially on the fact that the typed λ-calculus is equivalent to the theory of Cartesian closed categories. See Lambek (1980) and Scott (1980) for details of this equivalence. The categorical abstract machine (CAM) is described in Cousineau, Curien and Mauny (1985). Curien's work is refined in an excellent series of reports by Lins (1985a, 1985b, 1985c, 1986b), which—amongst other things—show how categorical combinators can be evaluated on a graph-reduction machine. Sander (1987) is also useful.

A close cousin of the CAM is the linear abstract machine, which is described in Girard and Lafont (1987) and which is based on the linear logic devised by Girard (1987). Avron (1987) investigates the relation between linear logic and relevance logics and these are thoroughly investigated in Anderson and Belnap (1975).

Yaghi (1984) shows how a functional language can be translated into a different intensional logic, this time one based on the work of Carnap and Montague.

Chapter 11: Reduction and Transformation

According to Hughes (1984a), Turner's implementation of KRC used the method of source reduction. Anane and Axford (1986, 1987) also use the technique in the implementation of ALGER.

Backus (1978) describes the FP system and Henson (1987) has a useful chapter on it. Wadler (1984) explains the listless transformer. The unfold/fold system of program transformation is used in Burstall and Darlington (1977) and in Darlington (1978, 1982, 1987); Bird (1986) and Bird and Hughes (1987) use a similar system, though other ideas are also incorporated. Wand (1980) develops continuation-based program transformations.

Ershov's interest in mixed computation started as a result of his study of optimizing transformations in compilers, in particular constant propagation and loop unloading. This early work is reported in Ershov (1977). After this he surveyed the literature looking for similar ideas and this is reported in Ershov (1978). The article Ershov (1982) is a good recent introduction. The work being done in Denmark in this area is reported in Jones, Sestoft and Søndergaard (1985) and Sestoft (1986). Futamura (1983) is an account from a Japanese researcher.

For the use of partial evaluation in Prolog—where it is sometimes called partial execution—see Shapiro (1987) and Pereira and Shieber (1987).

The technique of using partial evaluation to produce meaningful error-messages in a combinator-based compiler is discussed in Turner (1981a), Toyn and Runciman (1986) and Henson (1987). In such a connection it is usually called *symbolic evaluation* or *formal reduction*. Henson (1987) also mentions that it can be used to provide a pretty-printing facility.

Chapter 12: Strictness Analysis

Domain theory was developed in the context of giving the denotational semantics of programming languages. Scott provided the mathematics and Strachey the motivation and application. They wrote quite a lot and Scott and Strachey (1971) is a good early paper. More recent accounts are to be found in Bird (1976), Stoy (1977), Allison (1986) and Schmidt (1986). The last-mentioned book is the best.

The method of abstract interpretation was first studied extensively by the Cousots—see, for example, Cousot and Cousot (1977)—but Mycroft (1981) was the first to apply the method to functional languages. His work is restricted to functions defined by first-order recursion equations over flat domains, but later workers have generalized the method. See, in particular, Burn, Hankin and Abramsky (1985). Wray (1986) and Hughes (1987a) have extended the technique of abstract interpretation in other directions. Clack and Peyton Jones (1985) is a good straightforward introduction and

Abramsky and Hankin (1987) is a collection of recent papers on the topic.

Chapter 13: Type Systems

The theory of types was introduced into logic by Whitehead and Russell (1925). Andrews (1986) is a good recent exposition.

Hindley (1969) was the first to realize that the unification algorithm of Robinson (1965) could be used to assign types to CL-terms. (Paterson and Wegman (1978) present a linear first-order unification algorithm.) Milner (1978) extended Hindley's work to include **let**-clauses and provided a semantics for the type system he used. Damas and Milner (1982) and Damas (1985) tie up the loose ends. Holmström (1983) provides a proof-theoretic approach.

Peyton Jones (1987) and Henson (1987) both contain discussions of Milner's type-assignment algorithm from an implementation point of view, but Henson's treatment is only informal.

ML was the first functional language to incorporate Milner's ideas. It is described in Gordon, Milner and Wadsworth (1979) and Wikström (1987). Miranda—described in Turner (1985b, 1986)—and Orwell—described in Wadler (1985a, 1985b)—are recent examples of applicative languages whose type systems are based on Milner's work.

Appendix A: Simple Lispkit System

There are several good books available on the compilation of imperative languages which contain material on the techniques of character handling, lexical analysis and syntax analysis that are also necessary for the implementation of functional languages. Bornat (1979), Brown (1979) and Terry (1987) are all good, straightforward introductions. Aho, Ullman and Sethi (1986) is a thorough textbook—Aho and Ullman (1977) is an earlier version of this—and Aho and Ullman (1972, 1973) is an encyclopaedic coverage of the whole field. Backhouse (1979) is a very readable book which deals with the syntax of programming languages.

Petznick (1970) was the first to have the idea of using combinatory logic as the machine code of an abstract machine, but—being unable to devise an efficient abstraction algorithm—he was not able to turn it into a viable proposition. It was Turner (1979b) who did this, though he knew nothing of Petznick's work until later. Hughes (1982, 1984a) extended the idea to supercombinators. The books by Glaser, Hankin and Till (1984) and Henson (1987) both contain chapters on implementation issues, whereas Peyton

Jones (1987) is a thorough exposition which deals mainly with supercombinator methods and the G-machine.

References

The following abbreviations are used in this bibliography: *ACM* abbreviates *Association for Computing Machinery* and *LNCS* abbreviates *Lecture Notes in Computer Science*, and where would computer science be without this series of books?

Abdali, S.K., (1976), "An Abstraction Algorithm for Combinatory Logic", *The Journal of Symbolic Logic*, vol. 41, pp. 222–224.

Abelson, H., and G.J. Sussman, (1985), *Structure and Interpretation of Computer Programs*, London, The MIT Press.

Abramsky, S., and C.L. Hankin, (eds.), (1987), *Abstract Interpretation of Declarative Languages*, Chichester, Ellis Horwood.

Abramson, H., (1986), "A Prological Definition of HASL: A Purely Functional Language with Unification-Based Conditional Binding Expressions", in DeGroot and Lindstrom (1986), pp. 73–129.

Aho, A.V., J.E. Hopcroft and J.D. Ullman, (1983), *Data Structures and Algorithms*, London, Addison-Wesley.

Aho, A.V., and J.D. Ullman, (1972), *The Theory of Parsing, Translation, and Compiling*, vol. 1, *Parsing*, Englewood Cliffs (New Jersey), Prentice-Hall.

Aho, A.V., and J.D. Ullman, (1973), *The Theory of Parsing, Translation, and Compiling*, vol. 2, *Compiling*, Englewood Cliffs (New Jersey), Prentice-Hall.

Aho, A.V., and J.D. Ullman, (1977), *Principles of Compiler Design*, London, Addison-Wesley.

Aho, A.V., J.D. Ullman and R. Sethi, (1986), *Compilers: Principles, Techniques, Tools*, London, Addison-Wesley.

Allen, J., (1978), *Anatomy of Lisp*, Maidenhead, McGraw-Hill.

Allison, L., (1986), *A Practical Introduction to Denotational Semantics*, Cambridge, Cambridge University Press.

Anane, R., and T.H. Axford, (1986), *Description of the Functional Language ALGER*, Computer Science Report CSR–86–16, Centre for Computing and Computer Science, University of Birmingham.

Anane, R., and T.H. Axford, (1987), *Implementation of the Functional Language ALGER*, Computer Science Report CSR–87–3, Centre for Computing and Computer Science, University of Birmingham.

Anderson, A.R., and N.D. Belnap, Jr., (1975), *Entailment: The Logic of Relevance and Necessity*, vol. 1, Guildford, Princeton University Press.

Andrews, P.B., (1986), *An Introduction to Mathematical Logic and Type Theory: To Truth through Proof*, London, Academic Press.

Anscombe, G.E.M., and P.T. Geach, (1963), *Three Philosophers*, Oxford, Blackwell.

Augustsson, L., (1984), "A Compiler for Lazy ML", *Proceedings of the ACM Symposium on Lisp and Functional Programming*, Austin (Texas), pp. 218–227.

Avron, A., (1987), *The Semantics and Proof Theory of Linear Logic*, Report ECS–LFCS–87–29, Laboratory for Foundations of Computer Science, University of Edinburgh.

Axford, T.H., (1985), *Writing Re-usable Programs in a Functional Language*, Computer Science Report CSR–85–5, Centre for Computing and Computer Science, University of Birmingham.

Axford, T.H., (1986), *Lecture Notes on Functional Programming*, Computer Science Report CSR–86–13, Centre for Computing and Computer Science, University of Birmingham.

Axford, T.H., (1987), *Reference Counting of Cyclic Graphs for Functional Programs*, Computer Science Report CSR–87–1, Centre for Computing and Computer Science, University of Birmingham.

Backhouse, R.C., (1979), *Syntax of Programming Languages: Theory and Practice*, Hemel Hempstead, Prentice-Hall.

Backus, J.W., (1978), "Can Programming be Liberated from the von Neumann Style? A Functional Style and its Algebra of Programs", *Communications of the ACM*, vol. 21, pp. 613–641.

Bailey, R., (1987), "An Introduction to Hope", in Eisenbach (1987), pp. 21–43.

Bakker, J.W. de, A.J. Nijman and P.C. Treleaven (eds.), (1987), *PARLE: Parallel Architectures and Languages Europe*, vol. 2, *Parallel Languages*, *LNCS*, vol. 259, Berlin, Springer-Verlag.

Bakker, J.W. de, W.-P. de Roever and G. Rozenberg (eds.), (1985), *Current Trends in Concurrency*, *LNCS*, vol. 224, London, Springer-Verlag.

Barendregt, H.P., (1984), *The Lambda Calculus: Its Syntax and Semantics*, Amsterdam, North-Holland, 1981^1, 1984^2.

Barendregt, H.P., M.C.J.D. van Eekelen, J.R.W. Glauert, J.R. Kennaway, M.J. Plasmeijer and M.R. Sleep, (1987), "Term Graph Rewriting", in de Bakker, Nijman and Treleaven (1987), pp. 141–158.

Barendregt, H.P., and M. van Leeuwen, (1985), "Functional Programming and the Language TALE", in de Bakker, de Roever and Rozenberg (1985), pp. 122–207.

Bibel, W., and P. Jorrand (eds.), (1987), *Fundamentals of Artificial Intelligence: An Advanced Course*, London, Springer-Verlag.

Bird, R.S., (1976), *Programs and Machines: An Introduction to the Theory of Computation*, Chichester, Wiley.

Bird, R.S., (1986), *An Introduction to the Theory of Lists*, Technical Monograph PRG–56, Oxford University Computing Laboratory.

Bird, R.S., and J. Hughes, (1984), *The KRC Users Guide*, Oxford University Programming Research Group Memo.

266

Bird, R.S., and J. Hughes, (1987), "The Alpha-Beta Algorithm: An Exercise in Program Transformation", *Information Processing Letters*, vol. 24, pp. 53–57.

Bird, R.S., and P. Wadler, (1988), *An Introduction to Functional Programming*, Hemel Hempstead, Prentice-Hall.

Bornat, R., (1979), *Understanding and Writing Compilers: A Do-it-yourself Guide*, London, Macmillan.

Boutel, B., (1987), "Combinators as Machine Code for Implementing Functional Languages", in Eisenbach (1987), pp. 141–155.

Brady, J.M., (1977), *The Theory of Computer Science: A Programming Approach*, London, Chapman and Hall.

Brainerd, W.S., (1969), "Tree Generating Regular Systems", *Information and Control*, vol. 14, pp. 217–231.

Brauer, W., (ed.), (1985), *Automata, Languages and Programming, LNCS*, vol. 194, London, Springer-Verlag.

Brown, P.J., (1979), *Writing Interactive Compilers and Interpreters*, Chichester, Wiley.

Bruijn, N.G. de, (1972), "Lambda Calculus Notation with Nameless Dummies: A Tool for Automatic Formula Manipulation, with Application to the Church-Rosser Theorem", *Indagationes Mathematicae*, vol. 34, pp. 381–392.

Burge, W.H., (1975), *Recursive Programming Techniques*, Reading (Massachusetts), Addison-Wesley.

Burn, G.L., C.L. Hankin and S. Abramsky, (1985), *The Theory and Practice of Strictness Analysis for Higher Order Functions*, Research Report DoC 85/6, Department of Computing, Imperial College of Science and Technology, University of London.

Burstall, R.M., and J. Darlington, (1977), "A Transformation System for Developing Recursive Programs", *Journal of the ACM*, vol. 24, pp. 44–67.

267

Burstall, R.M., D.B. MacQueen and D.T. Sannella, (1981), *Hope: An Experimental Applicative Language*, Internal Report CSR–62–80, Department of Computer Science, University of Edinburgh.

Burton, F.W., (1982), "A Linear Space Translation of Functional Programs to Turner Combinators", *Information Processing Letters*, vol. 14, pp. 201–204.

Castan, M., M.–H. Durand and M. Lemaître, (1987), "A Set of Combinators for Abstraction in Linear Space", *Information Processing Letters*, vol. 24, pp. 183–188.

Church, A., (1951), *The Calculi of Lambda-Conversion*, Princeton, Princeton University Press.

Church, A., (1956), *Introduction to Mathematical Logic*, vol.1, Princeton, Princeton University Press.

Clack, C. and S.L. Peyton Jones, (1985), "Strictness Analysis—A Practical Approach", in Jouannaud (1985a), pp. 35–49.

Clark, R.G., (1985), *Ada as a Complement to Lispkit for the Prototyping of Software Design*, Computing Science Technical Report TR–21, Department of Computing Science, University of Stirling.

Cohen, J., (1981), "Garbage Collection of Linked Data Structures", *ACM Computing Surveys*, vol. 13, pp. 341–367.

Coppo, M., M. Dezani-Ciancoglini and B. Venneri, (1980), "Principal Type Schemes and λ-Calculus Semantics", in Seldin and Hindley (1980), pp. 535–560.

Cousineau, G., P.–L. Curien and M. Mauny, (1985), "The Categorical Abstract Machine", in Jouannaud (1985a), pp. 50–64.

Cousineau, G., P.–L. Curien and B. Robinet, (eds.), (1986), *Combinators and Functional Programming Languages*, *LNCS*, vol. 242, London, Springer-Verlag.

Cousot, P., and R. Cousot, (1977), "Abstract Interpretation: A Unified Lattice Model for Static Analysis of Programs by Construction or Approximation of Fixed Points", in *Proceedings of the Fourth ACM Symposium on Principles of Programming Languages*, Los Angeles, pp. 238–252.

Curien, P.–L., (1985a), "Categorical Combinatory Logic", in Brauer (1985), pp. 130–139.

Curien, P.–L., (1985b), "Typed Categorical Combinatory Logic", in Ehrig, et al., (1985), pp. 157–172.

Curien, P.–L., (1986), *Categorical Combinators, Sequential Algorithms and Functional Programming*, London, Pitman.

Curry, H.B., (1930), "Grundlagen der kombinatorischen Logik", *American Journal of Mathematics*, vol. 52, pp. 509–536 and 789–834.

Curry, H.B., (1932), "Some Additions to the Theory of Combinators", *American Journal of Mathematics*, vol. 54, pp. 551–558.

Curry, H.B., (1933), "Apparent Variables from the Standpoint of Combinatory Logic", *Annals of Mathematics*, vol. 34, pp. 381–404.

Curry, H.B., (1963), *Foundations of Mathematical Logic*, Maidenhead, McGraw-Hill.

Curry, H.B., and R. Feys, (1958), *Combinatory Logic*, vol. I, Amsterdam, North-Holland.

Curry, H.B., J.R. Hindley and J.P. Seldin, (1972), *Combinatory Logic*, vol. II, Amsterdam, North-Holland.

Damas, L., (1985), *Type Assignment in Programming Languages*, Internal Report CST–33–85, Department of Computer Science, University of Edinburgh.

Damas, L., and R. Milner, (1982), "Principal Type-Schemes for Functional Programs", in *The Ninth Annual ACM Symposium on Principles of Programming Languages*, Albuquerque (New Mexico), pp. 207–212.

Danicic, I., (1983), *Lisp Programming*, London, Blackwell Scientific Publications.

Darlington, J., (1978), "A Synthesis of Several Sorting Algorithms", *Acta Informatica*, vol. 11, pp. 1–30.

Darlington, J., (1982), "Program Transformation", in Darlington, Henderson and Turner (1982), pp. 193–215.

Darlington, J., (1987), "Software Development in Declarative Languages", in Eisenbach (1987), pp. 71–85.

Darlington, J., P. Henderson and D.A. Turner, (eds.), (1982), *Functional Programming and its Applications: An Advanced Course*, Cambridge, Cambridge University Press.

DeGroot, D., and G. Lindstrom, (eds.), (1986), *Logic Programming: Functions, Relations, and Equations*, Englewood Cliffs (New Jersey), Prentice-Hall.

Diller, A., (1985), *An Evaluation of Functional Language Implementation Techniques*, M.Sc. Dissertation, University of Oxford.

Duce, D.A., (ed.), (1985), *SERC Distributed Computer Systems*, Stevenage, Peregrinus.

Duijvestijn, A.J.W., and P.C. Lockemann, (eds.), (1981), *Trends in Information Processing Systems*, *LNCS*, vol. 123, London, Springer-Verlag.

Dummett, M., (1981), *Frege: Philosophy of Language*, London, Duckworth, 1973[1], 1981[2].

Ehrig, H., C. Floyd, M. Nivat and J. Thatcher, (eds.), (1985), *Mathematical Foundations of Software Development*, *LNCS*, vol. 185, London, Springer-Verlag.

Ehrig, H., R. Kowalski, G. Levi and U. Montanari, (eds.), (1987), *TAPSOFT '87*, *LNCS*, vol. 250, Berlin, Springer-Verlag.

Eisenbach, S., (1987), *Functional Programming: Languages, Tools and Architectures*, Chichester, Ellis Horwood.

Ershov, A.P., (1977), "On the Partial Computation Principle", *Information Processing Letters*, vol. 6, pp. 38–41.

Ershov, A.P., (1978), "On the Essence of Compilation", in Neuhold (1978).

Ershov, A.P., (1982), "Mixed Computation: Potential Applications and Problems for Study", *Theoretical Computer Science*, vol. 18, pp. 41–67.

Evans, A., (1968), "PAL—A Language Designed for Teaching Programming Linguistics", *Proceedings ACM National Conference*.

Even, S., (1979), *Graph Algorithms*, London, Pitman.

Fasel, J.H., and R.M. Keller, (eds.), (1987), *Graph Reduction, LNCS*, vol. 279, London, Springer-Verlag.

Feys, R., and F.B. Fitch, (eds.), (1969), *Dictionary of Symbols of Mathematical Logic*, Amsterdam, North-Holland.

Fitch, F.B., (1974), *Elements of Combinatory Logic*, London, Yale University Press.

Frege, G., (1893), *Grundgesetze der Arithmetik: Begriffsschriftlich abgeleitet*, Band 1, Jena, Pohle.

Friedman, D.P., and D.S. Wise, (1976), "Cons should not Evaluate its Arguments", in Michaelson and Milner (1976).

Futamura, Y., (1983), "Partial Computation of Programs", in Goto, *et al.* (1983), pp. 1–35.

Ganzinger, H., and N.D. Jones (eds.), (1986), *Programs as Data Objects, LNCS*, vol. 217, London, Springer-Verlag.

Geach, P.T., (1963), "Frege", in Anscombe and Geach (1963), pp. 127-162.

Geach, P.T., (1972), *Logic Matters*, Oxford, Blackwell.

Ghezzi, C., and M. Jazayeri, (1982), *Programming Language Concepts*, Chichester, Wiley.

Girard, J.–Y., (1987), "Linear Logic", *Theoretical Computer Science*, vol. 50, pp. 1–101.

Girard, J.–Y., and Y. Lafont, (1987), "Linear Logic and Lazy Computation", in Ehrig, *et al.* (1987), pp. 52–66.

Glaser, H., C. Hankin and D. Till, (1984), *Principles of Functional Programming*, Hemel Hempstead, Prentice-Hall.

Gordon, M., R. Milner and C. Wadsworth, (1979), *Edinburgh LCF*, *LNCS*, vol. 78, Berlin, Springer-Verlag.

Goto, E., K. Furukawa, R. Nakajima, I. Nakata and A. Yonezawa, (eds.), (1983), *RIMS Symposia on Software Science and Engineering, LNCS*, vol. 147, London, Springer-Verlag.

Hardin, T., and A. Laville, (1986), "Proof of Termination of the Rewriting System Subst on CCL", *Theoretical Computer Science*, vol. 46, pp. 305–317.

Hatcher, W.S., (1982), *The Logical Foundations of Mathematics*, Oxford, Pergamon.

Heijenoort, J. van, (ed.), (1967), *From Frege to Gödel: A Source Book in Mathematical Logic, 1879–1931*, London, Harvard University Press.

Henderson, P., (1980), *Functional Programming: Application and Implementation*, Hemel Hempstead, Prentice-Hall.

Henderson, P., (1984), **me-too**—*A Language for Software Specification and Model Building*, Functional Programming Note FPN–9, Department of Computing Science, University of Stirling.

Henderson, P., G.A. Jones and S.B. Jones, (1983a), *The LispKit Manual*, vol. 1, Technical Monograph PRG–32(1), Oxford University Computing Laboratory.

Henderson, P., G.A. Jones and S.B. Jones, (1983b), *The LispKit Manual*, vol. 2, *Sources*, Technical Monograph PRG–32(2), Oxford University Computing Laboratory.

Henderson, P., and S.B. Jones, (1984), *Shells of Functional Operating Systems*, Functional Programming Note FPN–4, Department of Computing Science, University of Stirling.

Henderson, P., and C. Minkowitz, (1985), *The me-too Method of Software Design*, Functional Programming Note FPN–10, Department of Computing Science, University of Stirling.

Henderson, P., and J.H. Morris, (1976), "A Lazy Evaluator", in *The Third ACM Symposium on Principles of Programming Languages*, Atlanta (Georgia), pp. 95–103.

Henson, M.C., (1987), *Elements of Functional Languages*, London, Blackwell Scientific Publications.

Hindley, J.R., (1969), "The Principal Type-Scheme of an Object in Combinatory Logic", *Transactions of the American Mathematical Society*, vol. 146, pp. 29–60.

Hindley, J.R., (1986), "Combinators and Lambda-Calculus: A Short Outline", in Cousineau, Curien and Robinet, (1986), pp. 104–122.

Hindley, J.R., and J.P. Seldin, (1986), *Introduction to Combinators and λ-Calculus*, Cambridge, Cambridge University Press.

Hindley, J.R., B. Lercher and J.P. Seldin, (1972), *Introduction to Combinatory Logic*, Cambridge, Cambridge University Press.

Hirokawa, S., (1985), "Complexity of the Combinator Reduction Machine", *Theoretical Computer Science*, vol. 41, pp. 289–303.

Hoare, C.A.R., and J. Shepherdson, (eds.), (1985), *Mathematical Logic and Programming Languages*, Hemel Hempstead, Prentice-Hall.

Holmström, S., (1983), *Polymorphic Type Systems—A Proof-Theoretic Approach*, Report 6, Programming Methodology Group, University of Göteborg and Chalmers University of Technology.

Huet, G., (1987), "Deduction and Computation", in Bibel and Jorrand (1987), pp. 39–74.

Hughes, J., (1982), *Graph Reduction with Super-Combinators*, Technical Monograph PRG–28, Oxford University Computing Laboratory.

Hughes, J., (1984a), *The Design and Implementation of Programming Languages*, Technical Monograph PRG–40, Oxford University Computing Laboratory.

Hughes, J., (1984b), *Why Functional Programming Matters*, Report 16, Programming Methodology Group, University of Göteborg and Chalmers University of Technology.

Hughes, J., (1987a), *Backwards Analysis of Functional Programs*, Departmental Research Report CSC/87/R3, Department of Computing Science, University of Glasgow.

Hughes, J., (1987b), *Managing Reduction Graphs with Reference Counts*, Departmental Research Report CSC/87/R2, Department of Computing Science, University of Glasgow.

Jensen, K., and N. Wirth, (1978), *Pascal: User Manual and Report*, Berlin, Springer-Verlag, 1975[1], 1978[2].

Johnsson, T., (1984), "Efficient Compilation of Lazy Evaluation", *Proceedings of the ACM Conference on Compiler Construction*, Montreal, pp. 58–69.

Johnsson, T, (1986), *Lambda-Lifting—Transforming Programs to Recursive Equations*, Report 24, Programming Methodology Group, University of Göteborg and Chalmers University of Technology.

Johnsson, T, (1987), *Target Code Generation from G-Machine Code*, Report 39, Programming Methodology Group, University of Göteborg and Chalmers University of Technology.

Jones, C.B., (1986), *Systematic Software Development Using VDM*, Hemel Hempstead, Prentice-Hall.

Jones, N.D., P. Sestoft and H. Søndergaard, (1985), "An Experiment in Partial Evaluation: The Generation of a Compiler Generator", in Jouannaud (1985b), pp.124-140.

Jones, S.B., (1983), *Abstract Machine Support for Purely Functional Operating Systems*, Technical Monograph PRG–34, Oxford University Computing Laboratory.

Josephs, M.B., (1986), *Functional Programming with Side-Effects*, Technical Monograph PRG–55, Oxford University Computing Laboratory.

Jouannaud, J.–P., (ed.), (1985a), (FPLCA) *Functional Programming Languages and Computer Architecture*, *LNCS*, vol. 201, London, Springer-Verlag.

Jouannaud, J.–P., (ed.), (1985b), *Rewriting Techniques and Applications*, *LNCS*, vol. 202, London, Springer-Verlag.

Joy, M.S., and T.H. Axford, (1987), *A Standard for a Graph Representation for Functional Programming*, Computer Science Report CSR–87–4, Centre for Computing and Computer Science, University of Birmingham.

Joy, M.S., V.J. Rayward-Smith and F.W. Burton, (1985), "Efficient Combinator Code", *Computer Languages*, vol. 10, pp. 211–224.

Kennaway, J.R., (1984), *The Complexity of a Translation of λ-Calculus to Combinators*, Internal Report CSA/13/1984, School of Information Systems, University of East Anglia.

Kennaway, J.R., (1987), "On 'On Graph Rewritings'", *Theoretical Computer Science*, vol. 52, pp. 37–58.

Kennaway, J.R., and M.R. Sleep, (1987a), *Director Strings as Combinators*, Internal Report SYS–C87–06, School of Information Systems, University of East Anglia.

Kennaway, J.R., and M.R. Sleep, (1987b), "Variable Abstraction in $O(n \log n)$ Space", *Information Processing Letters*, vol. 24, pp. 343–349.

Kernighan, B.W., and P.J. Plauger, (1981), *Software Tools in Pascal*, Wokingham, Addison-Wesley.

Kleene, S.C., (1952), *Introduction to Metamathematics*, Amsterdam, North-Holland.

Knuth, D.E., (1973), *The Art of Computer Programming*, vol. 1, *Fundamental Algorithms*, Reading (Massachusettes), Addison-Wesley.

Knuth, D.E., and P.B. Bendix, "Simple Word Problems in Universal Algebras", in Leech (1970), pp. 263–297.

Lambek, J., (1980), "From λ-Calculus to Cartesian Closed Categories", in Seldin and Hindley (1980), pp. 375–402.

Landin, P.J., (1964), "The Mechanical Evaluation of Expressions", *The Computer Journal*, vol. 6, pp. 308–320.

Landin, P.J., (1965a), "A Correspondence Between ALGOL 60 and Church's Lambda Notation: Part I", *Communications of the ACM*, vol. 8, pp. 89–101.

Landin, P.J., (1965b), "A Correspondence Between ALGOL 60 and Church's Lambda Notation: Part II", *Communications of the ACM*, vol. 8, pp. 158–165.

Landin, P.J., (1966), "The Next 700 Programming Languages", *Communications of the ACM*, vol. 9, pp. 157–166.

Leech, J., (ed.), (1970), *Computational Problems in Abstract Algebra*, Oxford, Pergamon.

Lins, R.D., (1985a), *The Complexity of a Translation of λ-Calculus to Categorical Combinators*, Computing Laboratory Report 27, University of Kent at Canterbury.

Lins, R.D., (1985b), *A New Formula for the Execution of Categorical Combinators*, Computing Laboratory Report 33, University of Kent at Canterbury.

Lins, R.D., (1985c), *On the Efficiency of Categorical Combinators as a Rewriting System*, Computing Laboratory Report 34, University of Kent at Canterbury.

Lins, R.D., (1986a), *Categorical Multi-Combinators*, Computing Laboratory Report 41, University of Kent at Canterbury.

Lins, R.D., (1986b), *A Graph Reduction Machine for Execution of Categorical Combinators*, Computing Laboratory Report 36, University of Kent at Canterbury.

MacLane, S, (1971), *Categories for the Working Mathematician*, Berlin, Springer-Verlag.

Manes, E.G., and M.A. Arbib, (1986), *Algebraic Approaches to Program Semantics*, London, Springer-Verlg.

Markov, A.A., (1961), *Theory of Algorithms*, Jerusalem, Israel Program for Scientific Translations.

Meira, S.R.L., (1983), *Sorting Algorithms in KRC: Implementation, Proof and Performance*, Computing Laboratory Report 14, University of Kent at Canterbury.

Meira, S.R.L., (1984), "Optimized Combinatoric Code for Applicative Language Implementation", in Paul and Robinet (1984), pp. 206–216.

Mendelson, E., (1964), *Introduction to Mathematical Logic*, London, Van Nostrand.

Menger, K., (1955), "On Variables in Mathematics and in Natural Science", *The British Journal for the Philosophy of Science*, vol. V (1954–1955), pp. 134–142.

Michaelson, S., and R. Milner, (eds.), (1976), *Automata, Languages, and Programming*, Edinburgh, Edinburgh University Press.

Milner, R., (1978), "A Theory of Type Polymorphism in Programming", *Journal of Computer and System Sciences*, vol. 17, pp. 348–375.

Minkowitz, C., (1984), *A Methodology for the Prototyping of Software Design*, Computing Science Technical Report TR–14, Department of Computing Science, University of Stirling.

Michie, D., (1968), " 'Memo' Functions and Machine Learning", *Nature*, vol. 218, pp. 19–22.

Monk, J.D., (1976), *Mathematical Logic*, Berlin, Springer-Verlag.

Mycroft, A., (1981), (AIOTAP) *Abstract Interpretation and Optimising Transformations for Applicative Programs*, Internal Report CST–15–81, Department of Computer Science, University of Edinburgh.

Mycroft, A., (1984), "Polymorphic Type Schemes and Recursive Definitions", in *Proceedings of the International Symposium on Programming*, Toulouse, pp. 217–239.

Naftalin, M., (1986), "An Experiment in Practical Semantics", in Robinet and Wilhelm (1986), pp. 144–159.

Naur, P., (ed.), (1963), "Revised Report on the Algorithmic Language ALGOL 60", *Communications of the ACM*, vol. 6, pp. 1–17; and *The Computer Journal*, vol. 5, pp. 349–367; and *Numerische Mathematik*, vol. 4, pp. 420–453.

Néel, D., (ed.), (1982), *Tools and Notions for Program Construction: An Advanced Course*, Cambridge, Cambridge University Press.

Neuhold, E.J., (ed.), (1978), *Formal Descriptions of Programming Concepts*, Amsterdam, North-Holland.

Nori, K.V., (ed.), (1986), *Foundations of Software Technology and Theoretical Computer Science*, *LNCS*, vol. 241, London, Springer-Verlag.

Noshita, K., (1985), "Translation of Turner Combinators in $O(n \log n)$ Space", *Information Processing Letters*, vol. 20, pp. 71–74.

Noshita, K., and T. Hikita, (1985), "The **BC**-chain Method for Representing Combinators in Linear Space", *New Generation Computing*, vol. 3, pp. 131–144.

O'Donnell, M.J., (1977), *Computing in Systems Described by Equations*, *LNCS*, vol. 58, Berlin, Springer-Verlag.

O'Donnell, M.J., (1985), *Equational Logic as a Programming Language*, London, The MIT Press.

Orgass, R.J., and F.B. Fitch, (1969a), "A Theory of Computing Machines", *Studium Generale*, vol. 22, pp. 83–104.

Orgass, R.J., and F.B. Fitch, (1969b), "A Theory of Programming Languages", *Studium Generale*, vol. 22, pp. 113–136.

Paul, M., and B. Robinet, (eds.), (1984), *International Symposium on Programming*, *LNCS*, vol. 167, Berlin, Springer-Verlag.

Paulson, L.C., (1987), *Logic and Computation: Interactive Proof with Cambridge LCF*, Cambridge, Cambridge University Press.

Paterson, M.S., and M.N. Wegman, (1978), "Linear Unification", *Journal of Computer and Systems Sciences*, vol. 16, pp. 158–167.

Pereira, F.C.N., and S.M. Shieber, (1987), *Prolog and Natural-Language Analysis*, Stanford, Center for the Study of Language and Information.

Petznick, G., (1970), *Combinatory Programming*, Ph.D. Thesis, University of Wisconsin.

Peyton Jones, S.L., (1986), "An Introduction to Fully-Lazy Supercombinators", in Cousineau, Curien and Robinet (1986), pp. 176–208.

Peyton Jones, S.L., (1987), *The Implementation of Functional Programming Languages*, Hemel Hempstead, Prentice-Hall.

Piperno, A., (1987), "A Compositive Abstraction Algorithm for Combinatory Logic", in Ehrig, *et al.* (1987), pp. 39–51.

Pitt, D., S. Abramsky, A. Poigné and D. Rydeheard (eds.), (1986), *Category Theory and Computer Programming*, *LNCS*, vol. 240, London, Springer-Verlag.

Raoult, J.C., (1984), "On Graph Rewritings", *Theoretical Computer Science*, vol. 32, pp. 1–24.

Robinet, B., and R. Wilhelm, (eds.), (1986), *ESOP86*, *LNCS*, vol. 213, London, Springer-Verlag.

Robinson, J.A., (1965), "A Machine-Oriented Logic Based on the Resolution Principle", *Journal of the ACM*, vol. 12, pp. 23–41.

Rosen, B.K., (1973), "Tree-Manipulating Systems and Church-Rosser Theorems", *Journal of the ACM*, vol. 20, pp. 160–187.

Russell, B., (1956a), "On Denoting", in Russell (1956b), pp. 41–56.

Russell, B., (1956b), *Logic and Knowledge: Essays 1901–1950*, London, George Allen & Unwin.

Rydeheard, D.E., (1981), *Applications of Category Theory to Programming and Specification*, Ph.D. Thesis, University of Edinburgh.

Sadler, C., and S. Eisenbach, (1987), "Why Functional Programming?", in Eisenbach (1987), pp. 9–17.

Sander, H.P., (1987), *Categorical Combinators*, Report 38, Programming Methodology Group, University of Göteborg and Chalmers University of Technology.

Schmidt, D.A., (1986), *Denotational Semantics: A Methodology for Language Development*, London, Allyn and Bacon.

Schönfinkel, M., (1924), "Über die Bausteine der Mathematischen Logik", *Mathematische Annalen*, vol. 92, pp. 305-316.

Schönfinkel, M., (1967), "On the Building Blocks of Mathematical Logic", in van Heijenoort (1967), pp. 357–366.

Schorr, H., and W. Waite, (1967), "An Efficient Machine-Independent Procedure for Garbage Collection in Various List Structures", *Communications of the ACM*, vol. 10, pp. 501–506.

Scott, D.S., (1980), "Relating Theories of the λ-calculus", in Seldin and Hindley (1980), pp. 403–450.

Scott, D., and C. Strachey, (1971), *Towards a Mathematical Semantics for Computer Languages*, Technical Monograph PRG–6, Oxford University Computing Laboratory.

Seldin, J.P., and J.R. Hindley, (eds.), (1980), *To H.B.Curry: Essays on Combinatory Logic, Lambda Calculus and Formalism*, London, Academic Press.

Sestoft, P., (1986), "The Structure of a Self-Applicative Partial Evaluator", in Ganzinger and Jones (1986), pp. 236–256.

Shapiro, E., (1987), "Concurrent Prolog: A Progress Report", in Bibel and Jorrand (1987), pp. 277–313.

Sridhar, S., (1986), "An Implementation of OBJ2", in Nori (1986), pp. 81–95.

Staples, J., (1980a), "Computation on Graph-Like Expressions", *Theoretical Computer Science*, vol. 10, pp. 171–185.

Staples, J., (1980b), "Optimal Evaluation of Graph-Like Expressions", *Theoretical Computer Science*, vol. 10, pp. 297–316.

Staples, J., (1980c), "Speeding up Subtree Replacement Systems", *Theoretical Computer Science*, vol. 11, pp. 39–47.

Stenlund, S., (1972), *Combinators, λ-terms and Proof Theory*, Dordrecht (Holland), Reidel.

Stoy, J.E., (1977), *Denotational Semantics: The Scott-Strachey Approach to Programming Language Theory*, Cambridge (Massachusetts), The MIT Press.

Sufrin, B., (1982), "Formal Specification of a Display-Oriented Text Editor", *Science of Computer Programming*, vol. 1, pp. 157–202.

Swamy, M.N.S., and K. Thulasiraman, (1981), *Graphs, Networks, and Algorithms*, Chichester, Wiley.

Tarjan, R.E., (1972), "Depth-First Search and Linear Graph Algorithms", *SIAM Journal on Computing*, vol. 1, pp. 146–160.

Terry, P.D., (1987), *Programming Language Translation: A Practical Approach*, Wokingham, Addison-Wesley.

Thompson, S.J., (1985), *Laws in Miranda*, Computing Laboratory Report 35, University of Kent at Canterbury.

Toyn, I., and C. Runciman, (1986), "Adapting Combinator and SECD Machines to Display Snapshots of Functional Computations", *New Generation Computing*, vol. 4, pp. 339–363.

Turing, A.M., (1937), "The p-Functions in λ-K-Conversion", *The Journal of Symbolic Logic*, vol. 2, pp. 164ff.

Turner, D.A., (1976), *The SASL Language Manual*, Technical Report CS/75/1, Department of Computational Science, University of St Andrews.

Turner, D.A., (1979a), "Another Algorithm for Bracket Abstraction", *The Journal of Symbolic Logic*, vol. 44, pp. 267–270.

Turner, D.A., (1979b), "A New Implementation Technique for Applicative Languages", *Software—Practice and Experience*, vol. 9, pp. 31–49.

Turner, D.A., (1981a), *Aspects of the Implementation of Programming Languages: The Compilation of an Applicative Language to Combinatory Logic*, D.Phil. Thesis, University of Oxford.

Turner, D.A., (1981b), "The Future of Applicative Programming", in Duijvestijn and Lockemann (1981), pp. 334–348.

Turner, D.A., (1981c), "The Semantic Elegance of Functional Languages", *Proceedings ACM/MIT Conference on Functional Languages and Computer Architecture*, Portsmouth (Massachusetts), pp. 85–92.

Turner, D.A., (1982a), "Functional Programming and Proofs of Program Correctness", in Néel (1982), pp. 187–209.

Turner, D.A., (1982b), "Recursion Equations as a Programming Language", in Darlington, Henderson and Turner (1982), pp. 1–28.

Turner, D.A., (1984), "Combinator Reduction Machines", in *Proceedings of the International Workshop on High-Level Computer Architecture*, Los Angeles (California), pp. 5.26–5.38.

Turner, D.A., (1985a), "Functional Programs as Executable Specifications", in Hoare and Shepherdson (1985).

Turner, D.A., (1985b), "Miranda: A Non-Strict Functional Language with Polymorphic Types", in Jouannaud (1985a), pp.1–16.

Turner, D.A., (1986), "An Overview of Miranda", *ACM SIGPLAN Notices*, vol. 21, pp. 158–166.

Wadler, P., (1984), "Listlessness is Better than Laziness: Lazy Evaluation and Garbage Collection at Compile-Time", *ACM Symposium on Lisp and Functional Programming*, Austin (Texas), pp. 45–52.

Wadler, P., (1985a), "An Introduction to Orwell", Oxford University Programming Research Group Memo.

Wadler, P., (1985b), "The Programming Language Orwell", Oxford University Programming Research Group Memo.

Wadsworth, C.P., (1971), *Semantics and Pragmatics of the Lambda-Calculus*, D.Phil. Thesis, University of Oxford.

Wadsworth, C.P., (1976), "The Relation Between Computational and Denotational Properties for Scott's D_∞-Models of the Lambda Calculus", *SIAM Journal on Computing*, vol. 5, pp. 488–521.

Wadsworth, C.P., (1978), "Approximate Reduction and Lambda Calculus Models", *SIAM Journal on Computing*, vol. 7, pp. 337–356.

Wand, M., (1980), "Continuation Based Program Transformation Strategies", *Journal of the Association for Computing Machinery*, vol. 27, pp.164–180.

Whitehead, A.N., and B. Russell, (1925), *Principia Mathematica*, vol. 1, Cambridge, Cambridge University Press, 1910^1, 1925^2.

Wikström, Å, (1987), *Functional Programming using Standard ML*, Hemel Hempstead, Prentice-Hall.

Wilensky, R., (1984), *Lispcraft*, London, Norton.

Wilf, H.S., (1986), *Algorithms and Complexity*, Hemel Hempstead, Prentice-Hall.

Wilson, R.J., (1985), *Introduction to Graph Theory*, Harlow, Longman, 1972[1], 1979[2], 1985[3].

Wittgenstein, L., (1922), *Tractatus Logico-Philosophicus*, (tr. C.K. Ogden), London, Routledge and Kegan Paul.

Wray, S.C., (1986), *Implementation and Programming Techniques for Functional Languages*, Computer Laboratory Technical Report 92, University of Cambridge.

Yaghi, A.A.G., (1984), *The Compilation of a Functional Language into Intensional Logic*, Theory of Computation Report 56, University of Warwick.

Yelles, C.B., (1979), *Type Assignment in the Lambda-Calculus: Syntax and Semantics*, Ph.D. Thesis, University of Wales.

Index